BEYOND THE ALTAR

BEYOND
THE
ALTAR

PERSPECTIVE
FOR
LITURGICAL WORSHIP

JOHN AINSLIE

First published in 2020 by Benedicamus
76 Great Bushey Drive, London N20 8QL, UK

Quotations from the Bible are taken – unless otherwise indicated –
from the New Revised Standard Version, Catholic Anglicised Edition,
copyright © 1999, 1995, 1989. Division of Christian Education of the
National Council of Churches of Christ in the United States of
America

Quotations from the documents of the Second Vatican Council are
taken – unless otherwise indicated – from the English translation of
the texts on the Vatican website

Other translations are by the author

ISBN: 978-0-9929050-5-7

Typeset by Benedicamus in 10/13 pt Cala
Printed by Book Printing UK, Peterborough

CONTENTS

PART II: REAPPRAISAL

EPILOGUE

APPENDICES

ILLUSTRATIONS

ACKNOWLEDGEMENTS

This book is a monograph. It is the fruit of many years of reflection on the presentation and celebration of the Church's liturgy. It expands and develops a three-part article I wrote in 2008-9 for *Music and Liturgy*, the journal of the Society of Saint Gregory, entitled 'A Question of Orientation', and also a keynote lecture I delivered to its 2011 Summer School with the title 'Beyond, but very near'.

In the preparation of this book, I owe particular thanks to Professor Emeritus Dr Rudolf Pacik of Salzburg, who has enabled access to a number of German literary resources and also advised me on some historical issues. I am also grateful to Canon Michael Cooley, Paul Inwood and Paul Moynihan, who have read the whole draft script, made some valuable suggestions and saved me from some egregious mistakes.

Photo permissions, with thanks: cover, under commons. wikimedia.org by Berthold Werner; 1, 2, 8 & 9 by licence and permission of shutterstock.com; 3 under commons.wikimedia.org by Durkadenz (CCo); 6 under commons.wikimedia.org by Norbert Schnitzler (CC BY-SA 3.0); 7: Kath. Kirchengemeinde Liebfrauen Trier, Foto: Rita Heyen; 10 Peter J. Harrison; 11 John Ainslie; 12 under commons.wikimedia.org by Groume; 13 Haus-Wasserburg, Vallendar; 14 Bernhard Lauer.

FOREWORD

On 4 December 1963, the bishops of the Catholic Church gathered at the Second Vatican Council approved its Constitution on the Sacred Liturgy by near-unanimous vote. It was greeted with great enthusiasm – I know, because I was a student in Rome at that historic time. There was a palpable impatience for its decisions and recommendations to be implemented.

On 26 September 1964, the first Instruction on the Implementation of the Liturgy Constitution, *Inter Œcumenici,* was duly published by the *Consilium* or commission set up for the purpose. The most anticipated of its directives concerned the introduction of vernacular languages in place of Latin; some simplifications of the Mass ritual were also prescribed – both these features had been ordered by the Liturgy Constitution. What was not expected (and nowhere mentioned in the Constitution) was this directive towards the end of the document:

> It is preferable for the main altar to be constructed separate from the wall, so that one can easily walk around the altar, and a celebration facing the people can take place on it.[1]

Despite the 'it is preferable' qualifier, the directive was universally interpreted as a virtual command, and temporary altars facing the

---

[1] *Inter Œcumenici*, no 91: my translation. The original Latin reads: 'Praestat ut altare maius exstruatur a pariete seiunctum, ut facile circumiri et in eo celebratio versus populum peragi possit.'

people sprang up everywhere almost overnight. This was in preparation for the implementation of the Instruction's decrees on the following First Sunday of Lent, 7 March 1965. On that day, people could (and did) say: "Yesterday you attended Mass said in Latin by the priest with his back to you; today you take part in the Mass in your own language with the priest facing you!"

Most priests at the time liked the change because they could see and directly relate to the people with whom they were celebrating. It must be remembered that hitherto the priest had celebrated the entire Mass at the altar, facing the sanctuary wall, his back to the people, turning towards them on only three occasions to greet them and once to bless them.

Most of the laity appreciated the new visual as well as aural sense of being involved in what had hitherto been regarded as 'Father's Mass'. It was seen as an important step forward in fulfilling the Liturgy Constitution's avowed intent to foster 'full and active' participation in the liturgy.[2]

But was this face-to-face configuration of priest opposite people the last word on the subject? Has not fifty years' experience of reform and renewal grown and matured the perception by priests and people of the meaning of the liturgy they celebrate?

The phrase Mass *versus populum*, 'facing the people', is unfortunate and seriously misleading. Who is celebrating the Mass towards the people? The phrase suggests that the 'real' liturgy is performed by the priest and his ministers in their dedicated area, the sanctuary or *presbyterium*, and the people are there in their area, the nave, initially as an audience or as spectators. There they are to be coaxed into participation in what is being performed in the sanctuary by the clergy and their ministers with or without them. This attitude underlies the texts of the 1963 Liturgy

---

[2] Cf *Sacrosanctum Concilium* (SC), nos 14, 21. Latin: 'plena et actuosa participatio'.

Constitution, which presume that the laity are not yet taking their due
part in the liturgy, and must be encouraged to do so.

The Catholic Church has long since outgrown that situation. Vocal
participation by people in the liturgy can now be taken for granted. But
there is a danger that the liturgy is seen as no more than fulfilling the
recitation of the Missal texts and the performance of its rubrics. The
mechanics of participation have been mastered. Fine. What about the
deeper purpose of the liturgical renewal – facilitating encounter with
God? Is not the visual focus of the entire celebration now the priest who
faces the congregation throughout? Where is God to be found?

Having the priest behind the altar, on the other side from the people,
far from uniting him with the people in the congregation, actually
separates him from them. There is a clergy side of the altar, and a laity
side. It is still 'Father's Mass'. Cardinal Joseph Ratzinger (later Pope
Benedict XVI) rightly lamented the new clericalization that had
entered on the scene because of this configuration.[3]

Of course the priest should face the people for dialogues with them, e.g.
'The Lord be with you' – 'And with your spirit'. And the reader and
deacon/priest should proclaim the Word of God to the people facing
them. That is not in dispute. But the Mass is above all an act of worship.
All praise and prayer in the Mass – particularly the Eucharistic Prayer
– is directed by priest and people together *through* Jesus Christ to God
the Father. And that should surely be expressed by a common direction
of worship, as was standard and almost universal throughout the
history of the Roman rite until 1965.

Dear reader, you may wonder whether what I have written is a prelude
to yet another appeal to reinstate altars and sanctuaries to the way they
looked before the Second Vatican Council. It is not. I acknowledge and

---

[3] RATZINGER 2000, 79-80. (Authors' names in SMALL CAPITALS refer to entries in the
Bibliography at the end of this book.)

appreciate the writings of Pope Emeritus Benedict XVI, and also of Fr Uwe Michael Lang of the London Oratory, author of *Turning towards the Lord*[4]. I share their criticism of celebration *versus populum*. But whereas they may dream of a revival of the *status quo ante*, there are other theologians today[5] who have, for the last thirty years, sought to develop new configurations of churches that are more expressive of the united worship by priest and people of the God, both transcendent and immanent, in whose life we are called to participate.

This book proposes the integration of sanctuary and nave, and the location of the altar in the midst of the congregation, so that the prayer offered and the sacrament shared at it may be more readily perceived as that of both people and priest. The sacrament is celebrated within the space, the prayer directed beyond it.

The text begins with an introduction into the nature of liturgy, and its expression by means of ritual and symbols. Part I is a historical overview, recalling how church architecture was in earlier centuries closely related to the liturgy, and tracing how the liturgical movement in the 1920s and 1930s laid the basis for the liturgical reform promoted by the Second Vatican Council. It then looks at the genesis and immediate aftermath of the decision to make Mass facing the people the norm. Part II examines the new relationship between priest and people in worship established at the Council, the significance of the altar, and the wider cosmic vision of the liturgy, before reviewing how post-Vatican II liturgy has changed the approach to the interior layout of new churches. On the basis of this, it proposes a concept model for potential further development. An epilogue reflects on the challenge of perceiving worship as directed 'beyond the altar'.

---

[4] LANG 2008.
[5] Of particular note are the writings of Professor Albert Gerhards of Bonn University. His paper "Look to the East!" ("Blickt nach Osten!" – GERHARDS 2001) together with his later article on liturgical spirituality (GERHARDS 2011b) reflect an agenda similar to mine.

This book offers no one-size-fits-all solutions. Every community has its own traditions of liturgical and devotional prayer. Every church space is different – and many, built before the liturgical renewal came to flower in the Second Vatican Council, could and can only be altered with difficulty. Moreover, parishes have spent much effort and money in the last fifty years making whatever adaptations have seemed appropriate.

Nevertheless, parish communities have changed over the years in size and scope, and, one would hope, enjoyed spiritual development. There may be hitherto unexpected opportunities for reviewing church layouts. Some churches have already undergone a second reordering.

This year marks 50 years since the 'new Order of Mass' was promulgated – now known as the Ordinary Form of the Roman Rite. In that time, there has been much prayerful experience and reflection on it. 'Active participation' in the liturgy is now taken for granted, a familiarity which can lead to thoughtless ritualism. A deeper appreciation of what we, priest and people, are doing when we celebrate the divine liturgy becomes even more necessary as time moves on.

Cardinal Joseph Ratzinger (Pope Benedict XVI as he later became) wrote in the foreword to Fr Lang's book in 2004: 'what is needed is a new mutual openness in the search for the best realisation of the memorial of Christ'[6].

That is the spirit in which this book also is offered.

John Ainslie
June 2020

---

[6] LANG 2008, 10.

INTRODUCTION

Chapter 1

LITURGY AND RITUAL

For the Liturgy, "through which the work of our redemption is accomplished", most of all in the Divine Sacrifice of the Eucharist, is the outstanding means whereby the faithful may express in their lives, and manifest to others, the mystery of Christ and the real nature of the true Church... [T]he liturgy is the summit toward which the activity of the Church is directed; at the same time it is the fountain from which all her power flows.[1]

What is the basis of this apparently extravagant claim for the liturgy?

Liturgy – the work of God

Liturgy is the work of God, by God, enabling communion in the life of the Trinity. It is made possible by the incarnation, death and resurrection of Jesus Christ, who shared our human nature to the full, that we might share his divine nature. Christians take upon themselves that divine nature by grace at baptism and renew that communion with him every time they celebrate and encounter him in his 'do this in

---

[1] Second Vatican Council, Constitution on the Sacred Liturgy (*Sacrosanctum Concilium* – henceforward *SC*), articles 2 & 10.

memory of me', in the Eucharist – a maturing process that will eventually be fulfilled at the 'end time' or *eschaton*, when God's kingdom will be complete.

Indeed, it is significant that the Catechism of the Catholic Church treats the liturgy as the prime ritual means of such encounter with God. The very first article under 'The Celebration of the Christian Mystery' is entitled 'The Liturgy – Work of the Holy Trinity', and consists of three sections, titled thus:

- The Father - Source and Goal of the Liturgy
- Christ's work in the Liturgy: Christ glorified... is present in the earthly liturgy... which participates in the liturgy of heaven
- The Holy Spirit and the Church in the Liturgy

'Downwards' from God the Father as source comes his salvation in Jesus Christ, and by the power of the Holy Spirit we celebrate the liturgy on earth as our 'upward' response in communion with Christ as High Priest, rendered to God our Father as our goal.

This communion in the life of God is only possible because of the saving work of Jesus Christ in the paschal mystery of his death and resurrection. That work was accomplished by him once in time, but it is 'aeviternal', for it marks 'the point of intersection of the timeless with time'[2]. It is his continuing saving work in the world through the Church, in which Christians, united to him as members of his Body, are participants.

Pope Pius XII in his 1947 encyclical *Mediator Dei* defines liturgy thus:

> The sacred liturgy is, consequently, the public worship which our Redeemer as Head of the Church renders to the Father, as well as the worship which the community of the faithful renders to its Founder, and through Him

---

[2] T. S. Eliot, *Four Quarters – Part III: The Dry Salvages.*

to the heavenly Father. It is, in short, the worship rendered by the Mystical Body of Christ in the entirety of its Head and members.[3]

We are thus united with Christ in his continuing, eternal act of self-offering to the Father. In the epiclesis of the Eucharistic Prayer we invoke the Holy Spirit to make holy the gifts of bread and wine, signs of creation and human work, signs of our self-offering, that they *and we* may be transformed and assimilated into the self-offering of Jesus Christ to his Father and ours.

It is all God's work, in which we are privileged to participate. Communities of Christians can determine *when* and *how* to celebrate a liturgy-event. But *what* it is exceeds their powers. Liturgy is 'first and foremost the work of grace, a bestowal of transcendence that (to be sure) *makes use of* human agents for its enactment but does not... *consist of* such agency'.[4]

Participation by perception

The 'active participation' of people in the liturgy, decreed as 'the aim to be considered before all else' in its restoration[5], has been widely misunderstood.

The original use of the phrase 'active participation' – *partecipazione attiva* – is found in Pope Pius X's decree *Tra le sollecitudini*, issued only months after he became Pope in 1903. Unusually for papal utterances of the time, it was issued in Italian, because it was principally directed at the Roman diocesan authorities, upbraiding them for their poor standards of music and liturgical celebration. When it came to be translated into Latin for publication in the official *Acta Apostolicae*

---

[3] *Mediator Dei*, article 20. This definition is the starting point of SC 7.
[4] NICHOLS 1996, chapter 2.
[5] SC 14.

Sedis, the word used to translate '*attiva*' was not '*activa*' but '*actuosa*', which means – according to respected Latin/English dictionaries – 'active, busy, energetic', even 'acting with extravagant gesture'. A more nuanced interpretation, derived from an 18th century Latin lexicon, is that *actuosus* means 'properly one who is totally engaged in the act or motion of the body...such as an actor and a dancer, who for this reason are called *actuosi*'.[6] From this one can derive 'fully engaged', 'involved', 'committed', such as an actor or dancer giving of their all to perform their required role. This is a much more demanding interpretation than 'active', 'actual' or 'effective', the usual attempts to translate *actuosa (participatio)*. It may even demand *less* outward activity; it certainly requires total commitment on the part of the participant.

'Participation' has also been widely misunderstood as something rational, the understanding of the sacred rites. Quite apart from the whole phenomenon of ritual, which exists precisely to express the *non-rational* – as we shall see shortly – poor translation of crucial texts in the Constitution has been an unfortunate source of misunderstanding.

An important paragraph reads, in its official translation:

> In this restoration, both texts and rites should be drawn up so that they express more clearly the holy things which they signify; the Christian people, so far as possible, should be enabled to understand them with ease and to take part in them fully, actively, and as befits a community.[7]

This gives the impression that intellectual 'understanding' of the texts and rites is what is required. But the Latin verb is *percipere*, so 'Christian

---

[6] From Forcellini's 18th century Latin lexicon, quoted in a website newsletter of the New Liturgical Movement dated 16 March 2015.
[7] SC 21. Original Latin: 'Qua quidem instauratione, textus et ritus ita ordinari oportet, ut sancta, quae significant, clarius exprimant, eaque populus christianus, in quantum fieri potest, facile percipere atque plena, actuosa et communitatis propria celebratione participare possit.'

people should be enabled to *perceive*… these holy things', discern their spiritual content, intuit, grasp or (even better) be grasped by the mystery that they signify.[8]

Similar poor translation affects another paragraph. It reads:

> The rites should be distinguished by a noble simplicity; they should be short, clear, and unencumbered by useless repetitions; they should be within the people's powers of comprehension, and normally should not require much explanation.[9]

But the Latin says nothing about 'powers of comprehension'. It reads: *sint fidelium captui accommodati* – 'they should be suited to the ability of the faithful to grasp them', even *without* understanding them intellectually. It has been said that when we truly enter the mystery of the liturgy, 'we understand that we do not understand'.[10]

An earlier paragraph makes the language of ritual clearer:

> In the liturgy the sanctification of man is manifested by signs perceptible to the senses, and is effected in a way which is proper to each of these signs.[11]

---

[8] 'Grace is an irreducible gift,…a fundamental openness, an attitude of listening and welcome toward something *ungraspable* by which we are already grasped; …a gracious attitude of *"letting be"* and *"allowing oneself to be spoken"* which requires [one] to renounce all ambition for mastery.' (CHAUVET 1994, 446.)

[9] SC 34. Latin: 'Ritus nobili simplicitate fulgeant, sint brevitate perspicui et repetitiones inutiles evitent, sint fidelium captui accommodati, neque generatim multis indigeant explanationibus.'

[10] CHAUVET 1994, 326-330, quoted in BALDOVIN 2008, 142.

[11] SC 7. '… in qua [liturgia] per signa sensibilia significatur et modo singulis proprio efficitur sanctificatio hominis…'

'Signs *perceptible* to the senses', by which 'the sanctification of man', incorporation into Christ and union with God, is effected, actually happens. That is the purpose of liturgy – and of participation in it.

Participation should therefore require little more than a willingness to let oneself be grasped by the mystery that is being manifested and accomplished by the sacred rites. "Bring your body; your mind will follow". Let go: let God! On the part of the participant, openness and receptivity to the mystery being made present in word and sacrament are fundamental. It is not what we do in ritual that is of prime importance: it is the divine action realized through the ritual within us, with our 'active participation'.

Good liturgy does not point to itself but to the One who is worshipped.[12] That is the way that participants can perceive, experience and become part of the mysterious reality they celebrate, and to which they belong.[13] Fully engaged participation is thus both a positive response to the perception of this indwelling and the means by which it is deepened.

How is that engagement by and with God to be executed? The language of the liturgy is one of signs and symbols – and ritual.

Becoming one with the symbol

Ritual, though apparently a strange concept in today's technological world, is in fact so embedded in human behaviour that Roy Rappaport, the author of a book that has become a classic in ritual studies, claims that ritual is 'the social act basic to humanity'.[14] Even in this post-

---

[12] BALDOVIN 2008, 98. 'The reforms brought attention to the liturgy itself, while the liturgy needs to point beyond itself' (id, 97).

[13] Cf GERHARDS 2017, 161. See also SEARLE 2007, 9-15, here 14.

[14] RAPPAPORT 1999, 31 & 107. His definition of ritual reads 'the performance of more or less invariant sequences of formal acts and utterances not entirely encoded by the performers' (24).

modern, technological age the basic human events of birth, betrothal, wedding and death continue to be celebrated ritually. Rappaport distinguishes two classes of rituals. One he calls 'self-referential', consisting of stylized ways of exchanging variable messages between individuals or small groups, e.g. shaking hands as a sign of greeting. The other class is that of 'canonical' rituals in which the entire assembly present perform together an inherited symbolic action, and it is here that the liturgy finds its place. In canonical rituals neither form nor content are created by the participants. There may be circumstantial features that are variable – place, style of music, size of gathering – but the kernel of the ritual is almost invariant, and is expected to be so.

All the participants in a liturgy celebrate it together, and are therefore co-celebrants of it, those who enact it, make it happen.[15] Most liturgical actions require an ordained priest to lead them and exercise his ministerial priesthood.[16] But he and other ministers are not the only actors. Priest and people together perform and make present, actualize the liturgical event. They help to create what they experience. If the Council was serious about active participation, then 'taking part' means 'entering into', 'becoming part of' the Mass or other liturgy being celebrated. The 1964 Instruction, *Inter Œcumenici*, talked of Mass *versus populum*, Mass being celebrated by the priest facing the people. In the 1970 Order of Mass, by contrast, we have *Missa cum populo*, Mass with the people, a single celebration by priest and people together.

To talk of 'performance' might well remind one of concerts or theatre productions. An important distinction must be made. A piece of music has been composed by its composer, a drama has been written by a

---

[15] Distinguish 'concelebrants', who are a sub-group of co-celebrants, being priests exercising their priestly ministry.
[16] A lay person may preside at the Liturgy of the Hours (the Divine Office) and, duly authorised, at weddings and funerals. As for the specific role of the priest, cf John Baldovin's comment: 'It is certainly clear that we can no longer speak of the priest 'doing something' in the liturgy independently of the people of God. The solution – theologically, anthropologically and pastorally – has so far eluded us' (BALDOVIN 2008, 94). See further in chapter 7 below.

playwright. It comes to life when it is expressed in performance, which on the one hand is a repetition, but on the other is a new event at each performance. People attend the concert or drama because it is an event, not just a repetition. But it is only acting, only a 'play'. When it is over, the players revert to their own identities.

In ritual, an event takes place, is performed, in which the participants make the prescribed ritual actions their own. The signs which they 'read' become real, and they become united with and part of the reality they represent. Ritual makes something happen. Engagement rings are signs that effect what they mean: the couple become engaged, hopefully permanently. The elements and ritual of Holy Communion are signs of the Body and Blood of Christ and by communion effect union in that Body, in all senses of the word – hopefully permanently and increasingly, time and time again.

Ritual is also dramatic, and the appropriate means of playing out what Hans Urs von Balthasar calls 'theo-drama'[17]. Here God the Father is the author, God the Son is the actor and God the Holy Spirit is the director of the action. Through Christ's Incarnation, death, resurrection and ascension, Man is inserted into the 'acting' of Christ, to play his/her personal role in salvation history in accordance with his/her divine calling. The stage for this drama is not the church building – still less its sanctuary – but the world as a whole. Nonetheless, it receives sacramental expression in liturgical celebration, when all its participants are united in the Body of Christ by the power of the Spirit in worshipping the Father. It is essentially a divine action played out for us and with us, into which we are invited to enter and wholeheartedly respond.

---

[17] BALTHASAR 1988. See also BALTHASAR 1990.

Symbols of mystery

The 'reading' of the liturgical symbols and perception of their significance is a crucial element and gateway into full participation in the liturgy. Pope Benedict XVI called for 'a greater *awareness* of the *mystery* being celebrated'.[18] The task of education for liturgical participation must therefore be one of *sensitizing* people to what is happening and its significance. Romano Guardini, the pioneer of liturgical renewal whom we will be meeting in chapter 3, was worried that, even after the reforms of the Vatican Council, people would still be incapable of grasping and making sense of the language of symbols, which is the language of the liturgy.[19] He provides an example:

> This [use of symbols] becomes clearest when it is a matter of 'doing', for instance, the offertory procession, where this is customary. It makes all the difference whether the faithful look upon this procession as a mere means to an end,... or whether they know that the act of bringing their gifts forward is a 'prayer' in itself, a readiness before God.[20]

At an earlier German Liturgical Congress, at Frankfurt in 1950, Guardini had read a paper entitled 'Liturgical Experience and Epiphany'.[21] In it he appealed for a rediscovery of a liturgical 'sense', an ability to perceive beyond mere explanations of the ritual, 'to open oneself to the liturgical action, to enter into its meaning, to let oneself be led by the logic of its images and its execution, to understand what it wishes to manifest'.[22] The execution of the liturgy should enable this perception. What Guardini is looking for in the liturgy is an 'epiphany',

---

[18] Encyclical Letter *Sacramentum Caritatis*, no 52. Original italics.
[19] See his Open Letter to the Third German Liturgical Conference, in Mainz in 1964: English translation in BRADSHAW 2007, here 8.
[20] Id., 6.
[21] GUARDINI 1950.
[22] Id., 94.

a perceptible manifestation of the Lord, "who has shone in our hearts to give the light of the knowledge of the glory of God in the face of Jesus Christ" (2 Cor 4:6).[23]

It is a challenge, vitally important, to present the liturgy in such a way that it is patent and expressive of the sacred mysteries it celebrates. The Vatican Council desired a liturgy in which participation is not only active but *conscious*. Conscious of what?[24] There should be a compelling sense of the God who is not only immanently present but also beyond perceptible presence, transcendent. The ritual, canonical shell is only the prescribed form of the liturgy – the musical score, so to speak. It is very easy – and, alas, too common – for priests and ministers to be satisfied with perfunctory fulfilment of the rubrics, despite the Vatican Council's insistence that 'more is required than the mere observance of the laws governing valid and licit celebration'[25]. To direct worshippers to the unseen One who is worshipped, the symbols that liturgy uses must communicate their significance as clearly as possible to its would-be participants.[26] The symbols include the whole *milieu* in which the liturgy takes place – the internal art, architecture and configuration of the church, which should reflect and foster the worship that takes place within it. The liturgy is both earthly and heavenly, both here and beyond the walls of the church and of the created universe. Since it is the offering of the whole Christ, Head and Body, it must signify that the Head, Christ himself, is both here and in heaven, sacramentally present and yet also beyond physical location, because now glorified.

---

[23] Id, 99.

[24] Owe Wikström, in a 1993 study of 'liturgy as experience', pointed out that (up to that time) 'no study has addressed the question of the relationship or distance between what professional religious *believe* or hope that liturgies convey and what those attending a church service *actually* understand and experience' (WIKSTRÖM 1993, 83-100, here 84).

[25] SC 11. Pope Francis, in a 2015 address to Roman diocesan priests, cautioned them against both rigidity to rubrics and showmanship; the priest must enter into the mystery and enable others to do so (*Catholic Herald*, 20 February 2015).

[26] 'To celebrate the liturgy means to do the action or perform the sign in such a way that the full meaning and impact shine forth in clear and compelling fashion' (*Music in Catholic Worship* (Washington, DC, 1972), nn. 6-7).

The Eucharistic liturgy is

> a corporate, ecclesial encounter with God that draws each participant towards the attainment of the reality it sets forth, and that attainment involves passing beyond everything we can conceive or understand, the rejection of everything that is simply *about* God, for the sake of an encounter in love with God Himself, an encounter in which we become transparent to God, and are deified.[27]

Everything, therefore, in the outward celebration of the liturgy, must be geared towards enabling this encounter. It does not require learning, but prayerful experience of the living God. The liturgical scholar Aidan Kavanagh invented a fictional parishioner, the devout 'Mrs Murphy'.[28] She is both a liturgist and a theologian – much to her surprise. Every baptised Christian who allows him/herself to enter into liturgy and be swept along by it towards encounter with God is a liturgist. And everyone who actively converses with or contemplates God in prayer exercises theo-logy, God-expression, whether or not he/she may be able to discourse *about* God. 'Theology is first a vision, then a cogitation.'[29] Liturgy itself is *of* God, not of those who perform it. 'It is only by accepting that the God we seek is the God as Other who acts within us that we can begin to see the liturgy shape us as we partake in it.'[30] The Roman rite would do well to take to heart the Orthodox terminology of '*Divine* Liturgy'. Even 'divine service' – German *Gottesdienst* – has a welcome double meaning: it is both God's service of his people by his presence among them, and their service of God by their response of worship.[31]

---

[27] LOUTH 1997, 6, quoted in FAGERBERG 2004, 16.
[28] KAVANAGH 1992, 146. David Fagerberg takes up the image of Mrs Murphy: cf *id*, 133-159.
[29] FAGERBERG 2010, 41-51, here 46.
[30] CAMERON-MOWAT 1995, 336.
[31] In Eucharistic Prayer II, the priest expresses thanks to God, on behalf of the entire congregation, 'that you have held us worthy to be in your presence *and minister to you*.'

Liturgy is a corporate, ecclesial encounter with God. The people's participation is to be communal and community-making. It is the worship by the gathered Body of Christ, not by a collection of pious individuals praying as if privately. That is why fully engaged participation requires the united responses, gestures and especially singing to symbolise and express that worship. And indeed such participation in united acts of worship is itself a means of perceiving and realising the encounter with God that they express.

Engaging participants

The paragraph in the Liturgy Constitution quoted earlier, advocating 'noble simplicity', a rite that is 'short, clear, and unencumbered by useless repetitions', reflects the functional outlook to ritual prevalent in the early 1960s. Academic studies since then have revealed that ritual is a complex human phenomenon in which recourse to symbols indicates that its scope extends beyond rational explanation.[32]

There is, of course, no necessary uniformity in the degree of perception and participation of those who witness a ritual.[33] Pope Benedict noted that 'by its very nature the liturgy operates on different levels of communication which enable it to engage the whole human person'[34].

Some parts of the rite (e.g. Scripture readings) may require a more audience-like attention. Other parts, however, even if spoken or performed by one person, represent actions being undertaken simultaneously by the entire body of participants (notably the prayers). In fact, it is in the parts of the liturgy where there are few or no symbolic actions but only words that the greatest difficulty with participation is experienced. However, it is important to realise – especially in this information-controlled age – that words in the liturgy are not just

---

[32] Cf NICHOLS 1996.
[33] Cf WIKSTRÖM 1993.
[34] Sacramentum Caritatis, 40.

statements of fact. They are 'performative'. The very command of Jesus to 'do this in memory of me' is performative: it does what it says. And it is not only performative: it is transformative. Holy Scripture is proclaimed so that the word of God may happen afresh: 'he spoke, and it came to be' (Ps 33:9). 'Liturgy belongs to the order of doing (*ergon*) not of knowing (*logos*).'[35]

Nonetheless, a valid criticism of the post-Vatican-II Order of Mass is that it is too wordy.[36] It had been hoped that the use of people's languages instead of Latin would make it easier for the people to pray the prayers of the Mass with the priest as he *prays* them. It is, alas, far too common for priests to simply read the texts from the missal as if mere recitation of the words fulfils the liturgical requirement, seemingly unaware that the whole point of saying the prayers aloud, and in the vernacular tongue, is to enable the people not only to hear them, but to pray them as they pray them. The commonly used Eucharistic Prayers are familiar enough, but still require the priest to utter them in a sensitive and prayerful manner so that they will *sound* like prayer[37]. Only then will listeners be enabled to enter into them and make them their own prayer.[38] The other principal prayers of the Mass (the Collect, the Prayer over the Offerings and the Prayer after Communion) present major challenges of translation, not least because, when most of them were originally written in the fourth to eighth centuries, they were never intended to be understood by the laity.[39]

---

[35] I.-H. Dalmais, as quoted by NICHOLS 1996.
[36] 'I have to agree that the problem with much contemporary liturgical performance... is with the over-verbalization of the rite... on account of which people are not invited to enter into the liturgy on its own terms' (BALDOVIN 2008, 97).
[37] The 'preponderance' of meaning in liturgy 'is transmitted... in what has been called 'the grain of the voice' – not just *what* is said but *the manner of its being said*' (HUGHES 2003, 5). *SC* 11 said of the faithful that 'their thoughts [should] match their words'. How much more necessary is it for priests to show this by how they express the texts they read!
[38] It would be a great help to foster a spirit of prayer if priests could take their eyes off the missal and say Eucharistic Prayers II and III by heart – and from the heart!
[39] 'Language in ritual is a sign and its task is to point beyond itself to a mystery beyond words and understanding' (O'LOUGHLIN 2016, 462). See also HUGHES 2003, 36-40.

One may, of course, stand back from participation, or even resist it. Or viewers may interpret it in different ways, especially if they are not acquainted with the ritual. A tourist may admire a priest's snazzy 'green suit', not realising the significance of a chasuble. The preparation of a liturgical celebration must take account of the differing levels of awareness of those attending it. Some may be newcomers searching for a God they have never yet encountered.

Ritual development

A strong sense of tradition is associated with rituals, and may even be considered as a constituent feature and expression of the culture that uses them. Indeed, repetition – and its regularity – are essential features. But they can also be dangerous: over-frequent repetition can lead to a ritualistic attitude by its performers. Each performance of a canonical ritual must be a distinctive event. Major festivals and one-off occasions are much easier to celebrate well than weekly or daily liturgies.

Repetition might suggest that ritual is necessarily unchanging. Experience of ritual in many fields shows that this is not so. One may distinguish a fundamental kernel from the particular historical and cultural performance of it.[40] The Mass celebrated in the early Church, often and necessarily in small groups because of the threat of persecution, was for that reason cast in the form of what we might today call a simple House Mass. The Roman papal Mass about the year 700[41] shows, by contrast, an astonishing complexity of ritual. The same Mass as described in the Pius V Missal of 1570 details what the priest must do, but the people have no prescribed part. Now we have the 1970 Order of Mass, in which Christian people are re-enabled to take that full part in the liturgy to which their baptism gives them the right and privilege. The Eastern rites continue to celebrate the Divine Liturgy in

---

[40] Rappaport calls such a kernel the 'Ultimate Sacred Postulate', see RAPPAPORT 1999, 335. On change in the liturgy, see BALDOVIN 2008, 36-64.
[41] The supposed year of *Ordo Romanus I*, the first detailed description of the papal rite.

their different ways. These are all different forms of the same obedience to Jesus' command, "do this in memory of me".

After the Council, there was a great willingness to 'do the right thing' in the revised liturgy, but little appreciation of why. The text of the Liturgy Constitution provided not only the principles of liturgical reform, but also the reasoning behind them. And it recognised that a process of education was necessary, beginning with pastors, who should 'become thoroughly penetrated with the spirit and power of the liturgy'[42]. But at that time there was as yet no experience of the liturgy as renewed by the Council.

The subsequent instructions from the *Consilium ad exsequendam Constitutionem de Sacra Liturgia*, the international body set up to implement the Constitution, did not always provide the rationale for their directives. Unfortunately, in the first Instruction, dated 26 September 1964, no reason at all was provided for the directive that 'it is preferable' for Mass to be celebrated by the priest facing the people, *versus populum*.

Ritual evaluation

We shall comment on this Instruction in detail in chapter 5. What we are emphasising in the current chapter, however, is the need to evaluate liturgical form and content from a ritual point of view, rather than a functional one. For we are concerned here with actions that are symbolic, that express worship of that higher reality that is God.

Guardini's description of an offertory procession, quoted above, makes the point succinctly; the widespread reintroduction of this simple symbolic gesture is one of the successes of the 1970 Order of Mass.[43]

---

[42] SC 14.
[43] Having the collection brought up at the same time as the bread and wine unites members of the congregation in the gesture of offering their own 'work of human hands'.

The establishment of a distinct location facing the congregation for the proclamation of the Liturgy of the Word is another – remember that the Scripture readings had hitherto been read by the priest in Latin at the altar, facing the sanctuary wall.[44] Now the proclamation of the word of God in the liturgy is honoured, as it should be, and given its own proper location at an ambo that, hopefully, is not just a portable lectern but something substantial and symbolic of its exalted function, for it is from there that God speaks his Word to his people through the ministry of its reader.

Communion of the laity under both kinds has been permitted once again precisely because of its sign value.[45] Jesus instituted the Eucharist under the signs of both bread and wine, both food and drink. He said "do this in remembrance of me" over both bread and cup. "For as often as you eat this bread and drink the cup, you proclaim the Lord's death until he comes" (1 Cor 11:26). Although Christ is indeed fully present sacramentally under either sign, it behoves us to accept this gift of himself under both signs, as he originally intended. The bread and wine presented by the people in the preparation of the gifts (even vicariously) are thus returned, sanctified, to sanctify those who gifted them.

Indeed, the liturgy expresses its content symbolically in many ways: its structure (word before sacrament), movement (processions, gestures), use of language (formal, not discursive), music, vestments, incense, etc. The gathering of the local community for celebration is itself a symbol of their unity in Christ.

The fact that these are in some way different from everyday usage and yet still bodily perceptible to the senses identifies them as being purposefully symbolic of a higher reality. The participant already takes

---

[44] At a High Mass, the older rubrics directed the subdeacon to sing the Epistle *contra altare* (facing the altar), but the deacon to sing the Gospel both *contra altare* and *versus populum*. This contradictory ruling resulted in the compromise custom of singing it towards the *north* wall. See JUNGMANN 1951, I, 412.

[45] *SC* 55; General Instruction of the Roman Missal (henceforward GIRM), no. 85.

part in that higher reality, in nearness to the immanent God, but still at a distance from ultimate union with His transcendence. Every earthly liturgy enjoys the presence of Jesus Christ through his Holy Spirit, but looks forward to eventual fulfilment in the heavenly liturgy.[46]

Gesture, direction and symbolism

So we should ask ourselves this question: what is the ritual and symbolic purpose of celebrating the Eucharist facing the people?

In 1965, the immediate impact of the implementation of the Roman Instruction was that of being able to see, for the first time, what the priest does at the altar, although in practice this is dependent on the horizontal distance of the altar from the congregation, and on any difference in vertical level. But the fact that the priest faced the congregation, instead of having his back to it, was intended to show that the celebration of the Eucharist was being shared with the assembly present at it, rather than being simply the priest's offering, with the people only attending it or 'assisting' at it. From this point of view, this simple reversal of orientation aimed at promoting the 'full, active and conscious participation' of the people.

However, the ritual of the Liturgy of the Eucharist had developed over more than sixteen centuries with the priest facing liturgical east, and therefore with his back to most attending congregations. There is a deep theological and liturgical significance in orientation, as we shall examine in the following chapters. And the priest's ritual gestures have hitherto presumed this orientation. The significance of at least two of these is seriously compromised by the reversal of direction.

One of them occurs at the Preparation of the Gifts. Representatives of the people have brought the bread and wine to the altar in the 'offertory

---

[46] SC 8; GERHARDS 2017, 180.

procession'[47]. In most churches they have processed in an 'eastward' direction to the altar, where the priest has received them. The procession is symbolic as an expression of offering to God, as we have learnt from Guardini. But the priest, instead of continuing this eastward direction of offering to God, and thereby turning his back on the people, now faces them when he lifts the offerings[48], appearing to offer the gifts towards them, as if giving them back to them. The ancient symbol of a gesture towards the unseen God is compromised.

A more important gesture occurs at the final doxology of the Eucharistic Prayer. This is the elevation of the host and chalice as a symbol of the offering of the sacrifice of the Mass 'by which the glorification of God is expressed'[49]. This elevation is not (and never was) for the purpose of showing them to the people[50]; however, the gesture as commonly practised gives the impression of being almost a repetition of the elevations at the consecration – unless the priest makes a conscious effort to lift his eyes upwards as he says or sings the words of the doxology. How well is the 'glorification of God' expressed?

Unlike the elevation at the doxology, the elevations at the words of institution are more devotional than symbolic. The elevation of the host was introduced in the thirteenth century to respond to the perceived devotional needs of the faithful at that time. The corresponding elevation of the chalice only entered the Order of Mass in Pope Pius V's 1570

---

[47] 'Offertory procession' is a popular description of this ritual, but the term is not officially sanctioned. The Missal rubrics and GIRM, under 'Preparation of the Gifts', simply say that bread and wine are 'brought forward' by members of the faithful, though this rite has 'spiritual significance' (GIRM 73).
[48] Slightly, Latin *paululum*: cf GIRM 141-142. Many priests make the mistake of lifting them too high, as if this gesture represents the offering of the Mass. The confusion is understandable, given that the 'Blessed are you...' prayers refer to the bread/wine 'we *offer* you'.
[49] GIRM 79h.
[50] Cf JUNGMANN 1951, I, 21, fn. 62 and II, 266.

Missal. Similarly the 'Behold the Lamb of God' before Communion, which was an innovation of the 1614 Roman Ritual[51].

One gesture that should be made visible to the participating congregation is the Fraction – the breaking of the consecrated bread(s) for distribution at Holy Communion, so symbolic that the earliest term for the Mass is 'the breaking of bread'.[52] The rubrics do not actually require this important symbolic action to be made visible to the people[53], though many priests laudably lift the (principal) host high enough for this gesture to be seen by them.

Of equal importance to these symbolic gestures is the manner in which the prayers are recited by the priest. He offers thanksgiving and prays to God the Father on behalf of the whole participating assembly, and should be perceived as doing so. Appearing to direct prayer towards the congregation in front of him is seriously misleading. This is evidenced by an answer given by an American priest to the question 'How is the Mass a meal?' As part of his answer to the enquirer, he feels compelled to state this:

> When the priest speaks the words of Consecration at Mass, he is not addressing the congregation. This is another common point of confusion today. Not only is the Mass not a mere re-enactment of the Last Supper; even when the priest speaks the words of Consecration at Mass, he is not addressing the congregation. These

---

[51] The 1570 Missal made no provision whatsoever for the distribution of Communion to the people during Mass. Latin missals right up to the time of the Second Vatican Council continued to omit any reference to people's Communion in the main *Ordo Missae*. In practice, the rite from the 1614 Roman Ritual for Communion of the Sick was simply slotted into the Order of Mass when the Communion of any laity was required.
[52] Cf Lk 24:35; Acts 2:42,46. See also below, chapter 8.
[53] Cf GIRM 83, 155.

words, like all the words of the Eucharistic prayer, are
directed to the Heavenly Father.[54]

That this needs to be said at all shows how the priest's quite distinct
roles as, on the one hand, addressing the congregation in dialogue with
them, and, on the other, addressing God in prayer, have been
drastically confused by celebration facing the people. 'Good liturgy
should do what it says and say what it does.'[55]

The Altar, uniting or dividing?

In the Eucharist – the Great Thanksgiving – the priest 'unites the
congregation with himself in the Prayer that he addresses in the name
of the entire community to God the Father through Jesus Christ in the
Holy Spirit'[56]. This comes to a climax in the concluding doxology of the
Eucharistic Prayer and the people's affirmation of it through their
'Amen'.

The priest's stance at this climactic point in the Eucharistic celebration
is deeply symbolic. Is the priest, vested in the distinctive vestments
symbolic of his office, *in persona Christi capitis*,[57] leading the people
entrusted to his pastoral care towards the God whom space cannot
contain? Is he visually and physically united with those on whose
behalf he enunciates the Eucharistic prayer addressed to God the
Father, and with whom he prays it? Or is he, uniquely standing on the
far side of the altar, representing God ministering to his people,
'imaginarily exalted to the point of being placed almost above the

---

[54] Mgr Charles Pope in 2016, on http://blog.adw.org/2016/08/understand-sacrifice-
mass-meal-must-clarify-sort-meal, accessed on 25 March 2020.
[55] O'LOUGHLIN 2016, 456. Also a mantra of one of the doyens of the liturgical renewal in
England, Clifford Howell SJ (1902-1981).
[56] GIRM 78; cf SC 48.
[57] 'In the person of Christ the head'. The addition of the attributive 'head' in more recent
Church documents refers the analogy specifically to Eph 1:22-23, and therefore in
relation to the Church, 'which is his body'. See more in chapter 7.

angels'[58]? Or does he represent both the people to God and God to the people?[59]

Previously the priest stood on the same side of the altar as the people (albeit with his back to them), and offered prayer to God in the same direction as they did. There was an implicit symbol of a united focus of prayer towards a 'vanishing point' behind and beyond the altar. The architectural orientation of the whole church supported and provided the context for this directedness of liturgical prayer towards and beyond the 'east' wall of the church. Stained-glass east windows expressed this well.

But now, at a time when the priest is bidden to unite the congregation with himself in the Eucharistic Prayer, he is standing in the opposite direction to them – and apparently praying at a 45° angle towards nothing more significant than the missal book from which he is reading. As a result, it is too easy for liturgy to be perceived as no more than the ritual – even ritualistic – utterance of prescribed texts. Moreover, as he says the prayers, the people may have their visual and aural attention transfixed on him rather than on the God to whom they are (or should be) praying with him. Instead of a God-human dialogue, there appears to be only a purely human interaction between priest and people. Joseph Ratzinger, later to be Pope Benedict XVI, complained that 'now the priest... becomes the real point of reference for the whole liturgy... Less and less is God in the picture.'[60] The purview and perspective of worship reaching beyond the altar has been compromised or lost. Where is the sense of the divine presence as something not only within but also transcending the worshipping community? Instead, the celebration has become self-enclosing,

---

[58] CHAUVET 2001, 86.
[59] WIKSTRÖM 1993, 94.
[60] RATZINGER 2000, 80.

inward-looking, even self-referential. The wider, cosmic dimension of every liturgy, which we will examine later, is not even hinted at.

Seeing what the priest is doing at the altar by having him face the people was intended to assist their participation. But seeing does not necessarily mean taking part in what is seen. For all their artistic embellishment, older sanctuaries never looked like stages because everyone within them had their backs to the congregation: the focus for everyone present was neither the sanctuary nor the altar but a point mysteriously beyond it. Now that he faces the people, the priest appears to be an actor on a stage; the people are his audience, two or more steps below him. The focus is foreshortened to him and to what he does and says. In the current entertainment-obsessed age, the liturgy must surely be perceived as something much more – indeed, quite other – than a live performance by an actor on a stage.

Moreover, the altar table has become a barrier, a counter-symbol of *apartheid* between priest and people, clergy and laity. At the very time that the Second Vatican Council was promoting shared liturgical participation by priest and people, the implementation of its reforms physically separated one from the other instead of uniting them. Is not the entire church space the 'stage' for the liturgical action in which all the participants are actors in the divine theo-drama?

We shall see in the following chapters of this book how the directive for Mass facing the people had lost touch with what the initiators of the liturgical renewal wished to promote, namely, the community celebration by priest and people together. Those pioneers wished to have the people around the altar – *circumstantes*[61] in the words of the Roman Canon (Eucharistic Prayer I) – or at least on three sides of it. As we shall see in chapter 4, the architect-theologian Rudolf Schwarz saw even 80 years ago that where the altar is not the common *centre* of the gathered

---

[61] The ICEL translation 'gathered here' is quite inadequate. The word means 'standing around'.

community, there could be a division of priest and people, and 'a "standing-opposite" develops, so that the mutilated form is no longer able to represent its true meaning'[62].

The celebrations of Mass 'in the round' in the 1920s and 1930s, with people standing around the altar, were almost entirely limited to small groups or closely-knit communities gathered for special events. Translating such a model into existing parish churches designed for a very different vision of liturgy and larger congregations was always going to be difficult, even impossible in some instances.

Going back to the *status quo ante*, with the priest's back visible at a distant altar, will not do.[63] Can we find a different approach to the configuration of priest and people which will signify better both their united celebration of the Church's liturgy and also its source in God and response towards God? That is what this book sets out to examine.

If celebration of the Liturgy of the Eucharist *versus populum*, facing the people, is now the *de facto* standard, how did it come about?

---

[62] SCHWARZ 1938, 62.
[63] 'When the altar was very remote from the faithful, it was right to move it back to the people.' RATZINGER 2000, 81. Despite this, in many reordered churches altars facing the people are as distant from the people as they ever were before the priest's about-turn.

PART I

HISTORICAL OVERVIEW

Photo 1 - Sant' Apollinare in Classe, Ravenna, Italy

Photo 2 – Monreale Cathedral, Palermo, Sicily

Photo 3 - Burg Rothenfels, Chapel

Photo 4 - Burg Rothenfels, Knights' Hall (as configured in 1928)

*Photo 5 - Heilig Kreuz,
Bottrop, Germany*

*Photo 6 - Fronleichnam,
Aachen, Germany*

Photo 7 - Liebfrauenkirche, Trier, Germany

Chapter 2

ORIENTATION

Theodor Klauser (1894-1984) was an archaeologist and historian of Christian antiquity. In this he followed his master, Franz Joseph Dölger (1879-1940), who had set out "to achieve a clear understanding of how early Christianity related to ancient culture". Klauser succeeded Dölger to the chair of Christian archaeology and history at Bonn, and founded an institute there, named after his predecessor. Later he became Rector Magnificus of the University of Bonn and a highly influential figure in German academic circles.

In 1943, in the midst of the Second World War, he published *A Short History of the Western Liturgy* as the 'Bonn Correspondence Course for Students on Active Service', i.e. prisoners of war.[1] The fifth edition of the book appeared in 1965, updated to reflect some of the decisions of the Second Vatican Council – it is still available.

Klauser reveals himself as a man of decided views. His studies had led him to believe that the standard practice in early Christian Rome and

---

[1] KLAUSER 1965, vii.

elsewhere was for the pope (or bishop or priest) to officiate from behind the altar, facing the people.[2]

In the immediate aftermath of the Second World War, with the rebuilding of churches in Germany a high priority, Klauser had been invited by the German bishops to write 'Guiding Principles for Designing and Building a Church in the spirit of the Roman Liturgy' – completed in 1947 and published in 1949.[3] Here he says: 'Ideally one would want a church fulfilling all these requirements of the Roman liturgy (i.e. priest and people situated directly opposite one another)'[4]. He continues: 'There are many indications today which point to the fact that in the church of the future, priests everywhere will once more celebrate from behind the altar, facing the people, as at one time they always did.'[5]

Klauser also supports the revival of the practice of easterly prayer in order to 'face God and His only begotten Son, who like the sun are thought of as enthroned in the East and coming from the East'[6]. But he continues: 'Now, however, this "coming" or "advent" of God in His Theophany takes place on our altars; hence in a Christian church, the object of turning East for prayer is to face the altar; and, therefore, both priest and people have to turn towards the altar.'[7] Given that countless churches have been built with beautiful apses and east-end windows beyond the high altar symbolising God's final theophany at the end of

[2] Id, 66. Stefan Heid (HEID 2019, 442) attributes Klauser's conviction to the beliefs of Franz Wieland (1872-1957), who had claimed in 1912 that celebration by priests with their backs to the people was completely unknown in the early Church.
[3] KLAUSER 1965, Appendix II, 161-169. The script also appears in TORGERSON 2007, 230-237; and in *Liturgy*, 19/3 (July 1950), 61-71.
[4] KLAUSER 1965, 164.
[5] Id, 165.
[6] Ibid.
[7] Ibid. Given the now-established convention of Mass facing the people, both Pope Benedict and Lang reluctantly accept 'orientation' as terminating at the altar (RATZINGER 2000, 83-84; LANG 2009, 136). However, Lang also states that, 'despite claims to the contrary, there is no explicit evidence from the early Church that the altar as such was considered the focus of orientation in the liturgy' (LANG 2009, 71).

time, Klauser's is a strangely stunted concept of orientation. If easterly *prayer* is indeed a valued tradition, why is the priest, the principal 'liturgist', expected to pray westwards opposite his eastward congregation, as if snubbing that tradition?

By 1965 Klauser could confirm that Mass facing the people in the early Church was also the conclusion of his pupils, Joseph Braun and Otto Nussbaum – and indeed the latter had just published a two-volume work of historical and archaeological research supporting this.[8]

During and immediately after the Second Vatican Council, there were two key words: *aggiornamento* and *ressourcement*. The first meant simply 'updating'; the second signified interest in going back to early resources of text and ceremonial in order to rediscover earlier liturgical practices that had become lost or forgotten in the course of time.[9] The results of the research by Klauser and Nussbaum fed neatly into and nourished this interest.

The renowned scholar of liturgy, Josef Andreas Jungmann, had already written in 1949 that 'it may be well to make clear that the historical precedent for the orientation of the altar [towards the people] is often highly exaggerated'.[10] Nevertheless, as the Second Vatican Council was about to start, the leaders of the liturgical renewal were unanimous in their opinion that celebrating Mass facing the people would be a return to the practice of the Church in antiquity. A Jesuit priest specialising in church architecture reported in 1961 that "there is a conviction that the early Christian practice will resume", adding that "the desire to celebrate facing the people is not just a fashionable archaic. One is convinced that this practice strengthens the experience of the eucharistic table-fellowship", citing Klauser in support of this.[11]

---

[8] NUSSBAUM 1965.
[9] For an extended treatment of *ressourcement*, see FAGGIOLI 2012.
[10] JUNGMANN 1949, 138. Cf also POCKNEE 1963, 88-100.
[11] MUCK 1961, 57.

But are the conclusions of Klauser and Nussbaum regarding early Church practice incontrovertible? We shall see that they are not.

Early Eucharists

The earliest attested account of a Eucharist is found in 1 Cor 10:16-22 and 11:18-33. There the context is that of a meal. St Paul draws a distinction between 'participation in the body of Christ' and pagan sacrifices, between 'the table of the Lord' and 'the table of demons'. The distinctive purpose of 'the Lord's supper' is not to eat one's own food and get drunk, but – when they eat *this* bread and *this* cup – to share fellowship-communion and 'proclaim the Lord's death until he comes'.

Meals took place at that time with the host and guests reclining on couches, food being placed on low tables in front of them. When the main meal was over, the tables were removed for the *symposion*, the drinking session. Stefan Heid claims[12] that, in early church practice, a distinct 'sacral' table was carried in at this point for the purpose of celebrating a Eucharist, but there is no evidence for this.

Although *anaphora*s – Eucharistic prayers – appear as early as the late-first-century Didache, the meal context for the celebration of the Eucharist lasted for a long time, 'the transition from full meal to symbolic rite... taking place before the middle of the second century in some places, after the middle of the third century in others, and probably chiefly related to the relative size of the congregation'[13]. In north Africa, Tertullian, writing c. 200 CE, talks of an evening *convivium dominicum* or *cena Dei* – God's supper[14]. But ten years later he describes a morning assembly at which the 'sacrament of the Eucharist' is distributed by the *praesidentes* – an occasion that must

---

[12] HEID 2019, 31.
[13] BRADSHAW 2012, 58.
[14] Tertullian, *Ad uxorem* II, 4, 2; 8, 8; *De spectaculis* 13, 4. There are conflicting views on whether these evening celebrations should be described as 'Eucharistic': cp BRADSHAW 2012, 31-32 with HEID 2019, 110-111.

have taken place without a meal, and in a more formal setting.[15] Cyprian of Carthage, writing some 50 years afterwards, insisted that the entire community gather for the Eucharist: 'we cannot celebrate the full truth of the sacrament if we do not have all the brethren present'. Therefore, he says, they must celebrate in the morning.[16]

As long as the Eucharist took place in connection with a meal, the orientation of its participants would have been centripetal. Once it became separate, it became more ritualized. Larger numbers celebrating under the leadership of a bishop would naturally have required some ordered configuration appropriate for worship. Cyprian refers to an area where the clergy gathered, and this may have also been where the movable altar was situated.[17] He also refers to a pulpit from which the gospel was read.[18]

Early Christian conventions of orientation

We can only conjecture that the first Christians may have adopted the prevailing Jewish custom regarding the direction of prayer. Earlier, when the Jews had been in exile, there had been a tradition of prayer facing Jerusalem – and indeed we read in Daniel of his prayer in exile, when 'he went to his house where he had windows in his upper chamber open toward Jerusalem; and he got down upon his knees three times a day and prayed and gave thanks before his God' (Dn 6:10). But there was also a tradition of praying towards the east, specifically of giving praise to God at the time of sunrise.[19] In Ezekiel's vision, 'the glory of the God of Israel was coming from the east' (Ez 43:2).

---

[15] JENSEN 2019, 41; cf. Cyprian, *De corona* 3, 3.
[16] JENSEN 2019, 42; cf Cyprian, *Epistolae*, 63, 16, 1.
[17] Cyprian, *Epistolae*, 54 (or 59), 18, 1. 'Quid superest quam ut ecclesia Capitolio cedat et recedentibus sacerdotibus ac Domini altare removentibus in cleri nostri sacrum venerandumque congestum simulacra atque idola cum aris suis transeant?'
[18] Cyprian, *Epistolae*, 33 (or 38), 2; 34 (or 39), 4.
[19] See WALLRAFF 2006, 155-165, here 157. See also WALLRAFF 2001 and LANG 2008, 35-47. BARKER 2003 claims (77) that facing east to pray dates back to the first Jerusalem

Naturally, in the city of Jerusalem, there needed to be some other focus
for orientation, other than the city itself. This was the Mount of Olives,
which is to the east of Jerusalem. There is evidence that the Essenes and
some other Jewish groups prayed facing east. After the destruction of
Jerusalem temple in the year 70 AD, the Jewish expectation of the coming
of Messiah shifted from Jerusalem to 'the east'.

With such an inconsistent Jewish background, it is not surprising that
there is no sure guide to Christian practice in the earliest Church, in
which the Jewish tradition of prayer naturally had a strong influence.
Jesus had ascended to heaven from the Mount of Olives and, with the
imminent expectation of his return, his Second Coming was expected
at that location. However, not only the destruction of 70 CE, but also
the gradual distancing of Christian prayer from its Jewish foundations,
led to a preference for the east over Jerusalem as the direction of prayer.
There was a corresponding reaction in Judaism to prefer a Jerusalem
orientation thereafter as a distinction from Christian practice.

The earliest specific mention of Christian prayer towards the east is
found in the apocryphal Acts of Paul, dating from c. 160 CE, where, in
the description of his purported martyrdom, he is described thus:

> Then Paul stood with his face to the east and lifted up his
> hands unto heaven and prayed a long time.[20]

Tertullian, writing in 197 CE, speaks of 'our well-known habit of
praying towards the east'.[21] From the third century onwards there is
little doubt about Christian prayer facing east. The clearest account is
from Origen, writing in the year 231:

---

temple, which was destroyed by Nebuchadnezzar in 587 BCE. See the whole of chapter 5
in her book, 'The Temple Roots of the Christian Liturgy'.
[20] Cited in KELLER 1989, 119-120.
[21] Tertullian, *Apologeticum*, 16.

And now we must add a few remarks on the direction in which we should face while praying... It should be immediately clear that the direction of the rising sun obviously indicates that we ought to pray inclining in that direction, an act which symbolises the soul looking towards where the true light rises.[22]

And indeed it was not lost on Christians in the long era of persecution that the time would come when 'the dawn from on high will break upon us, to give light to those who sit in darkness' (Lk 1:78-79).[23] As Origen expresses this hope:

Your propitiation came from the east. From there came the man whose name is the Dawn, who became the mediator between God and man. This invites you to keep looking to the east, where the sun of righteousness rises for you, where the light is always dawning for you.[24]

Of particular interest is the Syrian *Didascalia*, which dates from about 230 CE. This describes how priests, with the bishop in their midst, should sit in the easternmost part of the nave, then laymen behind them, then women at the back(!), so that when they stand up to pray together, the priests take the lead and the laity follow. 'For it is required that you pray toward the east, as knowing that which is written: "Give ye glory to God, who rideth upon the heaven of heavens toward the east" [Ps 67:34 LXX].'[25] Thus the whole congregation faced east, even the bishop in his *cathedra*, then located in the nave of the church.

---

[22] Quotation from Origen, *De oratione*, 32, as printed in LANG 2008, 46.
[23] The Greek word used in this sentence, *anatolē*, can mean both 'sunrise' and 'the east'. The corresponding Latin term is *oriens*; one of the great Advent 'O' antiphons addressed to Christ begins 'O Oriens'.
[24] Origen, *Homilia* 9,5.10: this is the Second Reading of the Office of Readings for Monday of the 4th week of Lent.
[25] *Didascalia Apostolorum*, tr. R. Hugh Connolly, Oxford: Clarendon Press, 1929, ch. 12. Literal translation of LXX.

The first churches

When Constantine recognised Christianity in 313 there was at long last the opportunity for public buildings to be used for Christian worship. And what building types were instantly available? Basilicas, used commonly for business and for settling legal disputes. These were long buildings, customarily oriented east-west, with the doors opening towards the east: even though Romans formally worshipped in temples, the veneration of the rising sun, common to many religions, was common practice here in Rome. The western end of basilicas was shaped into an apse, at the centre of which was a throne from which the magistrate would pronounce judgement.

Within weeks of Emperor Constantine's victory at the Milvian Bridge he commissioned the Lateran basilica in honour of the Emperor of Heaven. It was consecrated in 318. How easily the bishop, newly respected by the Roman state, assumed the throne in the apse vacated by the magistrate![26] The traditional position of the bishop's *cathedra* in the apse of his cathedral was thus established at this early date.

In 324, another new basilica, ordered by Constantine to be built over the tomb of St Paul the Apostle, was consecrated: St Paul's outside the Walls. Like the Lateran basilica, it used the Roman traditional east-west orientation with the doors at the eastern end. But veneration of the tomb was popular, and it proved far too small for the number of pilgrims visiting it. By the end of the century the original building had been demolished and replaced by a much larger one, this time oriented in the opposite direction in accordance with developing Christian practice.

---

[26] Earlier, about the year 265, Paul of Samosata, bishop of Antioch, 'was censured by his congregation because in both architecture and ritual he surrounded himself with the trappings of a Roman magistrate' (DOIG 2008, 19).

The vast original St Peter's basilica, also ordered by Constantine, was probably finished about 329.[27] It, too, had an east-west orientation with the doors at the eastern end; both the lie of the land and the fact that the doors faced the city of Rome have ensured that this orientation has remained to this day. But it was built over a cemetery, and it was always intended to be a *martyrium* in honour of the supposed burial place of St Peter, and therefore as a pilgrimage church, where the celebration of the Eucharist was secondary. 'The altar was not part of the apostle's shrine, and was probably a moveable table standing under the triumphal arch at the entrance to the nave.'[28]

In addition, Constantine also ordered the construction of a circular *rotunda* over the site of Jesus' tomb in Jerusalem – known thereafter as the 'anastasis rotunda' and the site of the Church of the Holy Sepulchre today. Another *martyrium* was the 5th century the Roman church of Santo Stefano Rotondo, which was also built to a circular design, with the altar over the tomb in the centre of the church. As at St Peter's, the liturgy there was secondary to veneration at the supposed tomb of St Stephen.

Nave altars

Contrary to popular misconceptions, altars were not always placed within the apse space of early churches. Indeed, nave altars are found in North Africa. A mosaic of the 'mother church' of Thabraca clearly shows an altar in the middle of the church (see below).[29] Augustine's cathedral at Hippo had an altar similarly located.[30] So also at Carthage where, in a sermon delivered there on 23 January 404, he describes how he would have preferred to have preached from the altar space, rather than from the pulpit situated in or alongside the apse, but the crowd

---

[27] DOIG 2008, 28.
[28] Id., 29.
[29] JENSEN 2015, 104-107; LANG 2009, 82. HEID 2019, 211 says that it is only a martyr's tomb. But altars were often built over them.
[30] JENSEN 2019, 52-54.

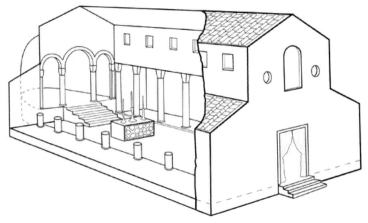

The church at Thabraca, North Africa, c. 400 – mosaic & reconstruction

was out of control, and he was unable to persuade those around the altar to come forward and fill the space between the apse and the altar.[31]

There is no doubt that Augustine subscribed to the established Christian tradition of praying towards the east.[32] It is often noted that many of his

---

[31] Augustine, *Sermon 359B*, 3-6 – HILL 1997, 332-335.
[32] Cf Augustine's 'On the Sermon on the Mount', 2, 18: 'When we stand at prayer, we turn to the east, whence the heaven rises: not as if God also were dwelling there, in the sense

sermons end with a prayer, introduced by *"conversi ad Dominum"*. This has been universally interpreted as a command to the congregation to turn and face the east, whichever direction that might be in relation to the orientation of the church. That would be awkward in Augustine's own cathedral at Hippo, which lay on a north-west–south-east axis: such a command, if understood literally, would have had them face diagonally across the back of the church. But the Latin words do not actually consist of a command; rather they address the people as those who have (already? recently?) been converted to the Lord. Nonetheless, Augustine states quite specifically:

> Doesn't God say, "Be converted to me"?... No, it isn't just saying that you, who were looking toward the west, should now look to the east – that's easily done. If only you also did it inwardly, because that is not easily done! You turn your body from one point of the compass to another; turn your heart around from one love to another.[33]

Note that *"conversi ad Dominum"* was an introduction to a prayer, with which Augustine concluded his sermon and/or introduced the dismissal of the catechumens or the Prayer of the Faithful.[34] It was not therefore an invitation to the people to turn east for the Eucharistic Prayer. It appears that at least some of Augustine's sermons were not preached in the course of a Mass. Even if they were, the people would have turned back to the face the altar for the following offertory of gifts.

---

that He who is everywhere present, not as occupying space, but by the power of His majesty, had forsaken the other parts of the world; but in order that the mind may be admonished to turn to a more excellent nature, i.e. to God, when its own body, which is earthly, is turned to a more excellent body, i.e. to a heavenly one.'

[33] Augustine, *Sermon 130A*, 12 – HILL 1997, 126.

[34] E.g. 'Turned to the Lord [*Conversi ad Dominum*], let us pray. May he look upon us and perfect us by his saving word...' (*Sermon 20B*, 11 – HILL 1997, 35). See also the commentary in the extended end-note printed in *id*, 128-130.

But on which side of a nave altar did the bishop/priest stand for the
Eucharistic Prayer? Augustine tells us that in Hippo the people would
stand all around the altar, which was surrounded by altar-rails (*cancelli*)
to keep them at bay, and over which the deacons would distribute
communion. It would have been easiest for the bishop and priests to
descend from their places in the apse and for the bishop to stand on that
side of the altar. But was the apse-orientation of the church considered
a virtual 'east', even if it was not geographical east?

Augustine is very aware that 'the one and only priest' is Jesus Christ
himself, and that he, as bishop, is, together with his people, a member
of the body of Christ. In the Old Testament, the high priest used to
enter the holy of holies just once a year, while all the people stood
outside. 'Are you nowadays outside, while the bishops stand at the
altar, and not watching inside, and hearing and attesting and
receiving?'[35] We can only surmise that Augustine's customary 'easterly'
orientation for prayer would have prevailed and that everyone would
have faced the apse with him for the Eucharistic Prayer.

Additional support for apse-directed celebration at the altar is found in
the remains of the a late fifth-century basilica at the ancient site of
Castellum Tingitanum in Mauretania Caesariensis. Discovered about
a third of the way down the nave, the mosaic's central panel depicts a
rectangular table set upon two columns within a field filled with vines,
fruit, and birds. Most scholars presume that the panel demarcated the
altar area, with the actual altar placed directly on the image of the table.
Its orientation indicates that only someone looking toward the apse
would view the table as upright.[36]

Nave altars may not have been an exclusively African practice. Eusebius
described the Tyre basilica's 'Holy of Holies' (constructed ca. 315) as in the

---

[35] Augustine, *Sermon 198*, 49, 53-54, 57 – HILL 1997, 218-224. 'Attesting' would be by
means of the Great Amen at the end of the Eucharistic Prayer; 'receiving' refers to Holy
Communion.
[36] JENSEN 2015, 110; JENSEN 2019, 56-59.

building's centre and protected by a wooden screen from the gathered congregation.[37] Rome's SS. Apostoli Basilica also had an altar in the centre until the sixteenth century, following a long-standing tradition that it had been in that place from its first construction in the third century.[38] Rome's Constantinian churches sited the altar at the chord of the nave and transept, or just at the opening of the presbyterium. The altar at the Lateran basilica was positioned at this juncture and still stands there today.

However, some ancient Roman churches (e.g. Santa Sabina and San Clemente) had an enclosed area built out from the apse and altar into the nave to accommodate the choir, with two *ambones* or pulpits built into the *cancelli* or walls of the area, for the reading of the epistle and gospel. This enclosing of the choir and clergy within a chancel (word derived from *cancelli*) resulted in and symbolised a clerical liturgy in which the laity took no active part.

Later, towards the early Middle Ages, there is evidence that in a few places a 'people's' altar in the centre of the church was occasionally used; there was one in the old cathedral at Cologne[39]. Another still stands to this day in the middle of the nave of Sant' Apollinare in Classe at Ravenna (see photo 1), purportedly over the place where St Apollinaris was martyred. It was restored in 1753[40]; there was an earlier altar 'in the middle of the lower choir'.[41]

It is noteworthy that where there were nave altars the bishop and his clergy would descend from their elevated seats in the apse to receive the people's gifts at the offertory, and would remain among them for the Liturgy of the Eucharist. The faithful would be ranged all about the altar – as the Roman Canon says, *circumstantes*, standing around.

---

[37] Eusebius, *Eccl. Hist.* 10.4.42.
[38] Hugo Brandenburg, *Ancient Churches of Rome* (Turnhout: Brepols, 2005), 64.
[39] GERHARDS 1999, 13-14.
[40] *Blue Guide: Northern Italy*, A & C Black, London, 1991, 417. Here it is called 'the altar of Archbishop Maximian', who built the church.
[41] HEID 2019, 278. The altar at San Vitale, Ravenna, is similarly placed today.

When in Rome...

Some early Roman churches followed the example of St Paul's outside
the Walls and had their original west-facing orientation reversed, e.g.
San Lorenzo outside the Walls and San Marcello al Corso. But in
remaining churches with a westerly orientation, the people began to
face the apse and only the priest, following the ancient tradition,
continued to face east, and therefore face the people. Pope Gregory the
Great (pope 590-604) somewhat confused the situation by building in
his St Peter's basilica a 'confession' – a burial crypt beneath the high
altar with its entrance directly in front of it, so that the celebrant was
obliged to celebrate facing the people over the altar and the crypt
entrance.

There is no detailed description of the Roman rite until the *Ordo
Romanus I*, dating from c. 700. Interpretation of this text is complicated
by later Gallican amendments to it. The earliest extant version states
simply that the pontiff faces east, which in a Roman west-oriented
church, would mean facing down the church towards the doors – note
that the privilege of a pontiff to celebrate facing the people is very
ancient and was once reserved to him alone.[42]

A later recension of *Ordo Romanus I* refers to east-oriented churches.
When the choir has finished singing the *Kyrie eleison*,

> the pontiff turns himself round towards the people
> (*dirigens se contra populum*), and begins, *Gloria in excelsis*,
> if it be the season for it, and at once turns back again to
> the east (*regyrat se ad orientem*) until it be finished. Then,
> after turning again to the people, he says, *Peace be to you*,
> and once more turning to the east, says, *Let us pray*, and
> the collect follows.[43]

---

[42] Cf LANG 2009, 92-93; HEID 2019, 332-338.
[43] *Ordo Romanus I*, para. 9. Translation by E. G. Atchley, Oxford University Press, 1905.

The pope would be standing at his cathedra in the centre of the apse for this, so in an eastward-facing church he would be praying towards the very close wall of the apse.

We can conclude that praying facing the people was an exception, not the norm, which contradicts the findings of Otto Nussbaum circulating at the time of the Second Vatican Council. Encouraged by his mentor, Klauser, he had researched the archaeological evidence of early churches on the basis that Mass facing the people was the standard unless proved otherwise, whereas more recent research has concluded that Mass with both priest and congregation facing eastwards for prayer was in fact the norm unless specifically contradicted.[44]

The apse and beyond, focus of liturgical worship

In any case, it was not the geographical direction of the church but the church's apse that would have determined the direction of prayer within it. In an exhaustively researched paper, Stefan Heid has shown that the elaborate apse mosaics of early Roman churches made prayer in their direction inevitable, whatever the topographical orientation of the church.[45]

It should also be noted that altars were generally located not within the semi-circular floor area delimited by the apse, but in front of it.[46] When the priest summoned the people to prayer with *"sursum corda"* ("lift up your hearts"), he would not be standing under the apse but would have it in front of him. The people would join him in raising their hands and eyes towards the cross in the apse mosaic standing on its heavenly blue

---

[44] LANG 2008, 61-65. He cites METZGER 1971, who had concluded that it was in only 20 out of 560 churches examined (not Nussbaum's 192) that the celebration *versus populum* is demonstrable. See also JUNGMANN 1951, I, 255-259; HEID 2019, 435-462. Nussbaum later (1971) accepted that both Mass with priest and people facing the same way, and Mass *versus populum*, were legitimate forms of Eucharistic celebration (GERHARDS 2001, 200).
[45] HEID 2006.
[46] See illustrations in HEID 2019, *passim*.

background (see photo 1): "We have lifted them up to the Lord". They would be joining the apostles or titular saints of the church depicted on the lower levels of the mosaic with their uplifted hands. Thus 'the apse dome became the most important element of church decoration in the most intimate, holiest moment of liturgical activity – prayer'. The earthly liturgy was aspiring to a heavenly liturgy. 'When Christ was portrayed here between the apostles and martyrs, it was not a mere representation of Christ but his epiphany presence as counterpart to the praying church.'[47]

The priest, conscious of standing with the heavenly mosaic in front of him, would say (as he still does in the Roman Canon): "with eyes raised to heaven to you, O God, almighty Father, command that these gifts be borne by the hands of your holy angel to your altar on high *so that* all of us, who through this participation at [this] altar receive the most holy Body and Blood of your Son, may be filled with every grace and heavenly blessing".[48] The people would not be bothering about what the priest was doing at the altar, for there was nothing to see there: the elevation of the host and chalice would not be introduced for many centuries.[49] But then as now the people wished to have something to see – especially as they could probably hear very little in a large church, and even then in Latin, a language which increasingly they did not understand. What they saw in the apse mosaic was a plain or gemmed cross against a blue sky. They prayed for the heavens to be opened as they were at Stephen's martyrdom (Acts 6) and for a vision of Christ in glory (see photo 2). Some churches had processions of saints displayed on the walls, all on their way towards the apse. The beauty of the church and its artistry were an integral part of the worship being offered.

---

[47] HEID 2006; see also HEID 2019, 354-359, 367-371.
[48] Original italics. Cf MAZZA 1986, 83.
[49] The elevation at the doxology dates from the seventh century, but its purpose was principally a gesture of oblation. The elevation of the host after the consecration only began in the early 13th century; that of the chalice only became obligatory in Pius V's 1570 Missal.

In churches with the apse facing east, there were windows in the apse to let in the light of the rising sun. St Ambrose said that the Christian may be like a house of God with windows open to the east, so that the eyes of the Lord may look in.[50]

The orientation of churches was taken very seriously in many countries. Practically every pre-Reformation church in England faced east, even athwart the lie of the land (e.g. Durham cathedral).[51] It was thought that in the opposite direction (west) was the devil[52], which helps to explain why cathedrals like that at Wells have such a splendid army of statues of saints adorning the west front to do battle with the devil's lot and keep them out. That is also reflected in the ancient baptismal liturgy, where the rite of *apotaxis* (renunciation of Satan) took place facing west, and that of *syntaxis* (acceptance of Christ) towards the east.[53]

The Cross and the Parousia

The earliest use of the cross as a Christian symbol is to be found not in a pictorial representation of the cross of Christ – whatever shape that might have been – but in the *orans* gesture of early Christians holding out their arms each side of them when they prayed.[54] The cross, painted on a wall as a sign of easterly direction may have been known in Syria as early as the second century[55].

The cross became a standard and significant feature in apse mosaics, as a symbolic gateway to heaven and imaged focus of priest and people as

[50] Ambrose, *Expositio in Psalmis*, 6,19. Quoted in HEID 2006.
[51] Cf KIECKHEFER 2004, 181.
[52] KUNZLER 1995, 147.
[53] GERHARDS 2017, 334. It is still the custom in the Church of England to turn and face east for the recitation of the Creed; this may originate from such a baptismal ritual.
[54] Cf HEID 2006.
[55] Cf KELLER 1989, 131-137, citing PETERSON 1959, 1-35. JENSEN 2015, 114 disputes the dating, and Keller acknowledges (132) that a fifth or sixth century date is better supported.

they prayed the liturgy. But it was also an integral part of the overall significance of church orientation, namely, as an eschatological symbol, a symbol of the *parousia* or Second Coming of Christ at the end of time. Cyril of Jerusalem (c. 350 AD) concludes one of his lectures on the Creed with these words: 'This [the cross] shall appear again with Jesus from heaven; for the trophy shall precede the king... that we may glory, exulting in the Cross...'[56]

Note that these apse crosses have no figure on them. A few have gems, some have a medallion of the head of Christ in the centre. But this usage is the origin of the altar cross. It only became obligatory for the altar cross to carry an image of the *corpus* of Christ in 1746.[57]

Apse and reredos

Erwin Keller nicely sums up the heritage of liturgical building we have been describing:

> The eastward direction of prayer as a visible outward gesture expressing the inner direction of prayer and worship of the coming Lord has also had an impact in Christian church building, from the orientation towards the east to the arrangement and meaning of the church as the image of the heavenly Jerusalem, in which the Church in her liturgy participates by signs and rites and in its sacraments, and which she herself actually is, until Christ comes and receives his own in fulfilled form into the heavenly Jerusalem.[58]

In eastern rite churches, the architectural and artistic context of the liturgy developed into a distinct sanctuary ('Holy of Holies') and nave

---

[56] Cyril of Jerusalem, *Catecheses*, 13, 41.
[57] Decree of Pope Benedict XIV, *Accepimus* (16 July 1746).
[58] KELLER 1989, 147.

('Holy Place') joined by the iconostasis, with the depictions of *Christus pantocrator* in the vault of the central dome, directing their prayers both eastwards and heavenwards, above their heads.

In the west, decorated apse vaults continued until the twelfth century.[59] But then architects became more interested in grandeur than liturgical artistry. 'The Gothic style has everything and nothing to do with the liturgy' for 'the functions and architectural forms of the Gothic great churches showed remarkably little interaction.'[60] The architects' concept was of soaring pointed arches reaching towards heaven, and of churches resplendent with light from the vast expanses of glass with which they filled the walls of their cathedrals.

At ground level, altars retreated closer and closer to the east wall. Dwarfed by the immensity of architecture around it, the liturgy was performed by the clergy in ever longer choirs from which the people were excluded, eventually closed off by rood screens through which they had to squint to see and adore the host being elevated at the consecration in the distance.

But the apsidal mosaics were not completely forgotten. Already, by the eleventh century, altarpieces were evolving in the form of reredoses or retables.[61] Early Italian examples showed an artistic continuity with Byzantine art, especially after the import of icons from the east after the fall of Constantinople to the Fourth Crusade in 1204. These often adorned the increasing number of side altars in larger churches, so were accessible to the people in a way that high altars in their distant sanctuaries were not. But side altars increasingly faced the nearest wall: the symbolism of orientation had been lost.

---

[59] And not forgotten thereafter: see the image of the victorious Christ in the apsidal vault of Christopher Wren's late-17th century St Paul's Cathedral, London.

[60] DOIG 2008, 69, quoting WILSON 1990, 9. For a more positive appraisal of Gothic architecture, see SEASOLTZ 2015, 120.

[61] JUNGMANN 1951, I, 109, note 37. A reredos is a floor-standing structure behind the altar; a retable stands on the rear side of the altar table.

In the fourteenth century this form of art developed into the triptych and polyptych. While many of these depicted the saint(s) to whom the relevant altar was dedicated, others developed wider themes. The famous 1432 van Eyck altarpiece in Ghent cathedral, with 12 internal panels, shows the feast of the Lamb in heaven, and above it a figure of Christ seated in majesty. The basic composition (the Lamb, the green fields, the blue sky, the victorious Christ) has much in common with the apse mosaics in Ravenna and elsewhere. It is a stunning vision of heavenly worship, of which earthly liturgy is but an anticipation. In both apse and altarpiece there is a sense of directing the celebration of the liturgy at the altar towards a God who is 'beyond', where the liturgy is destined to find its ultimate fulfilment.

From Counter-Reformation to Gothic revival

After the humanism of the Renaissance and the jolt given to the Catholic Church by the Reformation, a new imagery for 'heaven on earth' developed in the Baroque style, particularly in Rome itself. Away went the choir stalls and rood screens (retained by the Church of England and in Scandinavia) and instead there were vast open spaces with ceilings and domes decorated with angels pointing heavenwards, with the aid of *trompe l'œil*. The picture galleries in church ceilings were certainly uplifting, but had now lost all connection with the liturgy being celebrated at ground level. In any case, this was now celebrated in tiny sanctuaries from which the choir (if any) had been banished to remote musicians' galleries. The standard form of Mass had now become the Low Mass, or even a private Mass celebrated with a single server.

In England, the Catholic Emancipation Act of 1829 eventually permitted the public building of Catholic churches, and Augustus Welby Pugin promptly came upon the scene to promote a revival of Gothic architecture, Victorian style. But by then the Mass was understood as the holy sacrifice being offered by the priest *for* the people, present or absent, and as the means by which the Blessed

Sacrament, housed in the tabernacle in the centre of the high altar, could be 'confected' and made present, and exposed in a monstrance on a magnificent throne rising above and behind the altar.

The Development of the Tabernacle

In the early Church, deacons and commissioned lay people took the Communion bread to their homes to give to the sick, but after Constantine the preferred containers for the reservation of the Eucharistic bread were gold doves, either contained in a silver tower housed in a *sacrarium* (sacred place) away from the central body of the church, or suspended under the baldachino over the altar.

The theological controversies of the twelfth century regarding sacramental presence in the Eucharist resulted in a decree of the Fourth Lateran Council of 1215, stating that it should be reserved in a closed container. At first a wall-mounted aumbry sufficed, but by the fifteenth century, there were elaborate stone 'sacrament houses', of which examples can still be seen in Germany and Belgium, some of them restored more recently to their original use.

It was only at the beginning of the sixteenth century that this 'tabernacle' came to be placed on an altar – and indeed on the high altar. This occurred first in northern Italy, at Siena and Venice.[62] In 1542, the powerful bishop of Verona, Gian Matteo Giberti, alarmed by the Lutheran reform in northern Europe, decreed that a wooden tabernacle should appear on the high altar of every parish church of his diocese.[63] The Council of Trent emphasized the theological and sacramental properties of the Eucharist, but in reference to its reservation merely stated that it was to be kept in a *sacrarium*: the location of this sacred place was up to the local bishop. Then St Charles Borromeo, archbishop of Milan, approving of Giberti's initiative, decreed in 1577

---

[62] REISS 2005, 405.
[63] NAGEL 2011, 239.

that in more important churches such a tabernacle should be made of gilded silver or bronze, or of precious marble.[64] The new edition of the *Rituale Romanum* in 1614, for use throughout the Catholic Church, decreed that the tabernacle 'should be located on the high altar, or on another altar, more convenient (*commodius*) for the veneration and worship of such a great sacrament, but so that it did not constitute an impediment for other sacred functions and ecclesiastical duties'.[65]

Indeed, the tabernacle became the focal point of devotion – and of church design itself. The altar became a throne for it, and there are many examples of Victorian Gothic altars in which the apex of the design of the whole church is a throne for the monstrance, for Exposition of the Blessed Sacrament. Here was the presence of the Lord *versus populum*, facing the people for their adoration. At the annual Forty Hours devotion, organised on a diocesan rota system, Mass was said *coram Sanctissimo*, at the altar in front of the Blessed Sacrament exposed in the monstrance mounted above it, necessitating an extraordinary number of genuflections by the priest and ministers in the course of the Mass. Just as some liturgical celebrations at the time of Mozart and Haydn had become 'church concerts with liturgical accompaniment'[66], so here was devotional adoration of the Blessed Sacrament overreaching and obscuring its liturgical basis.

Liturgical Renewal from Guéranger to Parsch

A pioneer of liturgical renewal in the nineteenth century was Dom Prosper Guéranger (1805-1875), abbot of Solesmes. His revival of Gregorian chant and of the Roman liturgy at Solesmes had two consequences. One was Pope Pius X's decree *Tra le sollecitudini*, issued only months after he became Pope in 1903.[67] In it he declared his

---

[64] Charles Borromeo, *Instructiones Fabricae et Supellectilis Ecclesiasticae*, ed. Evelyn Carol Voelker, Book I, 35.
[65] *Rituale Romanum*, 1614 edition, 61. The wording is repeated almost exactly in the 1917 edition of the Code of Canon Law.
[66] JUNGMANN 1951, I, 149.
[67] See the letter he sent to the Vicar General of Rome along with *Tra le sollecitudini*.

earnest desire that the faithful should find the Christian spirit 'in its first and indispensable source, which is active participation in the most holy mysteries and in the public and solemn prayer of the Church'[68]. As an implementation of this, they were to join in the singing of the common parts of the Mass in Gregorian chant.

The other consequence – which Guéranger could not have foreseen – was the beginning of a wider movement for liturgical renewal. Two of the nineteenth-century visitors to Solesmes were the brothers Maurus and Placidus Wolter; they entered Beuron Abbey on Germany and became its first two abbots. Maurus initiated liturgical renewal and art at Beuron – and also at Maredsous in Belgium, founded from Beuron in 1872. There the first Latin-French missal was published in 1882; the first Latin-German missal, edited by a Beuronese monk, appeared in the following year. This was indeed progress: Pope Alexander VII had in 1661 condemned a translation of the Roman Missal into French and had forbidden any further translations under pain of excommunication; Pope Pius IX renewed the ban in 1857, but later thought better of it.

In 1906 Dom Lambert Beauduin entered Mont César abbey, founded from Maredsous in 1888. He had been a diocesan priest and labour chaplain, and was invited to speak at a conference held at Malines in 1909. His lecture was entitled 'The true prayer of the Church'. Its immediate impact encouraged him to launch a monthly periodical for clergy and laity in both French[69] and Flemish: this was a runaway success, such that Beauduin's lecture is considered as an early milestone of the liturgical movement.

---

[68] 'I fedeli si radunano per attingere tale spirito dalla sua prima ed indispensabile fonte, che è la partecipazione attiva ai sacrosanti misteri e alla preghiera pubblica e solenne della Chiesa'.
[69] *Questions liturgiques* (from 1922 *Questions liturgiques et paroissiales*). Beauduin himself was the first editor.

52

Another monastery founded from Beuron was at Maria Laach in Germany, where Ildefons Herwegen, abbot from 1913, encouraged both his own monks and visitors to study the liturgy and foster its renewal. Among them were Dom Odo Casel, author of the classic *The Mystery of Christian Worship*, and Romano Guardini, whom we shall meet in the next chapter.

In Austria, a major figure in the liturgical renewal was Pius Parsch (1884-1954), a Canon Regular of Klosterneuburg Abbey. He was an army chaplain in the First World War, and his experience of saying Mass for the troops on the battlefield led him to a commitment to promote the active participation of the laity in the liturgy. In his brief autobiography[70] he singles out Ascension Day 1922 as the launch of his apostolate. 'That was the first lay liturgical celebration of the Mass in German-speaking territory', he claims. It took place in the chapel of St Gertrude in the village of Klosterneuburg, which became the nucleus of his work.

It was not until 1935 that Parsch, working with architect Robert Kramreiter (1905-1965), had the opportunity to reorder the chapel and relocate the altar to make it possible to celebrate Mass facing the people. Even then the altar space was – and still is – very restricted, being enclosed behind a narrow triumphal arch.

Parsch founded a publishing company and published a weekly booklet in German enabling people to follow the Mass – a forerunner of today's 'missalette'. He also wrote and published a number of books on the use of the bible in the liturgy, and on the liturgy itself. One of these was translated into English as *The Liturgy of the Mass*, and was reviewed in the quarterly journal of the Society of Saint Gregory in 1940.[71] This may

---

[70] His autobiographical chapter was written expressly for *The Book of Catholic Authors* (online at catholicauthors.com).
[71] In *Music and Liturgy*, 9/1 (1940), 30-31.

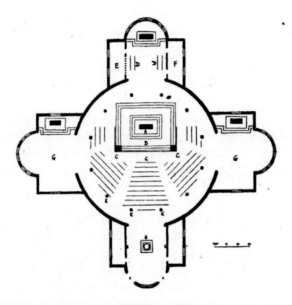

partly explain the appearance, three years later, of an article in the same journal by Fr James Crichton entitled 'A Dream-Church'.[72]

It was indeed a dream well before its time. The article included a floor plan (see above). The overall shape of the church may well have been inspired by Edwin Lutyens' design for a huge Liverpool Metropolitan Cathedral, on which building had already begun.[73]

> In my dream-church, of course, the altar is facing the people and the priest is facing the people.

---

[72] CRICHTON 1943.
[73] The building works halted for the Second World War and were abandoned after it. The crypt forms the base of the entirely different modern building completed in 1967.

'Of course'? His assertion must have caused much surprise at the time, though the article failed to generate any 'Letters to the Editor'.[74]

> There would be either no tabernacle [on the altar] (this might be accommodated on the retro-altar, used for weekday Mass and services) or a very low one.

The disposition of the people around three sides of the altar is notable.[75] There are two ambones at the corner of the altar space but no chair, since in the Order of Mass at that time the priest celebrated at the altar throughout.[76]

Needless to say, Crichton's 'dream-church' was never built. He was able to build a much smaller, square-dimensioned church for his parish at Pershore, completed in 1959. Even then, in the face of diocesan doubts, he had to insist on an altar facing the people (or rather, with the people arranged on three sides of the altar space), with a separate Blessed Sacrament altar for the tabernacle, and that was considered *avant-garde.*

Dialogue Mass

One feature of group Masses celebrated 'in the round' from 1921 by Abbot Herwegen, Pius Parsch, and – as we shall see in the next chapter – by Romano Guardini, was that they were 'dialogue' Masses. All present responded to the priest, instead of leaving it to the altar server. This vocal involvement of the congregation was somewhat grudgingly

---

[74] The same issue of *Music and Liturgy* contained articles for and against the use of English in the liturgy. Predictably, in 1943, these raised strongly emotional reactions.
[75] Eric Gill, for his church at Gorleston-on-Sea, built in 1938, envisaged people surrounding the altar on all four sides: see his article 'Mass for the Masses' in *The Cross and the Plough: The Organ of the Land Associations of England and Wales*, no 4 (1938). 'Wherever the altar is, there is the sanctuary, but as God came among men, so must the altar be...' (10).
[76] A *sedilia* was only used at Sung or High Mass for the priest to be seated while the singing of the 'Gloria' and 'Credo' was completed, or during a sermon given by another priest.

permitted by the Congregation of Rites in 1922, but Pope Pius XI celebrated a dialogue Mass in St Peter's basilica in that year, and wrote an encyclical in 1928, *Divini cultus,* recommending active participation in the liturgy. A warmer recommendation from the Congregation of Rites came in 1935. Dialogue Mass became the standard for communal Low Masses at Society of Saint Gregory Summer Schools from the following year,[77] but failed to 'catch on' elsewhere in England, and even in the 1950s was a rare event.

However, Dialogue Mass revealed a difficulty of communication. Even when the priest turned towards the congregation – at *'Dominus vobiscum'* – strict observance of the rubrics obliged him to keep his eyes to the ground.[78] For most other dialogues, he faced away from the people.

In 1943 Dom Lambert Beauduin assisted in the foundation of the Centre de Pastorale Liturgique in Paris, and was a member of the first editorial board of *La Maison-Dieu,* its quarterly journal which appeared for the first time in 1945. In the second issue of the journal there appeared an article by Canon M. Michaud of Lyon on Mass facing the people[79], which he advocated partly on the mistaken historical precedent examined earlier in this chapter, and partly for pastoral reasons. These were (1) to enable familiarity with the liturgy for children, (2) to enable the priest to face the people for all the dialogues in dialogued Masses. But he concludes that the use of an altar facing the people should be exceptional. The priest should not celebrate with his back to the tabernacle: the Blessed Sacrament should be temporarily moved to a lateral 'tower'. That raised another question.

---

[77] From the Society's minutes and brochures for its Summer Schools.
[78] *'demissis ad terram oculis', Ritus Servandus in celebratione Missae,* V, 1. This directive was often ignored by those priests who recognised what they were saying and why.
[79] MICHAUD 1945.

Altar v. Tabernacle

Is the central focus of a church the altar, or the tabernacle on it?

We have seen how Professor Klauser's 'Guiding Principles' were published by the German bishops in 1949, with its recommendation that Mass should be celebrated facing the people. There was, however, an obstacle to simply turning around the altar with its existing furniture: the presence of the tabernacle on it. Klauser's answer in his 'Guidelines' is twofold. First, he recommends that 'where possible, there is a place for the offering of the Eucharistic sacrifice separate from that where the Sacrament is venerated'[80]. A little later, he suggests that the altar 'may also have a tabernacle – all this should show clearly that the altar, perhaps emphasized by a ciborium [baldachino], is the holiest place in the church, the very heart and centre of everything in the church'[81].

Parsch was able to persuade his architect, Kramreiter, to mount the tabernacle in the lateral wall of the restricted altar space at Klosterneuburg. However, Kramreiter, although accepting that the altar was the principal focus of the church, insisted on having the tabernacle on it for all his other projects.[82] We shall see in chapter 4 that Rudolf Schwarz had the same conviction. Kramreiter's fellow-architect, Clemens Holzmeister (1886-1983), maintained to the end of his long life that the centre of a Catholic church is not the altar but the tabernacle.[83]

Pope Pius XII, in his allocution to the Liturgical Congress at Assisi in 1956, had this to say:

---

[80] KLAUSER 1965, 164.
[81] Id, 165.
[82] PACIK 2010, VII – XXVII.
[83] Id., fn. 57.

It is first of all through the sacrifice of the altar that the Lord makes himself present in the Eucharist and He is at the tabernacle only as *'memoria sacrificii et passionis suae'*. To separate the tabernacle from the altar is to separate two things, which must remain united by their origin and their nature. The manner in which the tabernacle may be placed on the altar without hindering the celebration of the people may receive various solutions upon which the specialists will give their opinion. The essential thing is to have understood that it is the same Lord who is present on the altar and at the tabernacle.[84]

This makes it clear that he had no objection to the celebration of Mass facing the congregation, but wished to retain the connection between altar and tabernacle.

The Congregation of Rites immediately took fright, and in the following year issued a decree entitled *'Sanctissimam Eucharistiam'*, in which it lays down the following:

A tabernacle should be firmly conjoined with an altar so that it is immovable. On an altar where the most Holy Eucharist is reserved, the Sacrifice of the Mass is to be habitually celebrated. In churches where only one altar exists, this cannot be constructed so that the priest may celebrate towards the people; but on that very altar, in the middle, a tabernacle for reserving the most Holy Eucharist should be located.[85]

The intention was clearly to enforce celebration on an altar with tabernacle, and thereby to discourage Mass facing the people. But some bishops insisted on a tabernacle placed on the main altar, and/or

---

[84] *Acta Apostolicae Sedis*, 23 (1956), 722. Author's translation from the original French.
[85] Sacred Congregation of Rites, Decree of 1 June 1957, no 2.

58   ORIENTATION

refused to allow Mass facing the people. In Basel-Riehen in Switzerland, the architect had provided a tabernacle in a niche behind the altar (facing the people). The local bishop demanded that it be replaced on the altar itself.[86]

Some churches in Germany tried to do their best with low tabernacles over which the priest faced the people:[87] As noted above, Fr Crichton envisaged one as a possibility in his 'dream church', but there were no such configurations in Britain. Clearly it was an unsatisfactory situation, and when the Vatican Council was called by Pope John XXIII in 1959, bishops looked for a more satisfactory solution to this, among many other matters of concern.

Towards the Second Vatican Council

Despite Pope Pius XII's warning about 'archaism' in his encyclical *Mediator Dei*[88], and Jungmann's reservations, published in 1949[89], the prevailing spirit of *ressourcement* encouraged the revival of liturgical practices supposed to be conventional in the Early Church.

In the 1950s, Mass facing the people became more common in France and Germany, even though hindered by the required presence of the tabernacle. We have seen one isolated instance in England; another was in the United States, where Archbishop Edwin O'Hara of Kansas City let it be known in 1951 that he would readily grant permission for 'field' Masses celebrated on temporary altars facing the people.[90]

However, as Dialogue Mass became more common, at least in some countries, it seemed more obvious that 'dialogue' required the addresser and addressee to face each other. While this was a welcome

[86] MUCK 1961, 60.
[87] Id., 57-63.
[88] Article 61.
[89] See note 10 above.
[90] ELLARD 1956, 114-115.

involvement of the people in the liturgy, did not the term 'Dialogue Mass' encourage the notion that the ritual of liturgy is primarily an interhuman dialogue between priest and people? Where is God?

What is surprising is the lack of critical analysis and evaluation of Mass facing the people in the 1950s.[91] The liturgical/theological journal *La Maison-Dieu* featured no articles on the topic between Canon Michaud's article in 1945 and the evaluation of the Vatican Council decrees. Nor is there any mention in *Liturgy*, the journal of the Society of Saint Gregory, which Crichton edited from 1945.

As we have seen, the experience of community Masses 'in the round' had been enjoyed since the 1920s, first by small groups at Maria Laach Abbey, and by larger groups of young people at Burg Rothenfels in the following years. The most influential pioneer of these was Romano Guardini, to whom we now turn.

---

[91] A letter by Paul Claudel protesting strongly at the growing use of Mass facing the people appeared in *Le Figaro* on 23 January 1955. Accessed 14 August 2019 on http://www.revue-item.com/12831.

Chapter 3

ROMANO GUARDINI

There is no doubt that one of the most significant precursors of the Second Vatican Council was Romano Guardini (1885-1968). Although he lived to witness the Council, his health did not permit him to take part in it.

He was hugely influential in academic circles from beginning his doctoral studies in 1912 to his retirement from Munich University in 1963, writing over seventy books and a hundred learned articles. For the purposes of this book, it is his contribution to the liturgical renewal that is of particular interest, especially regarding his theology of church community and its realisation in liturgical celebration.

Early awakening[1]

Guardini was born to an Italian family in Verona, Italy, in 1885, but within a year his family moved to Mainz, where his father was employed in the export-import business. He excelled at school and began his life at university studying chemistry. But it did not suit him,

---

[1] The principal sources for biographical detail in this chapter are Guardini's own memoirs, 'Berichte über mein Leben', written in 1945 and re-published in 5th edition most recently as GUARDINI 1995. Cf also KRIEG 1997 and DEBUYST 2008.

so he moved on to economics. When he failed to thrive at this, he fell into depression and also suffered a crisis of faith – a matter of great concern to his pious family. One of his friends from his school days, Karl Neundörfer, helped him, and out of their discussions, he underwent a conversion which he later compared with Augustine's. Within a matter of months he decided to become a priest. After a semester at the University of Freiburg, he began theological studies at Tübingen in October 1906.

More significantly, in 1907 he and Neundörfer paid a visit to the Benedictine abbey of Beuron. In his 1945 memoirs he describes it thus:

> My first visit there remains vivid in my memory. It was evening. We went from the railway station immediately to the monastery and received our rooms not in the guest wing, which was not yet built, but in the enclosure itself. Staying in the enclosure made our visit warm and living. In their simplicity the rooms were like home, with a great deal of dark wood and an indescribable element which made one feel a deep sense of well-being. We received something to eat and then went to Compline. The church was already dark with only a few candles in the choir. The monks stood in their places and prayed by heart the beautiful psalms of Compline which were then always monotoned. Through the whole church moved mystery, sacred and at the same time sheltering. I eventually saw that the liturgy has a great deal of power and glory, but at the beginning it was the simple door of Compline rather than the portals of majestic liturgical action [at Mass] that led [me] more intimately into the heart of the liturgy's holy world...

> I had learnt of the German mystics and loved them; but I had always thought that there must be another 'mystique' in which the intimacy (*Innigkeit*) of the mystery would be

combined with the vastness (*Grösse*) of the objective
forms. In Beuron and its liturgy I found it.[2]

He was so captivated that he registered as an oblate of Beuron and
maintained his connection there throughout his life. In subsequent
visits he questioned the monks about their life of liturgical prayer.

He later reminisced:

> These first impressions have continued through the
> whole of my life. They were all the more profound when
> the experience of the liturgy combined the knowledge of
> what the Church is and the further insight that Christian
> proclamation is effective in proportion to its expression
> of the sacred message, without compromise or
> adaptation.

> At the time we [Karl Neundörfer and I] adopted a plan,
> which we would sometime later fulfil, to present what
> 'Church' means: he would treat it from the side of canon
> law,... I would start with the liturgy, as the source and
> fundamental form (*Gestalt*) of contemplative life. As far
> as I was concerned, it didn't result in the grand 'theology
> of the liturgy' that I had projected, but all the same there
> were some writings such as *Vom Geist der Liturgie* [The
> Spirit of the Liturgy], *Liturgische Bildung* [Education in
> Liturgy] and some others...[3]

It is important to note that he intended to write about the Church by
writing about its liturgy.

---

[2] GUARDINI 1995, 85.
[3] GUARDINI 1923b, 20-21, and GUARDINI 1995, 86. Neundörfer was tragically killed in a
mountain accident in 1925.

On completion of his studies at Tübingen, he and Neundörfer entered the seminary at Mainz. At once they found the neoscholastic course in theology stuffy. Remonstrating with their superiors did not enamour them to the authorities, and their priestly ordinations were deferred by six months as a sign of disapproval – a disciplinary measure still in use in seminaries in the 1960s.

After ordination in 1910, Guardini served in parishes in Mainz before going to Freiburg to study for his doctorate, for which he chose to examine the thought of St Bonaventure. Doctorate completed in 1915, he thought he would be expected to teach theology in the Mainz diocesan seminary. But his diocesan authorities were concerned about the orthodoxy of his theology, and he was once more assigned to pastoral work in parishes. This time he had the opportunity for the pastoral care of young people in the Juventus movement, which led him to an important development, as we shall see.

His experience of the liturgy in his parishes was almost soul-destroying. While he celebrated Mass – and before the Blessed Sacrament exposed[4] – the faithful would silently pray the rosary or engage in their own devotions. He describes his reactions in his memoirs:

> The senselessness of this activity was unbearable, and I was able to avoid inner harm [only] by making myself insensitive to it.[5]

---

[4] This entailed placing the Eucharistic Host in a monstrance and setting it in a throne above the tabernacle, where it stood throughout Mass being celebrated on the altar in front of it. Guardini was obliged to say Mass in this way every day for two years, despite later admitting to personal difficulties regarding the devotional practice of Exposition of the Blessed Sacrament (cf GUARDINI 1995, 93, 97, 159). This practice survived in connection with Quarant' Ore (the Forty Hours' Devotion) until the Second Vatican Council. Quarant' Ore continues, but Mass in front of the Blessed Sacrament exposed is now forbidden (Instruction of the Sacred Congregation of Rites, 25 May 1967, *Eucharisticum Mysterium*, no 61). However, this ruling does not apply to Mass said according to the Extraordinary Form.

[5] GUARDINI 1995, 93.

It wasn't that he was unappreciative of private prayer and devotion, but the lack of a sense of community celebration hurt him deeply. It formed the backdrop and a motive for his first and most well-known book on liturgy, *Vom Geist der Liturgie*, published by the abbey of Maria Laach in 1918 as the first in a series, *Ecclesia Orans*. Its English translation, *The Spirit of the Liturgy*, was published in 1935.[6]

The Spirit of the Liturgy

When examining this short book, it is important to recognise the time in which it was written and Guardini's distinctive philosophical approach.

The Catholic Church had taken a very defensive, almost inquisitorial line against modernism after Pope Pius X's 1907 decree *'Lamentabili'*. Any deflection from a strict neoscholastic orthodoxy was frowned upon. Guardini was well aware that, after being sidelined into parish life in 1915, he would have to be careful about what he wrote and how he wrote it.

He had espoused an inductive approach to reality, based on the phenomenology of Edmund Husserl. Going beyond empirical reality, it investigates the essence of things and their interrelationships. These may be complex and involve opposing polarities – for example, the individual and his place in community, 'head' and 'heart', rational deduction and intuition.[7] At Tübingen he had also encountered the ecclesiology of Johann Adam Möhler (1796-1838), for whom 'there exist polarities between the individual believer and the whole assembly of the faithful, between the church's inner reality and its outer manifestations, its institutions and its rituals'.[8]

---

[6] GUARDINI 1935.
[7] Cf KRIEG 1997, 2-16.
[8] Id., 53.

So he paints his 'canvas' of the liturgy as he observes it and reflects on its inner essence. Abbot Ildefons Herwegen wrote in his Foreword to *Vom Geist der Liturgie*: 'The author does not want to start from the scientific concept of the liturgy, but from the concrete man and his "capacity for liturgy (*Liturgiefähigkeit*)". Above all, he intends to prepare a favourable ground, to make the soul receptive to all that the liturgy has been able to store up in its treasures.' The ability of modern man to worship by means of liturgical symbols was a continual concern of Guardini's. At the end of his life, he even wondered whether it was possible at all.[9]

In the first chapter of *The Spirit of the Liturgy* he carefully distinguishes liturgy as the public and objective worship of the Church as distinct from the private and more subjective prayer of the individual. Both are necessary. And both concern the individual, for 'it is of paramount importance that the whole gathering should take an active share in the [liturgical] proceedings'.[10] He credits Pope Pius X with the statement, "You should not pray at Mass; you should pray the Mass."[11] The liturgy is the expression of both the prayer life of the Church (*lex orandi*) and of belief (*lex credendi*).

He begins the second chapter thus: 'The liturgy does not say "I" but "We". The Church is more than the mere body of the faithful.'

> The faithful are actively united by a vital and fundamental principle common to them all. That principle is Christ Himself; His life is ours; we are incorporated in Him; we are His Body, '*Corpus Christi mysticum*'. The active force which governs this living unity, grafting the individual on to it, granting him a share in its fellowship and preserving this right for him,

---

[9] See above, 11.
[10] GUARDINI 1935, chapter 1.
[11] Ibid, footnote 1. The original authorship of this axiom is disputed.

is the Holy Ghost. Every individual Catholic is a cell of
this living organism or a member of this Body.[12]

In this short paragraph, Guardini anticipates by 25 years Pope Pius
XII's 1943 encyclical, *Mystici Corporis*.

He must have raised more than a few eyebrows by the title of the fifth
chapter, '*Liturgie als Spiel*' – literally 'Liturgy as a Game', more chastely
rendered in the English translation as 'The Playfulness of the Liturgy'.
What he is saying in this chapter is that the liturgy is creative, rather as
a child plays a game – that is, it has no functional purpose but is a free
act of praise. In the 1920 and subsequent editions of the book, Guardini
inserted an additional chapter after this one, entitled '*Vom Ernst der
Liturgie*', 'The Seriousness of the Liturgy', which gave him the
opportunity to make the important point that participation in the
liturgy is not an esoteric technique for the aesthete but a simple
openness to the mystery of the liturgical action being presented.[13]
Liturgy may indeed be beautiful, but 'it is only when we participate in
liturgical action with the earnestness begotten of deep personal interest
that we become aware of true liturgical beauty'.[14]

The meaning of the Church

In the autumn of 1920, with the permission of his bishop, Guardini
moved to the university of Bonn to write his '*Habilitationsschrift*', the
additional thesis required of German academics to qualify them for
teaching in universities. He again studied St Bonaventure, and in
January 1922 completed his work. His time at Bonn brought him into
contact with a number of top-level thinkers, including Max Scheler,
whom he received into the Catholic Church.

---

[12] Id, chapter 2.
[13] See above, chapter 1.
[14] GUARDINI 1935, chapter 6.

By then, Guardini was also involving himself in the liturgical scene. In 1921, Abbot Ildefons Herwegen founded at Maria Laach an association for the promotion of liturgical studies, which published its first yearbook in the same year. Guardini wrote an article for it on 'Systematic Method in Liturgical Studies'[15]. These, he says, are not just concerned with the history of liturgy, but have as their object of research 'the living, sacrificial, praying Church, which accompanies the mysteries of grace in its actual worship and in its binding statements in relation to it'.[16] As at Beuron, Guardini was seeing the liturgy as the Church in action, even defining the Church.

He then prepared and delivered in the summer of 1922 a course of lectures, immediately published as *Vom Sinn der Kirche*, 'On the meaning of the Church'[17] – dedicated, significantly, to 'Catholic youth'.

In his first lecture, he laments the perception of the Church exclusively as an authoritarian body, seeking to regulate the lives of its members as individuals – as Guardini had witnessed in his parish appointments in Mainz.

How little in divine worship were the faithful aware of themselves as fellowship! How inwardly disintegrated the fellowship was! How little was the individual conscious of the parish community, and in how individualistic a spirit was the very sacrament of fellowship – Communion – conceived![18]

---

[15] GUARDINI 1921.
[16] Cf HERMANS 1987, here 349-350.
[17] GUARDINI 1922; English translation included in GUARDINI 1935.
[18] GUARDINI 1935, Chapter 1; GUARDINI 1922, 22. The English translation translates *Gemeinschaft* throughout as 'community'. It is better translated as 'fellowship' in the sense of the New Testament's *koinōnía*. I have corrected subsequent quotations from *The Church and the Catholic* accordingly. 'Community' translates *Gemeinde*.

Man is naturally a social person. The Church builds on this to incorporate its members into the mystical body of Christ. 'It is not merely a fellowship, but a community.'[19] That is how we should understand the liturgical movement.

> The liturgy is reality through and through. It is this that distinguishes it from all purely intellectual or emotional piety... [It] is a process of fulfilment, a growth to maturity. The whole of nature must be evoked by the liturgy, and the liturgy, seized by grace, must take it all, refine and glorify it in the likeness of Christ... The liturgy is creation, redeemed and at prayer, because it is the Church at prayer.[20]

Thus *Vom Sinn der Kirche* sees the liturgy and its fellowship as the prime manifestation of the Church. 'The Holy Mass is an act of fellowship through and through.'[21] We shall see how he translated this conviction into practice.

On the strength of this book, the University of Bonn offered him the chair of Practical Theology and Liturgical Studies, which he declined. Then the University of Berlin invited him to assume its new chair of Philosophy of Religion and Catholic *Weltanschauung*, which he accepted. He began his life in Berlin in 1923.

Sacred Signs

After the end of the First World War, there was a great yearning in Germany for rebuilding social groups. Youth movements experienced an influx of new members. Among them was Quickborn, a Catholic movement which bought the castle at Rothenfels, between Fulda and Würzburg, in which to hold its meetings. Its first conference was in 1919;

---

[19] GUARDINI 1922, 28: 'Nicht Gemeinschaft bloß, sondern Gemeinde.'
[20] Id, 32. The quotation begins: 'Liturgie ist ganz Wirklichkeit.'
[21] Id, 86: 'Die heilige Messe ist ganz Gemeinschaftswerk.' This chapter (5) is entitled 'Gemeinschaft'/'Fellowship'.

in the following year, 1500 young men gathered under the title 'Christ, our Leader', and Guardini was invited as a speaker. In the evenings, 200 or 300 of the youngsters would gather in the Knights' Hall to engage in discussions with the shy priest from Mainz. Guardini and his listeners captivated each other.

A journal ('*Schildgenossen*') had already been inaugurated as a means of communication between 'friends of Rothenfels', but Guardini recognised that the young people needed catechetical material to introduce them to the language of liturgy, its symbols. He gradually produced short essays, no longer than 600 words each, on the principal symbols and gestures used in the liturgy: the sign of the cross, the hands, the knees, standing, candles, incense, bread and wine, the altar, even the altar linen, and finally the name of God. The collection of these beautiful vignettes was published in 1923 as *Von heiligen Zeichen*, 'Holy Signs'.[22] An English translation appeared in 1956, reprinted in 2015.[23]

Encouraged by the reception of *Vom Sinn der Kirche*, and aware of his educational responsibilities at different levels both in Berlin and at Rothenfels, Guardini then wrote *Liturgische Bildung*, 'Education for Liturgy', published in 1923 at Rothenfels. It is, so he says[24], a deeper treatment of his *The Spirit of the Liturgy*. The liturgy engages the whole person, body and soul, but the first task of education in liturgy is to render him capable of dealing with symbols (*symbolfähig*), for it is in the liturgy that the symbols that he had sketched in *Von heiligen Zeichen* are fulfilled as such. But he is soon back to his principal concern: the relationship between the individual and community fellowship. 'Full Christian humanity is only present where the Church and the individual personality are in a relationship in conformity with their nature.'[25] And where is the Church? In the diocese, and in the parish

---

[22] GUARDINI 1923a.
[23] GUARDINI 1956.
[24] GUARDINI 1923b, 23.
[25] Id, 63.

community.[26] True education for liturgy is to awaken the consciousness of fellowship-community. 'I' must become a 'fellowship-I' until it becomes the greater 'we' as the subject of prayer and offering.[27] And the Church is the fellowship that Christ willed, and she is that fellowship in her historical-actual living being.[28]

Guardini was aware that, in treating of education for liturgy, he had not dealt with what the liturgy actually is. This he remedied in 1925 with a lengthy article in *Schildgenossen*, entitled '*Vom liturgischen Mysterium*'[29]. He develops Odo Casel's sense of mystery in his own way. He examines what the liturgy is: not a dramatic representation or repetition of the past, but an actual event in the present. The Mass is a memorial that transposes the historical-realistic event of the Last Supper into liturgical-cultic present action. Jesus Christ is 'aeviternal' – existing both in time, then and now, and in eternity.

> He is not in time, but he is Lord of all time. After He has gone home with all his being into eternity, He is again directed to the whole of history. And then immediately there is his *parousia*, his return. He comes again, at every historical moment, whenever there is one who believes, who 'is in Christ and Christ in him'.[30]

Therefore, every celebration of the liturgy is an event of history for both the individual and the community that celebrates it – and it *makes* history (we would say today 'salvation history'). The text concludes:

> The mystery comes from the coexistence of the 'aeviternal' work of God. It has the sense of always taking history and drawing it into eternity, to lift it out of mere

---

[26] Id, 65, 75.
[27] Id, 76.
[28] Id, 99-100.
[29] 'Regarding the Liturgical Mystery'. Reprinted in id, 111-155.
[30] Id, 146.

uniqueness into the eternal reality of salvation. Thus the individual person and individual congregation take up the mystery into their actual lives, and bring their lives into the mystery, and thus into the communion of God.[31]

The Rothenfels Experience

By 1922 Guardini had become a permanent member of the Rothenfels management and took part in all its summer meetings. In 1927 he became its director. This provided him with a golden opportunity to realise at Rothenfels his ideal of community-celebrated liturgy. He stated later in his memoirs that he intended to record his reflections on Quickborn, on Rothenfels and on the liturgical movement, but in fact he never did so. Fortunately, a few contemporary articles in Quickborn publications give an insight into what happened there.

Foremost among his colleagues at Rothenfels was his architect-friend Rudolf Schwarz, whom we will meet again in the next chapter. The two men began in 1924 to redesign the existing baroque-overlaid chapel. It was to be simply refurbished with white walls, a single new altar with tabernacle – still attached to the wall, like its predecessor – and a silver *corona lucis* above the centre of the room (see photo 3). The communion rails were to be removed 'to make the space freer'[32] – a daring innovation at the time. The pews, instead of being arranged in a single block, were to be disposed on three sides of the sanctuary steps. Already the ideal of community worship was being implemented. The work on the chapel started in 1927 but was not completed until 1931.[33]

More significant was the refurbishment of the Knights' Hall (*Rittersaal*) elsewhere in the castle (see photo 4). This was a room 19.20 × 11.45 metres in floor space. It was also redecorated in white, in contemporary

[31] Id, 155.
[32] Cited from a Quickborn publication reprinted in ZAHNER 1992, 112.
[33] Id, 120.

Bauhaus style. A hundred small wooden stools were installed – and nothing else by way of furniture. 'The community must create the other, living space, by gathering there.' This was the assembly hall for all kinds of gatherings, discussions, entertainment – and worship. Later, Schwarz described it thus:

> It was not a church, and one was envious of the fact that it remained secular, but for that hour it became a church. An altar was built in the middle of a long wall. The priest stood behind it, and the people were grouped together into three blocks on the other three sides. So they were all together a ring of table-fellowship, which succeeded particularly well if each held a burning candle and thus contributed to a ring of light.

> This form of worship is exceedingly intimate, about the common centre, the We-form opened to the chalice. The priest also contributes to it by joining the ring. He prays to the centre, and speaks out into the community when he speaks to the people.[34]

The celebration of Mass facing the people had taken place at Rothenfels since 1921 or 1922, contemporaneous with similar celebrations at Maria Laach abbey, and at Pius Parsch's parish at Klosterneuburg in Austria and other pioneer sites of the liturgical movement.[35] Now, in the Knights' Hall, there was complete flexibility of liturgical layout.

The room came into use in 1928, with the altar at first in front of one of the shorter walls, as Schwarz recommended, but in 1930 its location was altered to front the longer east wall.[36] Schwarz wrote in the same year:

[34] SCHWARZ 1960, 37.
[35] DEBUYST 2008, 55-56.
[36] Cf id, 103.

Rothenfels is known as one of the centres of the
'Liturgical Movement', which is something alive among
these young people. The meaning of this spontaneous
and broad movement is the realization of the liturgy as a
work of fellowship, that is, the activation of the
community. Since the community actually had this co-
operative function in the past, it is merely a reform that
does not wish to change the worship, but to restore it.
And yet much is changed when certain actions are
undertaken by the whole community, when the medieval
division of space, which is almost a complete separation,
is replaced by an organic and hierarchical space-step,
when the altar-space is situated in the middle of the
congregation instead of in its own particular space, closed
off by a rood screen. Thus, for instance, the choir is
contained within the faithful instead of in a gallery, and
the inner form of the liturgy changes from forms of
solitude and distance into the form of a benevolent
nearness (where this other form is not to be deprecated,
but only as not being presented in a way appropriate for
the current time). All this certainly does not mean a
change in the cultic elements, which cannot be altered as
elements, but it is a change in the appearance of these
elements, and thus part of the task of construction.[37]

Thus the liturgical space in the Knights' Hall was configured with the
congregation on three sides and the priest alone on the fourth. (Do not
forget that the Order of Mass at that time obliged the priest to stand at
the altar for the entire Mass.) Later on, Schwarz was to make the point
that the priest/people dialogues and the reading of the Scripture lessons
require the responders/listeners to be in front of him; on the other
hand, both priest and people together pray to God. It is why he rejected

---

[37] SCHWARZ 1930.

the concept of the closed circle and opted for one that is open on one side.[38]

There is no doubt that the summer youth weeks at Rothenfels every year from 1919 to 1938 were inspirational for both leaders and participants. They taught fellowship-community by experiencing its creation and celebration, culminating in the liturgies in the Knights' Hall.

As we shall see in the next chapter, Schwarz had reservations about the application of the Rothenfels configuration elsewhere. Even Guardini had reservations, which he eventually overcame when he became chaplain to Berlin university in 1928. He described the chapel there thus:

> The chapel consisted of three rooms, the partition walls of which were removed, and two adjoining rooms. As it lay lower than the entrance to the house, one had the impression of descending into a catacomb. It was quite simple. The walls are white, without any decoration except for the consecration crosses. The altar stood free on an elevated platform built of bricks, on the steps of which the faithful knelt down to receive communion. It was also made of bricks, with a simple white sandstone slab, with only the crucifix, two candlesticks, and horizontal cloths. The Holy Mass could be read [from the missal] on both sides [of the altar], thus facing the people. Behind the altar, on the wall, was an image of Christ in copper. From the year 1928 until the summer of 1943, only interrupted by holidays, I said and preached Holy Mass on Sunday.

---

[38] SCHWARZ 1938, 62-68. See more in the next chapter.

The worship was always a Latin 'missa recitata', strictly adhered to without any concession to popularism. This could happen, as the faithful were, for the most part, academics, and the Latin language was powerful. The pastor, Dr Pinsk, had from the outset read Holy Mass facing the congregation. It was the time when one could still do something of this kind without having to justify oneself, and so it remained. For a while I had resisted this, for I thought that to see me praying during the sacred action would be insufferable, but then I gave in, and regretted not having done so before. Especially in a small room, this is the only natural way of celebrating Holy Mass. Through it a real coherence arises. All see what happens and can follow every detail.[39]

Meditations before Mass

In two parts, in 1936 and 1939, Guardini published *Besinnung vor der Feier der Heilige Messe*, translated into English as *Meditations before Mass*.[40] It was intended for popular reading – and succeeds admirably in this. Its purpose is 'to reveal what the Mass demands of us and how those demands may be properly met... It is time that the Mass become again for the faithful what it is and was instituted to be: the sacred action of Christ's community.'[41] Thus the community is placed in prime position from the very first page of the book.

In its first chapter, on 'Stillness', we read:

---

[39] GUARDINI 1995, 103-104.
[40] GUARDINI 1936. The English translation by Elinor Castendyk Briefs was first published by Newman Press, Westminster MD in 1956. Currently available in two English editions, one by Sophia Institute Press, Mansfield NH (1993 – but incomplete), the other by Ave Maria Press, Notre Dame IN, 2014. Quotations henceforward will be from the latter edition (GUARDINI 2014).
[41] GUARDINI 2014, xiii.

What then is a *church*? It is, to be sure, a building having walls, pillars, space. But these express only part of the word 'church', its shell. When we say that Holy Mass is celebrated 'in church', we are including something more: the *congregation* (*Gemeinde*). A congregation is not merely people. Churchgoers arriving, sitting or kneeling in pews are not necessarily a congregation; they can be simply a roomful of more or less pious individuals. Congregation is formed only when those individuals are present not only corporally but also spiritually, when they have contacted one another in prayer and stepped together into the spiritual 'space' around them, and, strictly speaking, when they have first widened and heightened that space by prayer. Then true congregation comes into being, which, along with the building that is its architectural expression, forms the vital church in which the sacred act is accomplished.[42]

Guardini goes on to describe the attitude required of the churchgoer to the liturgy: not just stillness, but silence and listening before the Word of God, and composure – in which he quotes a beautiful Italian phrase: '*farò atto di presenza*': 'I will make an act of being present'[43]. And it is within 'composure' that he situates 'participation'. 'To participate means to share the task of another. Here that other is the priest.'[44] At the Canon of the Mass:

What happened in the room of the Last Supper is taking place here: Christ comes. He is present in his salutary love and in the destiny it met. The priest acts, but we must

---

[42] Id, 5-6. Italics original.
[43] Id, 23. Later he describes the congregation as 'the sacred coherence which links person to person as it links God to men and men to God. It is the unity of men *in Christ*...' (89-90).
[44] Id, 30. Cf Vatican II, Constitution on the Liturgy, art. 48: "...by offering the Immaculate Victim, not only through the hands of the priest, but also with him...'.

act with him by being inwardly present, by watching him
every moment at the altar table, identifying ourselves
with his every gesture... Naturally we must be genuinely
active, not simply watchful.[45]

This watchfulness at the altar table almost presupposes the facility of
seeing the priest's every action close-up – and therefore of Mass facing
the congregation. But Guardini concedes, significantly: 'as long as
congregations have the size they must have at present, the possibility
of direct participation will necessarily remain limited.'[46]

A little later in *Meditations before Mass*, he comes to treat of the altar in
two chapters: first 'The Altar: Threshold', then 'The Altar: Table'. 'As a
threshold, the altar creates first the border between the realm of the
world and the realm of God... The thoughtful believer does not have to
be taught that it is a border, that "above it" stretch inaccessible heights
and "beyond it" the reaches of divine remoteness.'[47] And he continues:

Threshold is not, however, only borderline; it is also
crossing over. One can step over it into the adjacent
room, or standing on it, receive him who comes from the
other side. It is something that unites, a place of contact
and encounter. This too is contained in the symbol of the
altar. The essence of revelation is the news that God loves
us... Now he is with us, 'on our side'... All this is
expressed by the altar. It reminds us that God turns to us;
from his heights he steps down to us; out of his
remoteness he approaches us... We can cross the border
only because God crossed it to come to us. His descent
draws us upward.[48]

---

[45] Id, 32-33.
[46] Id, 30.
[47] Id, 42-43.
[48] Id, 44.

And he concludes: 'the altar-threshold is also the crossing-over *par excellence*, because God became man so that we might become "partakers of the divine nature".[49]

This symbol of threshold is clearly something of great importance for Guardini. Visually, it accords well with traditional east-end high altars, beyond which is nothing but an apse or stained-glass window representing an unreachable beyond. But it is difficult to reconcile with his championing of Mass facing the people, for when the priest faces the people, or they encircle the altar, that visual symbol of altar as threshold and boundary is lost.

In fact Guardini betrays some uncertainty here. In his chapter 'Mimicry or Liturgical Form', he explains in layman's terms what he wrote in *Vom liturgischen Mysterium*:

> [T]he memorial of the Mass is celebrated not in the form of a play but of a liturgy. The object commemorated is not imitated but translated into symbols... The original form has vanished. No longer is there a table around which the faithful gather; in its place stands the altar, and however close architectural arrangement has permitted, it still remains essentially separated from the believer. At the altar stands the priest; opposite him, united as a congregation, the faithful.[50]

That was how Guardini saw the situation at the time of the first edition of the second part of his book in 1939. But in the fourth German combined edition published in 1947, there is no mention of the congregation facing the priest. Instead, we read:

---

[49] Id, 46.
[50] Id, 156-157.

> Whatever may be the disposition of this altar, however
> near it may be to the faithful, it nevertheless remains a
> principle of separation of the priest and the faithful.[51]

Guardini must have seen this as an unresolved problem. For the altar
is also the point of community and communion uniting priest and
people with God and among themselves. It is 'the table to which the
heavenly Father invites us... At the altar we enjoy the intimate
community of his sacred table'. Both threshold and table are 'images' of
'the mystery of the altar' which he does not attempt to inter-relate.[52]

Returning to the chapter 'Mimicry or Liturgical Form', Guardini warns
against ritualism, when 'the essential can be discerned only with
difficulty through a tangle of forms'. The signs of the liturgy must be
transparent of the reality they represent: 'the business of liturgical work
today is to do everything possible to present the original form in its full
clarity and power'.[53]

> The believer is faced with an important task: that of
> discerning the essential in what meets the eye. In the altar
> he must see the table; in the priest, the head of the
> congregation; in the host, the bread; in the chalice, the
> cup... It is not enough, however devoutly, to 'keep up
> with' a mysterious celebration's prayers and hymns,
> readings and acts of consecration and offering. The
> believer must also follow the 'translation' into symbols of
> everything that is taking place. When we watch a person
> we love, we do not merely observe his expression and
> gestures; we try to interpret those external manifestations
> of what is going on within. Here we have something
> similar, only greater.[54]

---

[51] Translation from the French edition (GUARDINI 1957), 178.
[52] GUARDINI 2014, 50.
[53] Id, 159.
[54] Id, 159-160.

It is instructive to note that the original 1939 edition contained a chapter that does not appear in either of the English editions or in the French edition. It was entitled: 'The Form of the Memorial: the Meal'. In the preface to the second edition, published in 1947, he explained that this chapter had been misunderstood as a reduction to a protestant view of the Eucharist. He was only trying to present the *form* of the Mass as being that of the meal, not its essence. However, to avoid further misunderstanding, he was withdrawing the entire chapter. It did not reappear until the 1961 and 1965 German editions.[55]

In the 'missing' chapter he explains that it is the form that is the means of participation:

> The altar is a table, even if, thanks to certain styles and religious attitudes it hardly appears as such any longer... There comes the moment when the memorial is accomplished, when the living reality of Christ becomes present. Then the Father, by the hand of the priest, offers his own the divine nourishment.

> It is from this that Communion receives all its urgency. One takes part in a meal by eating and drinking it. Communion is not a separate element... Without Communion, participation in the Mass is unfulfilled.[56]

The final chapter of *Meditations before Mass* is entitled 'The Mass and Christ's Return'. He refers to Mt 26:29: 'I will never again drink of this fruit of the vine until that day when I drink it new with you in my Father's kingdom'. And he comments:

> Jesus seems to be gazing through and beyond the hour of the Last Supper to the coming of the kingdom... The

[55] DEBUYST 2008, 44-48.
[56] GUARDINI 2014, quoted in French translation in DEBUYST 2008, 47-48.

passage tinges the whole memorial with a singular radiance which seems largely to have faded from the Christian consciousness.[57]

The Mass is a 'constant reminder of his glorious promise' of his return.

Holy Mass is distinctly eschatological, and we should be much more concerned of our forgetfulness of the fact... Now we must really acquire the truth of the world's 'passing', must practice watching, waiting, and persevering 'until the Lord comes'.[58]

The Second Vatican Council rediscovered the eschatological nature of the Mass.[59] The debate about liturgical orientation has largely revolved around the preservation of its sense of expectation. Guardini does not consider how this might be symbolically expressed.

From 1939 onwards

In 1939 he was dismissed from his post at Berlin University by the Nazi regime, which also commandeered Rothenfels that summer. Guardini stayed in Berlin until 1943, when he took refuge in a friend's house at Mooshausen in southern Germany until the war ended. While he was there, he wrote his memoirs.

In 1945 he was immediately appointed professor of Philosophy of Religion and Christian *Weltanschauung* at Tübingen; in 1948, a chair of the same title was erected for him at Munich and he became its first holder, a position he retained until his retirement through ill health in 1963. He was appointed a member of the Second Vatican Council's Preparatory Commission for the Liturgy, but was unable to take part

---

[57] GUARDINI 2014, 192.
[58] Id, 194, 201.
[59] Cf SC 2, 8; Eucharistic Prayers II, III & IV; first and second Eucharistic Acclamations.

in it. In 1965 he was offered a cardinal's hat by Pope Paul VI, but declined it. He died on 1 October 1968.

During this final period of his academic life, he did not seek to revive his pre-war pastoral work at Rothenfels. Indeed, in his 1953 diary, he saw the liturgical movement as consisting of four periods: the restorative (Solesmes), the academic (Maria Laach, Beuron), the 'realistic' (Rothenfels, Klosterneuburg) and now the pedagogical – 'would anyone be able to realise at all the texts and agenda that had been handed down?'[60]

Although he preached occasionally, his academic work in theology gave him no opportunities for pastoral work. One of his few post-war interventions on specifically liturgical topics occurred at the German Liturgical Congress at Frankfurt in 1950. There he read the paper entitled 'Liturgical Experience and Epiphany' that we encountered briefly in chapter 1. It merits our further attention.

Here he notes how, as recorded in the bible, God has always manifested Himself to the human senses in order to reveal Himself – to the eye by brightness, to the ear by his word, to the hand by his touch. God is at once inaccessible yet made palpable – and realised in the supreme manifestation that is the person of Jesus Christ, the 'true Epiphany', about whom John is so excited in the opening words of his first letter:

> That which was from the beginning, which we have heard, which we have seen with our eyes, which we looked upon and have touched[61] with our hands... (1 Jn 1:1 – ESV)

And Guardini asks: 'What happened to this epiphany after the ascension of the Lord?' He replies: 'Epiphany is not something that

---

[60] GUARDINI 1995, 154-155.
[61] Greek *epsēlaphēsan*, a rare intensive verb meaning 'handled, felt by touching'.

happens once only, but is a fundamental event in the life of the
believer, as God would wish it to be.'[62] And he continues:

> Consciously or unconsciously, one seeks epiphany in the
> liturgy, the luminous apparition of the holy reality in the
> worship event, the resonance of the eternal Word in what
> is said and sung, the presence of the Holy Spirit in
> graspable 'fleshly' realities.[63]

Apropos 'where two are three are gathered in my name, there am I in
the midst of them' (Mt 18:20), he comments:

> Is this presence of the Lord enclosed in faith alone? Could
> it not be in some way an experience? Shouldn't we apply
> the old adage according to which *'pistis'* – without ceasing
> to be the obedience of faith – ought to become *'gnosis'*,
> knowledge within faith? And, within faith, should there
> not already begin a 'vision' which does not suppress faith
> but deepens it, and which will one day become fulfilled
> vision?[64]

If this seems beyond human reach, Guardini reassures the reader:

> The Lord of glory, if he wills it by his grace, can make his
> glory visible in the liturgical symbol, for God 'has shone
> in our hearts to give the light of the knowledge of the
> glory of God in the face of Jesus Christ' (2 Cor 4:6).[65]

What makes the eye capable of seeing, the ear of hearing, the hand of
grasping? It depends on the object seen, heard, grasped. It is the Creator
who has made the organ in view of the object, and it finds its fulfilment

---

[62] GUARDINI 1950, 75-76.
[63] Id., 90. '...la présence de l'Esprit-Saint dans des réalités "charnelles" saisissables.'
[64] Id, 92-93.
[65] Id, 99.

in being united with it. So when the eye, ear, hand is used in the liturgy
as a means of perceiving the reality beyond what it sees, hears, touches,
it achieves its highest purpose.[66]

It is little wonder that he saw the ability of man to 'read' the symbols of
the liturgy as being vital for the success of the liturgical renewal. As
reported in chapter 1, he rather shocked the Third Liturgical Congress
in Mainz in 1964 by asking the question 'Is man still *liturgiefähig*
(capable of liturgy)?'

In his open letter to the congress – he was unable to attend personally
– he summarises his concept of the symbol as the vehicle of liturgical
participation, as the basic liturgical 'act':

> The symbol should be 'done' by the performer as a
> religious act and those observing it should 'read' it by an
> analogous act, the inner meaning displayed in the
> outward sign. Without this everything would be a waste
> of time and energy and it would be better simply to 'say'
> what was meant.[67]

His fears come to a head in the final paragraphs of his letter:

> How is the basic liturgical act constituted?... How are its
> demands related to the make-up and life-consciousness
> of modern man? What must be done so that he can really
> and truly learn it?... Would it not be better to admit that
> man in this industrial and scientific age, with its new
> sociological structure, is no longer capable of a liturgical
> act?[68]

---

[66] Id, 103-104.
[67] BRADSHAW 2007, 6, translation revised from the original German in GUARDINI 1923b,
13.
[68] BRADSHAW 2007, 8.

The Church of the Lord

Guardini's final thoughts on the Church consisted of five meditations 'on the nature and mission of the Church', entitled 'Die Kirche des Herrn' ['The Church of the Lord'][69]: it was published in 1965. The collection was dedicated 'in deep respect' to the memory of Pope John XXIII. In his foreword to them, Guardini asks why the Church had remained so exclusive for so long. Among examples he gave was this one:

> Wasn't it something like exclusion inside the church itself when, for example, the faithful saw the priest in front at the altar, turned to the wall, muttering what he had to, whereas they themselves had to be tormented by some "Mass devotions"? Was there here that great openness and unity which showed that the experience of 'Church' had been awakened within it?[70]

Here he is reflecting his pastoral experience in Mainz in the 1910s, but he knew well enough that this situation could be corrected – at least under Rothenfels conditions. Indeed, he had a sense of a church community (and Church) that is much wider in its embrace than the local *Gemeinde*. This is what he wrote in his 1936/9 *Meditations before Mass*:

> The concept [of congregation] must include also those outside any particular building, even outside the Church; for congregation reaches far beyond. It is no closed circle, no organization or union with its own centre; each congregation is part of a whole that far surpasses any Sunday gathering. It embraces everyone who believes in

---

[69] Reprinted in GUARDINI 1965, 101-197.
[70] Id, 109: '...wenn zum Beispiel der Gläubige in der Eucharistiefeier den Priester vorn am Altar, zur Wand gekehrt, murmelnd sein Werk tun sah, und er selbst sich mit einer „Messandacht" plagen mußte?...'

Christ in the same city, the same country, over the whole
earth.[71]

Guardini's disciples

Guardini's leading disciples, Heinrich Kahlefeld and Aloys Goergen,
were convinced that the Rothenfels *Rittersaal* template could be
translated into parish churches.[72]

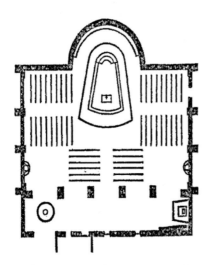

Kahlefeld (1903-1980), who
revived the congresses of
young people at Rothenfels
and led them from 1948 to
1959, created a country retreat
for the young people of his
Leipzig parish, in which the
church space had exactly the
same dimensions as the
Knights' Hall. Behind the altar
was an entirely white wall,
'reserved for the invisible
presence of Christ' – just like
Guardini's church at Aachen.

But his greatest achievement was his collaboration with Emil Steffann
in the design of the church of St Laurentius in Munich (see above),
opened in 1955.[73] Significantly, his aim was to enable the people to be
real 'table-companions' at the altar-table. 'Their number is very
important to enable them to "sit" at the table' – but this inevitably
restricts that number, and is impractical for a large congregation.

---

[71] GUARDINI 2014, 96.
[72] Cf DEBUYST 2008, 101-119.
[73] The bench in the apse is the priest's *sedilia*, though in the older rite he hardly ever used
it, since he led the entire Mass from the altar. The tabernacle is at the lower right of the
plan, the font at the entrance (lower left).

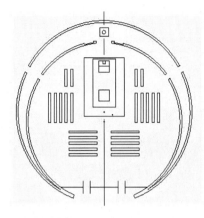

Goergen (1911-2005) saw Rothenfels – which he attended for the first time when he was just 14 years old – as the birth of a 'new community'. With the architect Sep Ruf he designed the circular church of St John Capistran in Munich (1958-1960 – see left).[74] Like Kahlefeld, he also founded a country retreat, this one at Rattenbach, principally as an academic centre, and here he created a Rothenfels-type culture and liturgy.

But how realistic was this imitation of the Rothenfels experience in quite different pastoral situations? Experts after Vatican II failed to evaluate this adequately. They should have considered the thinking of Rudolf Schwarz, to whom we now turn.

---

[74] The main altar is almost central. Behind it is the Blessed Sacrament altar. Behind this again in a recess, curiously, is the baptismal font.

Chapter 4

RUDOLF SCHWARZ

Rudolf Schwarz was born in Strasbourg in 1895 and grew up in a pious Catholic family.[1] Visits to Beuron Abbey were permanent features of his summer holidays, where his father knew Dom Ildefons Herwegen, later to be abbot there. It brought him into contact with Beuron's artistic tradition. In early 1919, he registered in Bonn for a course in Catholic theology, and spent the following two semesters studying philosophy and theology, when he read Romano Guardini's *The Spirit of the Liturgy*, and became one of his disciples. By 1922 he had met him and in 1924 went on an Italian holiday with him.[2]

But architecture was his chosen profession. He had already completed an architectural course at the Berlin High School and obtained a diploma in engineering in 1918, and it was there that he obtained his doctorate in 1922 with a dissertation on 'Early Types of Rhineland Churches'.

---

[1] Biographical details in this chapter have been mainly sourced from ZAHNER 1992.
[2] In 1935 he designed a house for Guardini: Niklasstraße 50 in Berlin-Zehlendorf – from its entry in the list of Berlin historical monuments: see Wikipedia article 'Rudolf Schwarz (Architekt)'.

Beginnings

'Architecture', he wrote much later in retrospect, 'was for me the setting up of forms in which people may be together'. And what was the purest form (*Gestalt*) that he could find?

> My reflections fell on sacred building, for it stands at the frontier, and – it seemed to me – even before a threshold where nothing remained that could be claimed as purpose or service, but just architecture itself. I sought, therefore, whether there was a class of forms in which people tend to meet God, and indeed found such people among mystics... but that was a lesson for solitary people, not for communities. I found such forms only in the liturgy, which contains a series of spiritual spaces. I tried to sketch the inner spaces of the liturgy and what flows from them.[3]

In 1924 he spent six months at Burg Rothenfels. This castle had been acquired in 1919 by Quickborn, the German Catholic youth movement, as a residential centre for courses. But it had as yet no money for alterations to the building, so Schwarz had to bide his time. He embarked on a very simple project – the design of a Mass chalice. It took him a few hours every day of his six-month stay. He described it as a form 'destined to be filled... directed to man... open to God but created by man'. He called it 'his first church'.[4]

In 1925, he moved on to the School of Architecture and Art at Offenbach and was taught there by Dominikus Böhm, who shared his church building projects with him. One on which they worked was very simple: a rectangular floor plan in which the altar, though raised by a flight of steps, was not separated from the congregational space as

---

[3] SCHWARZ 1960, 9-10.
[4] Id, 12.

chancel from nave. Schwarz had understood liturgical celebration as
being the worship of the community:

> The ground plan of the building consists of the ordered
> people on their way to the altar, and just these people.
> The liturgical renewal had taught us that a community is
> more than a sum of individuals; it is a body, and one with
> a definite form, a 'we'-form, which an individual has
> never produced.

It was a new concept, and that was enough for the church authorities to
reject it.

In 1927 Schwarz became head of the Aachen Art Academy, and shortly
afterwards was invited to design the church of Corpus Christi there.
Here he was able to implement the earlier rejected design. The
Fronleichnamskirche (Corpus Christi church) is a vast cuboid, entirely
white inside (see photo 6). Here is how he describes his approach:

> The builder has the earth to fashion into a landscape for
> worship. It consists of three areas. The first is the space of
> this world, whose house consists of pure creativity, and is
> open to God. The second region is the threshold, where
> Christ lives as mediator, and the third is the absolute
> open, and that is heaven. In this landscape of prayer, the
> builder has to transform the world. He has to lay the
> threshold which divides people on the one side from
> God's inaccessible space on the other, and which also
> opens the one to the other. The builder has to gather the
> people before the threshold into a great body and to open
> them up to the beyond. Prayers enter the threshold from
> this side, God's answer enters it from the other.[5]

---

[5] Id, 24.

The altar marks the threshold. Whereas earlier German churches built after the First World War, while detaching the altar from the 'east' wall, had mounted sorrowful crucifixion scenes behind it, witnessing post-war grief, here at Fronleichnam there was nothing at all behind the altar but a white wall. The altar itself stands as the threshold between man and God, the place of Christ, High Priest and mediator.

He makes this insight fully trinitarian a few pages later:

> So there are three areas in a church building: the area of open space, the area of the threshold and the inaccessible area behind it. The first is the real sphere of the Spirit, the other Advocate; the second is that of Christ, the mediator; the third is the region of the Father, and also of Christ, who has gone before us.[6]

In 1925 Pope Pius XI had added the feast of Christ the King to the Catholic calendar. Four years earlier, Johannes van Acken had written a booklet entitled 'Christocentric Church Art'. It had emphasised the altar not only as a symbol of Christ but also as the end-point of worship. Schwarz invokes the opinions of his lifetime friend, Romano Guardini, to correct this:

> There was at that time [of the construction of Fronleichnam] the concept of Christocentric church building, which meant that the altar was the place of Christ, and the church was to gather around him to celebrate the Lord's Supper. This concept was dangerous, because it contained only half of the truth, and has caused much mischief right up to today. Guardini has pointed out that the prayer of the Church is not Christocentric, for all prayers go 'through Christ' to the Father.[7]

---

[6] Id, 27.
[7] Id, 28-29.

And, in defence of the stark clinical whiteness of the 19m-high wall
behind the altar, he quotes Guardini's assessment of it:

> What the lack of pictures in holy space expresses, its
> emptiness, is in itself a picture... It expresses something
> of the holy which is beyond form and concept. Visitors to
> the Hagia Sophia speak of the immense religious
> impression that its emptiness makes.[8]

Rothenfels

In 1927 Guardini had become director of Burg Rothenfels and, having
obtained funding, was able to implement the plans to refurbish the
chapel and Knights' Room (*Rittersaal*) that he and Schwarz has been
working on since 1924.

These have been described in the previous chapter. From Schwarz's
point of view, in both rooms there was a very different use of space,
compared with Fronleichnam at Aachen. There it was longitudinal,
even two-dimensional, with a specific tripartite, indeed trinitarian,
division of space. Here at Rothenfels, the direction is centripetal. It is
clearly an entirely different liturgical experience, but Schwarz
immediately issues a warning:

> Like Corpus Christi, the hall of Rothenfels has
> unmistakable consequences. Actually, I ought to be glad
> about it, but I am not, because the conditions of
> Rothenfels are not transferable. The ring of the
> community comes about only where individuals can give
> themselves up to fellowship; the altar becomes a centre
> only where the community has the power to have such an
> interiority. But where average people do not have this
> great power of creating space and of interiorization – and

---

[8] Id, 29.

this seems to me the average situation of the parishioner – this form of construction very easily fails; it becomes a kind of organizer, and can even be an irritation, in that the centre moves from the altar to the priest. In Rothenfels the soul of the individual was hidden in the fellowship, and such concealment is needed.[9]

This is a vital distinction between the ethos of a Mass celebrated by a fellowship-group of limited size, who are already united as a community and are celebrating that unity in communion, and a congregation that only comes together once a week for Mass, whose participants may not even know each other. Schwarz realized this from his experience with the Fronleichnamskirche. In 1930, the year of its opening, he wrote:

> The church of Corpus Christi was begun this Easter and is to be consecrated for Christmas. The conditions there were quite different [to Rothenfels], and I had to accept them. Our task was to build a church to hold about 2,000 people, mostly workers of an industrial suburb. This meant that the task was [to cope with] a great *mass* of people, because *'fellowship'* of several thousand people cannot be achieved under normal circumstances. So many people in a space remain a mass, and each one remains an individual. It must, however, be known that this fact, though new in all its severity, has strongly impacted the forms of worship and evoked a peculiar form of the liturgy, which is characterized by great anonymity, objectivity and silence. There is much room for the individual, and there is only the consciousness of standing in a large crowd and being connected through the sacrifice [of the Mass]. It is all influenced by the fact

---

[9] Id, 37-40. Aloys Goergen described Schwarz's opinion as elitist and 'a tragic mistake' (DEBUYST 2008, 113).

that everything that is necessary for 'fellowship' is
unfeasible.[10]

This is a question that is still highly relevant today. How does one
mould a large crowd of parishioners gathered for Mass into a
community?

Developing principles

In 1936, Schwarz attended the consecration of the new church of Sankt
Annen at Berlin-Lichterfelde. He had not been involved in its design
or construction – his own design, developed with Emil Steffann, had
been rejected[11] – but the occasion prompted him to write a lengthy
'memorandum' for the Rothenfels journal, *Schildgenossen*.[12]

In this text, he expounds his concept of the church as a liturgical
community:

> The basic form of Christian worship consists in the fact
> that a priest comes before God in front of the community
> and turns to Him *'per Christum Dominum nostrum'*. This
> worship is not christocentric, but theocentrically built,
> and the congregation, which is indeed the Lord's body,
> closes on itself, but never closes itself as a ring; it cannot
> do so because man is a creature that never remains within
> himself, but is a directed and open being. Expressed and
> represented in the human form is its reference to a
> distance, whether it is a step forward, or, standing still,
> looking out, standing facing the distance which calls for
> silence.

---

[10] SCHWARZ 1930, 554-555. Original word highlights.
[11] SCHWARZ 1960, 59.
[12] Reprinted as SCHWARZ 2004.

We regard the appropriate form in which the praying community stands before God, as neither the ring, in which one remains imprisoned, nor the separation of the Middle Ages with its remote God, but the *'open ring'*.

This is a form in which the church truly surrounds the altar and truly finds its centre in it. But it only surrounds it on three of its four sides, and the fourth side remains open. The eyes are gathered on the altar, but they pass through it and beyond it.

This form unites both the possession and the absence, the inner fullness and the incompleteness of man, his state of holiness and his state of expectation; it is the true expression of the two forms of life, between which the life of Christians is stretched, the *imitatio Christi* and the change into the presence of God. The congregation surrounds the altar, and in its open attitude one can well compare it to one of those old praying figures who stand with their arms raised, and simultaneously both surround a space and make a prayer into the distance.

It is therefore proposed that the people in the three 'quarters' should be placed closely around the altar. This can be done in practice by arranging it in three groups at its steps.

The communion rails are the place of communion. It would be wrong, then, to give them the form of a barrier, since they then separate what is there to combine. It would be best to bring the people into an open ring around the altar and to present them to it on a broad, lowest step.

The priest's position at the altar requires special consideration. It is well known that part of the liturgical movement, and the abbey of Maria Laach, preferred the position of the priest behind the altar (*'versus populum'*), since it hoped to achieve such a close connection between the people and priest. However, we do not wish to follow this proposal. Sometimes, in a small community with few people, it may be the right one. Otherwise we would like to see the priest rise *from the people* to the altar. He is not to be opposed to them, to come from elsewhere, and then to confront them from elsewhere; instead, he should step out of their midst, and stand in front of them, as the first of the people, and be together with them before God. The priest and the people stand together before God and before the altar: their theological situation is essentially the same.[13]

This 1936 text of Rudolf Schwarz sums up a principal thesis of this current book. See more in chapter 7 below.

On Building the Church

The two different directions of focus of the two churches he had built – longitudinal in Aachen and centripetal in Rothenfels – led Schwarz to his concepts of *Wegkirche* ('path church') and *Ringkirche* ('ring church') respectively, and indeed on to his other models. These were never intended to be finished designs, but to function 'as a certain creative incompleteness', to use Schwarz's own phrase about his sketches[14]. They were published in 1938 as *Vom Bau der Kirche*[15]. This German title is interesting: it translates as 'On Building the Church', not 'On Building Churches'. The theologian Henri de Lubac would later coin

---

[13] Id., 10-11.
[14] '...schöpferische Unvollständigkeit...': SCHWARZ 1960, 10.
[15] SCHWARZ 1938.

the phrase "it is the Eucharist that makes the Church"[16] – evidently through its celebration in churches all over the world and throughout time. Schwarz, like Guardini, had a more visceral sense that it was the people worshipping in churches that realised 'Church' in a higher sense than individuals or even individual communities, that there was a single offering of worship and prayer to God being shared by all these churches, the worship and prayer of a single body, the Church.

And it was Guardini who was invited to write the Foreword of *Vom Bau der Kirche*[17] – and he evidently found it a difficult task. He sounds quite surprised by the book, which is strange, given their friendship and the frequent in-depth conversations they must have had. He says that it is 'more a theme than a book: a set of themes full of light and fruitfulness'. He sums up the book like this:

> The forms of church architecture appear as interfaces of man and world, of human history and divine action, as illustrations of that mysterious procession in which the people of God journey through time, as giant symbols in which the Christian being is visible in time, and in the forms in which it is cultivated.

Schwarz begins his book by looking at the medieval concept of body, as portrayed in art, and finds it so rich in imagery and meaning that he can claim that 'the congregation or the church building itself are the mighty holy body of the Lord'.[18] He sees in the eye and the hand the creative potential for the artist and architect to paint and sculpt and build.

> There are levels of doing. At the highest step in this order stands that work in which man spends himself utterly in

---

[16] DE LUBAC 1986, 134. Cf also the encyclical letter of Pope John Paul II, *Ecclesia de Eucharistia*, chapter 2 entitled 'The Eucharist builds the Church'.
[17] This Foreword is unfortunately missing from the English translation.
[18] SCHWARZ 1938, 8.

order to consummate the world as sacred likeness... If you like, this is the worship, the service of God.[19]

Schwarz then describes and explains his seven 'plans'. In *Kirchenbau*, written 22 years later, he summarises them with the aid of a lifetime of experience, and we shall use these summaries as well as the original explanations in *Vom Bau der Kirche*.

The first plan is 'the ring'. The structure emanates from a central altar, around which the people gather in concentric rings. 'Christ is in the centre and it is for his sake that the people stand about it.'[20] Schwarz sees this centre as an opening into the eternal, like – to use a modern image – a 'black hole' drawing all into itself beyond the horizon of the physical universe in constant sacrifice. At the same time that circle is the ground of a hemisphere, the vault above it being held in God's hands: God is at the centre and also all around it. And just as 'black

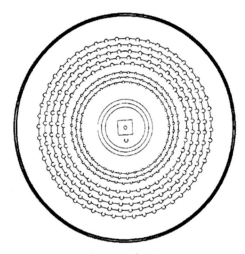

Plan 1 – The Ring

---

[19] Id, 31.
[20] Id, 38.

holes' are the creation cradles of new stars, so that centre is the point of 'silent divine birth in the midst of creation'.[21] That 'giving birth' might be illustrated in three dimensions as a gushing fountain playing up from the centre until it hits the hemispherical roof and flows down on the inside of the roof to the edges of the ground circle.[22]

The closed hemisphere is superseded in the second plan, 'the open ring'. If the first ring is one of giving birth to the Christ child, the second takes him through his passover, and to the church 'between times', looking forward to his final return. The Lord is still here, but he has also gone out beyond the comfort of the circle and passed over to the Father. 'Christ is in the same room with his own and yet he is not – he belongs at the same time to another space, he is at once centre and mediator.'[23]

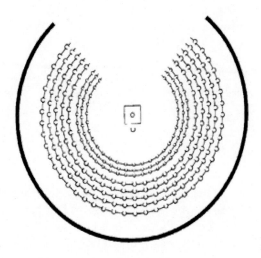

Plan 2 – The Open Ring

---

[21] SCHWARZ 1960, 77.
[22] SCHWARZ 1938, 59-61.
[23] SCHWARZ 1938, 68.

> The people are standing around in the circle, and this is
> still the holiest place in the world, but it is open in front,
> and the rings no longer close, they are gaping. From the
> front, through a huge leak, the emptiness penetrates into
> the space towards the middle, and there is clear, holy
> emptiness. The earth is broken open, and the dark
> enclosing circle in the back pushes the people into the
> open space. The earth is bleeding itself to death into the
> unsealed wound which the Lord left behind when he
> passed on, but it is renewed again and again by grace out
> of the open, so that it remains in existence, the primordial
> shape of the one who prays, who stands before God with
> arms spread out.[24]

Schwarz clearly has in mind the traditional Christian *orans* gesture
portrayed in ancient mosaics, originally shared by priest and people
alike.

This plan, Schwarz claims, 'is intended to be valid for the average
situation of every day and every year'.[25] It is what he refers to as his
Ringkirche.

From among the people, the priest goes forward and stands on their
side of the altar.

> And then, across the altar, that is to say across the holy
> earth with all her gifts, he begins to invoke the Father, to
> praise him and to beseech him. In the priest, the
> congregation and Christ within it face across the earth
> into the openness. They go to the innermost brink of the
> world to the place where her shore curves in an open arc
> about the eternal. The congregation goes to the threshold

---

[24] SCHWARZ 1960, 78.
[25] SCHWARZ 1938, 68.

of its house and calls out into God's eternity... The people are borne forward through the priest as they step to the threshold and then "look out into the distance". They pour themselves out in the invocation of God and surrender themselves into the infinite direction.[26]

And God gives his answer out of his remoteness:

It comes back as streaming light out of the direction into which the people have surrendered themselves. Thence the Word is sent anew into the universe. The light falls upon the altar, thence to stream out into the interior.

Now the figure turns around and comes back once more. The priest becomes the ministrant through whom the Word is communicated. In the consummate answer the new form of grace is given as the sacred form of new history. The people are dismissed back into the world.[27]

Nowadays we would invert the order of service: first comes the Liturgy of the Word, God addressing his people through his priest/reader facing them, then comes the answer of the priest and people in thanksgiving and prayer (the Eucharistic Prayer) in response, into the open, infinite space.

Thus we have, even in this ring configuration, a tripartite division of spaces.

The people's space is the intermediate space, the space in which the earthly church stands in this present life, between providence and light. The space of this world arches over it and God's holy government bounds it. For

---

[26] Id, 78.
[27] Ibid.

the earth and the world, the altar is at once the centre and
the threshold. Earth and world gather in the altar, and in
it they reach their end. The altar belongs to two realms: it
belongs to the realm of earth in which we can walk and it
belongs to the realm of light which we cannot enter; on
three sides it faces the world and on the fourth heaven.
Thus it is the place where "earth and heaven kiss", the
spot where the earth, turned to face eternity, remains
behind. Out from this spot a "sacred way" begins. We can
follow it for a little while with our eyes but our feet
cannot tread it: it runs its course on beyond the
universe... At the point where the centric movement
veers out into the infinite stands the impassable portal of
heaven: window, threshold, shining negation, the
piercing of the world — and, seen from the world, the
shining void, God's other dwelling.

God's radiant dwelling is at the same time his heaven and
this is Christ's truer home. The Lord and the saints have
entered into it: they have entered into the light. And thus
our everyday situation is not exactly like that of the last
supper before the Lord's death. The Lord is with us;
Christ lives in the people, he sits with them at table and
in their name he speaks with the Father. It is the Lord in
the people who goes to the brink of the earth and looks
out into the far distance. But in very fact he is no longer
present; he is "at the right hand of the Father" in heaven
and thence he comes across the threshold to the earth.
Our supper is the true Lord's supper, and yet at the same
time it is only its "commemoration". The Lord himself
indicated that this was so when he said that he would no
longer celebrate this supper on earth, but that he would
indeed celebrate it in eternity. And the Apostle, too,
indicates this when he says that through the celebration
we should proclaim the death of the Lord "until he

comes". And thus the empty side is also Christ's empty
seat at the table of this world. The death of the Lord and
his going forth are the wound where history bleeds.
When the Lord departed, he left the world open behind
him.[28]

There is an amazing understanding here – 25 years before the Second
Vatican Council – of the eschatological fulfilment of the liturgy
hereafter.

Schwarz concludes his chapter on the 'open ring' with a lengthy
excursus on the impossibility of architects or anyone else to 'represent
heaven' in artistic imagery. 'In the end, God is utterly different. And
while the ascetic is scaling the lonely peaks perhaps God is in the valley,
playing with the children and the flowers.'[29]

Instead, 'the open place would remain the meaningful break in the ring.
This could be intimated by leaving a part of the wall behind the altar
utterly white' – as Schwarz did at Fronleichnam. Alternatively, he
proposes a plain window, and outside it a space that is 'utterly empty
and utterly white', and a mirror image of the space of the ring.
'Although we cannot "reproduce" heaven, we may still reverently
"name" it' – as we do when we say "Our Father, who art in heaven".[30]
Encouraged, he continues:

> But perhaps, empowered only by the tidings about the
> fatherliness of the eternal, we can, through the images,
> "name" what lies beyond, instead of trying to reproduce
> it. Perhaps we may achieve this if we give, as it were, a
> silhouette of the sacred...

---

[28] Id, 80-81.
[29] Id, 88.
[30] Cf id, 91-92.

Perhaps the mosaics in the choirs of the early churches were conceived in this way. The apse represents a spiritual horizon filled with the gold of the heavenly light and in it the holy figures appear. They are bathed in God's golden effulgence... And so these representations are, as it were, gates of heaven: through their outlines we see eternity. The likeness of heaven became shining and translucent in fact when the walls of the choirs vanished and their place was taken by the stained glass windows. The sunlight shone through them and in them it took on colour... The concave sweep of the apse points into the distance; out of the apse the church shines like a radiant star. But this same apse embraces and shelters – it is the image of the distant heaven but also of its imminent approach. Apse, altar wall and chalice are the steps on which heaven descends.

All these images stand directly on the threshold. They fill the windows with colours and outlines through which the sun shines in. They are transient forms, heaven on the point of entering the world or world on the point of leaving the earth. No mortal eye has seen what happens beyond them.[31]

This is a remarkable description, both artistic and liturgical, of the sense of 'distance beyond', of the hint of transcendence that is gained from the gazing 'eastward' from within the finest examples of Christian church architecture, as described already in chapter 2. The significance of the altar as threshold to this 'beyond' is fundamental.

The third plan is the 'Sacred Parting'. This is in effect a three-dimensional projection of the second plan, in which there is a central opening above the congregation. It is like looking upwards into the

---

[31] Id, 93-94.

dome of an Eastern Church with its icon of *Christus pantocrator*. Like the apostles at the Ascension, the Church can gaze upwards after her departing Lord. However, 'man as an open form is placed in a path, towards a goal that lies ahead; the glance upwards can only be exceptional'.[32] Christian architectural tradition, in both east and west, has always wanted to extend churches horizontally, even centrally focused ones, by adding an apse, and thus giving them a sense of direction. In the west, the Church took over the basilica form, 'an obstructed centric structure'. The 'secret' form of the church 'is contained neither in the closed comprehensiveness of the dome nor in the long ranging of the nave. Bursting the one and closing the other, she stands between them in a state of inwardness and yet of displacedness, of having and not having, of sheltering and of summoning'.[33]

The 'goal that lies ahead' gives direction to the fourth plan, the 'Sacred Journey' or 'the Way' – Schwarz's *Wegkirche*. Here the people of the second plan, having been already broken apart by the irruption of God's light, form into the 'ranks of an army on the march' towards their heavenly goal. Each person looks directly ahead: the interpersonal warmth of the ring is no longer present. It is in fact the conventional longitudinal pew-filled nave.

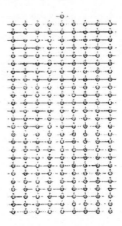

Schwarz concedes that 'this people has a hard lot'. It is a 'pilgrim's progress' in which there are only two options: struggle forward into the light beyond the altar that is the threshold to it, or give up and turn back. But one can interpret this ineluctable process as being that of human life, of history – and indeed, of

Plan 4 – The Way

[32] SCHWARZ 1960, 78.
[33] SCHWARZ 1938, 113.

salvation history. We are a historical people, and our destiny is to move through time to the timelessness of eternity.

Surprisingly, Schwarz stated categorically (in his 1958 book) that his longitudinal Fronleichnamskirche is 'not really a "way" church'.[34]

> Here is nothing but the silent presence of the Church and of Christ, the goal has been attained, and all the way is satisfied in pure existence in a common, bright, high, and very simple space; the people and the Lord are together, one body in a festive form of building, the higher body of their holy existence.[35]

Unlike his classic 'way' plan, in which the people struggle forward, the 'ring' form of this church is 'satisfied in the goals achieved'.

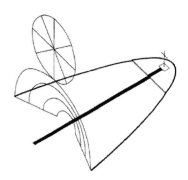

Plan 5 – The Dark Chalice

The fifth plan, the 'Sacred Projection' or 'dark chalice', is best understood as the reverse of the second plan – not the people looking towards the Lord, but the Lord looking back at his people. Imagine a mosaic of Christ in an apse extending his arms outstretched to embrace the people coming towards him – like the apse mosaic in Monreale cathedral, Sicily (see photo 2).

What does the iconic Christ in the mosaic see, looking down and 'westwards' towards his people? At the front is the altar at the focus of a parabola. Further back it gets progressively darker as the space draws

[34] SCHWARZ 1960, 20.
[35] Ibid.

away from Christ the Light. In the distance, the parabola is partly closed off by a west-end wall, in the upper part of which is a rose window of deep red, but the portal below it is still open.

There is now an ebb and flow in the movement of the people. They reach the altar, but as yet their meeting with the Lord is unfulfilled. They are turned back towards the portal, their shadows before them, to meet their Lord in death and then judgement. Jesus has been there before them, at his own crucifixion, at his own "thy will be done". But it is the gateway to eternity. Architecturally, it is like a tympanum of Christ seated in judgement over the west door of Gothic cathedrals, instead of – or in tension with – the Christ in glory depicted in the eastern apses of earlier Romanesque basilicas.

The sixth plan is entitled 'Sacred Universe: The Dome of Light'. It is an apocalyptic moment of promised transfiguration, when the whole world is bathed in divine light, a world that "has no need of sun or moon to shine upon it, for the glory of God is its light, and its lamp is the Lamb" (Rev 21:23).

There is a seventh plan, 'the cathedral of all times', which is the amalgamation and consummation of the previous six plans, and of time itself. It is the city of God. All the previous plans were like limbs of the body, but 'only the cathedral is true body'.

> At no time in history can the last plan be realized, but in many varied ways it shines through the architecture of the epochs, showing itself now in this way, now in that. The 'whole' is to be discovered in one thing above all others: in the act of divine service.[36]

The 'whole' can also become visible in the liturgical year from Advent to Pentecost, in the day from morning to evening, and even in every

---

[36] SCHWARZ 1938, 196.

breath, 'for it, too, is an entering and a departing and has a profound meaning'.[37] It is like a DNA helix.

> Each plan is valid only for its time, and is not intended to be retained beyond it, even the short hour of the blessed vision, where enlightenment breaks out of the murky earth ... But there may be times when the whole meaning of the historical, spread over these plans, is present as a 'cathedral of all times'. This was my last plan, the plan of all the plans.

He adds:

> The book appeared before the war in Rothenfels, and many people told me that it was a comfort and guide.[38]

As a summary of these plans, we may reprint one of Schwarz's own:

> [A]rchitecture is not geometry. It is the forming of our own destiny. We cannot turn its plans this way and that and look at them from above and from the outside, for we are ourselves worked into them. We ourselves, our own life, our soil, our people, God as he is to us here and now – that is what these plans are.[39]

The remainder of *Kirchenbau* contains Schwarz's own appraisals of some 30 of his most important churches built after the Second World War. Many are of elliptical ground plan, a few are parabolic, as suggested by his fifth plan. All have high, sheer walls, with light mostly entering at clerestory level. At Heilig Kreuz in Bottrop, the window

[37] Ibid.
[38] SCHWARZ 1960, 80.
[39] SCHWARZ 1938, 99.

high above the altar contains an eye (see photo 5), and there is a rose window at the other end.[40]

Altar and tabernacle

One relevant factor even in the 1930s was the position of the tabernacle, as related already in chapter 2. In the 1936 memorandum referred to earlier, Schwarz struggles with the notion of an altar without a tabernacle.

> It is understandable that the liturgical movement desires a simple altar, perhaps only the simple table of the Lord's Supper with candles and crosses. It would not have a tabernacle on it. The presence of the Eucharist as early as the beginning of the action, it says, removes part of her sense of change, which consists in the fact that the gifts offered are 'changed'.[41]

This is a prophetic insight into liturgy as dynamic 'act', which would be canonised after the Second Vatican Council so many years later.[42]

He would like to see the revival of medieval 'sacrament houses', separate from the altar. Besides 'the process' (the Mass) there is also 'the existence' of the abiding presence of the Lord in churches. This is evident in the 'Most Holy Place' in Eastern Rite churches behind their iconostases.

> Christian church buildings will have to contain and connect both. They will be the body of Christ, and at the same time the place of redemption, if they are to be the parable of the *whole* of holy history. Whether it is now

---

[40] Sadly, this church was taken out of use and deconsecrated in 2016. It has been preserved as a cultural monument.

[41] SCHWARZ 2004, 12.

[42] 1967 Instruction Eucharisticum Mysterium, art. 55.

more the one, now more the other, they must always keep
both, the permanent in the temporary, and change within
the permanent. Perhaps it would be best to form two
spaces, the bright and visible battlefield and the dark
tabernacle. Perhaps, in small churches in particular, it
might be possible to penetrate both in the same space, so
that the place where the Eucharist is offered would be
deeply imbued with the eternal presence of the Lord.
However, we do not yet see clearly the further path.[43]

Nearly all the many illustrations in Schwarz's 1960 book show
tabernacles on the rear side of the altars – evidence that he expected the
priest to pray *versus orientem*, in the same direction as the people he
leads, as indeed his 'plans' anticipate. Of the tabernacle he says:

I do not like to take the sacrament away from the altar.
What is meant by this is already mentioned in the context
of Rothenfels, the emptiness of the table and space, and
the Eucharist as nourishment for the way, the separation
of existence and progression (*Vorgang*). But it seems to
me that what the Eucharist means and is, the flesh-
making of God and the God-making of flesh, is pushed to
the brink of Christian reality as far as dogma is
concerned; the opposite would be better, namely, the
widening of the Eucharistic presence into incalculable
incarnations, the great marriage of the world with the
Lord, in which everything becomes a body. It is not at all
true that Christ is only in the host; he is, in many ways, a
body, in the poor, in the priest, in the husband, in the
child, in the needy, in the church, even in the altar and in
the house. The essence of the Church is incarnation... I
am concerned that the world, from its most intimate
place, will be completely filled with the Eucharistic state,

[43] SCHWARZ 2004, 13-14.

and will again, in the same most intimate place, re-establish its holy state in the sacred progression.[44]

Altar and apse

Already in the 1950s, two questions were coming to the fore: where should the priest have his presidential chair, and should he face the people at the altar, or have his back to them? As we have seen, Klauser's guidelines made it clear that the priest should celebrate facing the people; he also strongly recommended that he should preside from the centre of the apse, as bishops in ancient basilicas used to – and Roman civil magistrates before them.

Schwarz has a completely different and contrary viewpoint[45]. All his plans see the altar as a threshold to the beyond, to the indescribable empty space for God, for which only a white wall might suffice as a symbol. In his post-war churches, Schwarz relented on the white wall, but his 'east' ends are all of plain brick or, at most, an abstract painting.

When he was rebuilding the church at Cologne-Niehl[46] in 1947-1950, it was proposed to have choir stalls for a boys' choir in the apse. There were fears that this would distract the faithful, but in the event 'it was not a problem'. But it did raise the question of the significance of the space between the altar and the apse.

An apse is nevertheless a heavenly background, the world horizon and the coasts of eternity; for the curved wall is this place, because it can be thought of as transparent. In the Gothic, it is transparent in windows; in Byzantine light it shines in golden mosaic with the

---

[44] SCHWARZ 1960, 72.
[45] Briefly dismissed by Klauser: KLAUSER 1965, 151-152.
[46] This church still stands. However, it has been reordered by an Eastern rite community. Debuyst (DEBUYST 2008, 67) comments: 'cette église est malheureusement occupée aujourd'hui de manière très inadéquate...'

great image of the pantocrator. Sant' Apollinare in Classe
[Ravenna] is double-stepped, from the entrance to the
choir and in zones from bottom to top. The bishop and
the clergy sit in the apse on their round bench as a
sublime heavenly college.[47]

Where, then, is the threshold between the earthly and the heavenly, if
it is not the altar? He admits that he has found difficulty with such
issues, and even dodged them, but finds a solution by bringing the altar
forward of the apse hemisphere, and considering the space between the
altar and the diameter of the apse as 'walkable, shaded earth: the
heavenly firmament illuminates it. The apse can be compared with a
magnifying glass, whose focal point lies where the altar stands.'[48]

The presidential chair for the priest, then known as the *sedilia*, did not
then have the same liturgical function as the place of leadership as it
does now in the revised Order of Mass. In Germany, the custom of
locating the priest's chair directly behind the altar was and is much
more widespread than in England. It is clearly incompatible with the
concept of altar as threshold in Schwarz's sense of the word.

Altar and priest

This incompatibility is more pronounced when it comes to the matter
of celebration *versus populum*.

The priest in front of the altar is the spokesman and agent
of the congregation, for whom he comes to the threshold,
suspended on the last stretch of accessible earth, from
where, as from one last vantage point, he looks into the
horizon of eternity. There he prays. The priest behind the
altar on the side of the apse, on the other hand, stands in

---

[47] SCHWARZ 1960, 133.
[48] Ibid.

the other space, and is the messenger of heaven to man, a *persona* who is not alive among the people, but stands in *persona* of the Christ who has gone before us. Both are theologically conceivable; whether both are equally welcome, whether in the priest we should rather see the brother or the 'angel', whether the position of the priest behind the altar seems to contain the danger that the altar, which is both centre and threshold, is 'looked over' and 'spoken over' – that it something not for discussion here.[49] It is important, however, that the priest, by simply taking a fixed position in front of the altar[50], fundamentally changes the theological meaning of the building...

In reality [this] is about how he [the priest] stands before God and presents the prayer of the people. When a priest who stands behind the altar turns to God, he has to turn his back to its origin, the apse. But as it is evidently not the case that he speaks the prayers towards the apse, with the altar behind him, one must create another theological focal point for him. On these questions, the liturgists have occasionally replied that they should furnish the building with a dome as well as an apse. The priest then faces away from the apse and could look up into the dome. This is obviously not the case: the apse and the dome do not give a meaningful polarity either structurally or theologically. The dome is a world firmament, and as a response the centre is the most intimate place of the world. This could result in a genuine doubling of the 'heavenly place', but it can only be represented in a very small church. A real polarity, on the other hand, may arise between the apse and the west,

---

[49] See the question asked above in chapter 1, 22.
[50] 'Der Liturge... vor dem Altar Stellung nimmt'. Or did Schwarz intend 'behind the altar'?

between origin and end – in the language of the mystic, morning outlook and evening outlook.

If the priest in Bottrop stands behind the altar – which is architecturally possible – then he can pray over the heads of the congregation towards the great sign of God in the rose window [at the 'western' end]. In any case, it is remarkable how the ancient question of the double eternal place, between which the people are set, suddenly reappears. Already in [St] Michael's church [in Frankfurt], the choral apse had created a response in the contra-apse.[51]

Here he is invoking his fifth plan, as explained above. St Michael's church in Frankfurt, which he designed, is basically of elliptical shape, with the sanctuary at one of the foci, and the baptistery at the other. The people seated between these two extremities are thus located between the two 'eternal places'.

He is doing his best to reconcile his long-held *versus orientem* axiom with the growing practice, even in the 1950s, of Mass celebrated *versus populum*. But in most older churches, in Germany and elsewhere, if the priest facing the people looks up from the missal and over the heads of his congregation to pray, he finds himself praying towards... the west-end gallery and organ!

Liebfrauenkirche, Trier

The vast majority of Schwarz's work after the Second World War consisted of entirely new buildings. Only occasionally did he accept commissions to redesign configurations within existing structures, and most of these were small-scale constructions. But there is one interesting exception – the radical redesign of the altar-space in the

---

[51] SCHWARZ 1960, 245-246.

unusual Gothic Liebfrauenkirche in Trier, which Schwarz achieved between 1946 and 1951 (see photo 7).

It is basically a cruciform building with its longest arm extending east rather than the traditional westward 'nave'. The external angles of the cross are built out to form a twelve-bay rounded ground-plan, with an eastern extension. In earlier times it may have had a central altar, but for centuries the high altar had been located deep in the eastern apse. Schwarz restored the altar to the crossing in the architectural centre of the building, with benches for the people on three sides, leaving the eastern side open. So far, it sounds very much like his standard *Ringkirche* plan.

But although the raised circular sanctuary platform stands at the centre of the crossing, the altar itself is displaced slightly to the east, as if pointing in that direction, leading the worshippers' eyes beyond it along a gradually narrowing eastward extension of the sanctuary platform to a tabernacle-pedestal under a baldachino some 15 metres away.[52] Behind the tabernacle by another 10 metres are the stunning stained-glass windows of the eastern apse.

Thus the space on the fourth side of the altar is not entirely empty, as Schwarz would have wished, at least in theory. He commented: 'But, after all, Desiderius Lenz has already put together the "draft of a liturgical church" from the Mass altar as the "throbbing heart" and the tabernacle as the "resting head" of the Lord, and this may be the case here once more.'[53]

The whole configuration is a remarkable – and rare – example of a 'directional' *Ringkirche*. It stands as a milestone in the application of the

---

[52] The German bishops' 1949 guidelines on liturgical configuration, written by Klauser, were issued while Schwarz was at work on the Trier project. They recommended the installation of a baldachino (see above, 56).

[53] SCHWARZ 1960, 113. Desiderius Lenz (1832-1928) was the leader of the artistic school at Beuron.

principles of the liturgical renewal to church spaces long before Vatican II. After the Council, the Church authorities in Trier resisted the temptation to place the priest's chair between the altar and the tabernacle, instead accommodating it against one of the bounding pillars of the crossing, leaving Schwarz's original line of sight unaltered.[54]

Conclusion

Dr Albert Gerhards, professor of liturgical studies at the University of Bonn, wrote the following in his introduction to the 2007 reprint of *Kirchenbau*:

> Rudolf Schwarz's reflections... show an astonishing topicality, even forty years after the liturgical reform of the Second Vatican Council. The more recent discussions about the appropriate spatial design as well as the orientation in prayer can attain a width of perspective and mental clarification by confronting his writings.[55]

Schwarz died on 3 April 1961, the year before the Vatican Council started. If he had survived, how would he have viewed, architecturally and theologically, the relevant paragraphs of the Instruction *Inter Œcumenici*? To this document we now turn.

---

[54] Schwarz's 'graceful' altar was later replaced with a heavy block designed by a local sculptor: the current tourist guidebook apparently regrets this.
[55] SCHWARZ 1960, xvi.

Chapter 5

ROMAN INSTRUCTIONS

Although the matter of orientation was aired in committees preparing the text of the Second Vatican Council's Constitution on the Liturgy, the eventual text of its article 128 only laid down that there was to be an 'early revision' of legislation relating to the construction of sacred buildings, 'the shape (*forma*) and construction of altars, the nobility, location and security of the Eucharistic tabernacle' and allied matters. 'Laws which seem less suited to the reformed liturgy are to be brought into harmony with it, or else abolished; and any which are helpful are to be retained if already in use, and introduced where they are lacking.' In addition, authority was granted to bishops' conferences 'to adapt matters to the needs and customs of their different regions'.

This article is, more or less, that proposed by the relevant sub-commission of the Preparatory Commission on Liturgy in its third revision, in January 1962. Like some of the other articles submitted at this time for the approval of the whole Council, there was also a *declaratio* or commentary from the sub-commission, which would eventually form the substance of post-conciliar measures to implement the relevant articles.

Inter Œcumenici

Let us remind ourselves of article 91 of *Inter Œcumenici*, the first Instruction of the *Consilium* for the implementation of the Liturgy Constitution, issued on 26 September 1964, for implementation on 7 March 1965.

The whole article reads:

> It is preferable for the main altar to be constructed separate from the wall, so that one can easily walk around the altar, and a celebration facing the people can take place on it. Its location in the place of worship should be truly central so that the attention of the whole congregation naturally focuses there. Choice of materials for the construction and adornment of the altar is to respect the prescriptions of law.
>
> The *presbyterium* is to be spacious enough to accommodate the sacred rites.

It is remarkable that the weighty tome of documentation of the liturgical reform compiled by Annibale Bugnini, the secretary of the *Consilium*, commenting on this paragraph, refers to the altar being detached from the wall, but makes no mention of the phrase 'celebration facing the people' nor any reference to Mass *versus populum*.[1]

Let us compare this article 91 with the Preparatory Commission's commentary on the Constitution's article 128[2]. The first of 14

---

[1] Cf BUGNINI 1990, 835. Nor is paragraph 91 mentioned in MARINI 2007, even though it contains a whole chapter on *Inter Œcumenici*.
[2] The texts of this *declaratio* have been translated from the original Latin provided by PACIK 2012. See also VAN BÜHREN 2013.

explanatory notes is entitled 'On the right ordering of the church for the sacred *synaxis* (liturgical gathering)'. It begins:

> The church building should be so set out, that the arrangement of everything and of their location should be a clear sign and, so to speak, a faithful echo (*repercussio*) of the sacred *synaxis*, which is the assembly (*congregatio*) of the people of God, hierarchically constituted and duly gathered from the 'servants of God' and as 'the holy people' (cf Roman Canon).

This is an excellent statement of the theological principle of church configuration, sadly lacking in *Inter Œcumenici*.

The next note concerns the presidential chair, and states that in cathedrals, the bishop, 'as presider and overseer', should have his chair in the centre of the apse, 'which is the head of the church, that is, of the *synaxis*'. And it is permitted for a parish or other priest who presides at the *synaxis*, to have his chair in this position, in the name of the bishop. This is immediately followed up by a note regarding the main altar (*de altare maiore*):

> The main altar, which for this reason (*ea ratione*) is to be separated from the wall, so that it can be walked around, should be conveniently erected in a place between the *presbyterium* and the people, namely, in the middle of the *synaxis* ('middle' being ideally, not mathematically understood).

This can be interpreted in two ways. If one takes 'the middle of the *synaxis*' as the ideal, this could mean the gathering of priest and people surrounding the altar, or of the people being situated in three of its sides, with the priest on the fourth – as at Rothenfels. On the other hand, if the priest's proper area is the *presbyterium*, the altar placed between it and the people implies that he and his quasi-clerical ministers stand on one side of the altar and the laity on the other – as indeed was the most common result.

Now compare this with article 91's statement that 'the altar... is to be truly central', presumably with reference to the entire church building, but 'the *presbyterium* is to be spacious enough to accommodate the sacred rites', whether it is central or not. The thinking is confused, as witnessed by the question (*dubium*) put to the Congregation for Divine Worship: 'is it permissible to construct an altar in the middle of the church, so that Mass is always celebrated *versus populum*?'[3] The answer came back: 'The Instruction does not talk of the 'mathematical centre' of the church, but only of the 'ideal centre', such that 'the attention of the whole congregation naturally focuses there' – which refers back to the unpublished *declaratio* but scarcely answers the question. More interesting is the following question put to the Congregation for Divine Worship, and its answer:

> Until the church is duly reordered, is it permissible to locate a portable altar, in the form of a simple table, in front of the fixed altar made of precious marble, so that it can be used for the celebration of Mass *versus populum*?

> *Answer:* Yes, (a) provided that a truly notable space intervenes between the two altars; (b) it is to be strongly desired that the portable altar is placed outside the *sanctuarium*, in which case it should have sufficient space around it, like a *presbyterium*, suitably distinct from the nave (*aula*) of the church.[4]

So here we have an official recommendation for the location of at least a temporary altar outside the previously existing sanctuary and in its own distinct area in the nave of the church.

---

[3] *Notitiae* 31 (1975), 137-138.
[4] Ibid.

It is worth pointing out that the term '*presbyterium*' hardly figures at all in official documents prior to *Inter Œcumenici*. In the 1917 Code of Canon Law and other documents published thereafter, it was only mentioned in relation to the exclusion of civic authorities and women from the area dedicated to the clergy and their all-male servers. Now, ironically, just at the time when the concept of a united liturgical gathering space incorporating both priest and people was being introduced, we find for the first time this definition of the *presbyterium* as 'the place wherein the sacred rites are to be accommodated'. Its continued and officially intended *apartheid* from the space for the laity was to be confirmed in the 2004 Instruction of the Congregation for Divine Worship, *Redemptionis Sacramentum*, which instructed the priest to remain in the sanctuary at the Sign of Peace.[5]

At least *Inter Œcumenici* uncoupled the freestanding of the altar from the required position of the chair, which is defined in the following article (art. 92):

> In relation to the plan of the church, the chair for the celebrant and ministers should occupy a place that is clearly visible to all the faithful and that makes it plain that the celebrant presides over the whole community.

> Should the chair stand behind the altar, any semblance of a throne, the prerogative of a bishop, is to be avoided.

This opens up the possibility of the priest's chair being related to the location of the people in the church rather than to the existing church architecture.

The other contents of this section of *Inter Œcumenici* are less radical. The title of the section is 'Designing Churches and Altars to Facilitate Active Participation of the Faithful', and it elaborates on this in article 98:

---

[5] Art. 72.

> Special care should be taken that the place for the faithful
> will assure their proper participation in the sacred rites
> with both eyes and mind... Care is also to be taken to
> enable the faithful not only to see the celebrant and other
> ministers but also to hear them easily, even by use of
> modern sound equipment.

Regarding the reservation of the Eucharist, article 95 states:

> The Eucharist is to be reserved in a solid and secure
> tabernacle, placed in the middle of the main altar or on a
> minor, but truly worthy altar, or, in accord with lawful
> custom and in particular cases approved by the local
> Ordinary, also in another, special, and properly adorned
> part of the church.

> It is lawful to celebrate Mass facing the people even on an
> altar where there is a small but becoming tabernacle.

The first paragraph is virtually unchanged from its original formulation
in the *Rituale Romanum* of 1614. The second paragraph is an indication
of doubts expressed about the practical and theological difficulties
encountered in celebrating the Eucharist 'over' a tabernacle. New
'people's altars' were set up in front of the existing high altars
everywhere with remarkable speed – and without tabernacles, which
were left 'high and dry' on the old high altars in the background.

To be quite certain of the visual relationship of the tabernacle to the
celebrant standing in front of it, this *dubium* (question) was submitted
to the Congregation:

> When Mass is celebrated on an altar placed between the
> high altar and the people, can the Blessed Sacrament be
> reserved on the high altar, even if the celebrant turns his
> back to it?

Answer: Yes, as long as (a) a truly notable space intervenes between the altars; (b) the tabernacle on the high altar is located at such a height that it is higher than the head of the celebrant standing at the foot of the intermediate altar.[6]

Contrary to this answer, there are, unfortunately, many churches where minimal reordering has simply detached the altar from its previous reredos and tabernacle, and moved it forward only a few feet, so that the priest celebrating at it *versus populum* is hardly any nearer the people, but now has the tabernacle immediately behind his head. It is scarcely surprising that some priests feel uncomfortable with such a situation. By having tabernacle and altar so close together, it also confuses devotion to the Blessed Sacrament with attention to the consecrated altar and the liturgy celebrated on it.

The General Instruction of the Roman Missal

When the first *editio typica* of the revised Roman Missal appeared in 1970, it contained an invaluable rationale and commentary in the General Instruction that acted as its Foreword. Subsequent editions admitted some detail revisions – from the third (2002) edition, the paragraphs were also renumbered. Some episcopal conferences succeeded in having their own national variations included in their own editions of the General Instruction.

Of interest to this book is the chapter on the arrangement and furnishing of churches for the celebration of the Eucharist. At the end of the first section of this chapter, 'General Principles', we read:

Hence the general arrangement of the sacred building must be such that in some way it conveys the image of the assembled congregation and allows the appropriate

---

[6] *Notitiae*, ibid.

ordering of all the participants, as well as facilitating each
in the proper carrying out of his function.[7]

Even the hierarchical elements expressed by the sanctuary ministries
'should nevertheless bring about a close and coherent unity that is
clearly expressive of the unity of the entire holy people'. Nevertheless,
the sanctuary should be 'appropriately marked off from the body of the
church either by its being somewhat elevated or by a particular
structure and ornamentation'.[8] The disposition of the furniture should
be such that the people should be able 'to participate in the sacred
celebrations, duly following them with their eyes and their attention'.[9]

The preference stated in *Inter Œcumenici* that the altar should be
detached from the wall and enable Mass facing the people has since
been hardened. In the first edition of GIRM (1970), the text dropped
the initial words 'it is preferable', making the recommendation a virtual
command. In the 2010 edition of the General Instruction, an additional
clause was added, saying that this is 'desirable wherever possible'[10].
Here again, no rationale is provided for this directive.

Later Roman clarifications

On two subsequent occasions, the Roman Congregation for Divine
Worship and the Discipline of the Sacraments provided guidance on
the topic of orientation.

---

[7] *General Instruction of the Roman Missal* (henceforward GIRM), from the 3rd typical
edition of the Roman Missal, 2010, art. 294.
[8] Id., art. 295.
[9] Id., art. 311.
[10] Id, art. 299. The whole sentence reads: 'The altar should be built separate from the wall,
in such a way that it is possible to walk around it easily and that Mass can be celebrated
at it facing the people, which is desirable wherever possible.' This has been commonly
understood to refer to the desirability of Mass facing the people, but the Congregation for
Divine Worship has clarified that it actually applies to the provision of a freestanding
altar.

The first was an editorial that appeared in *Notitiae* in 1993.[11] Entitled 'Praying toward the East', it begins by pointing out that

> In fact, for the Church, the celebration of the Eucharist is putting into action something not earthly, but rather heavenly, because she has the awareness that the main celebrant is the Lord of Glory. The Church celebrates the Eucharist necessarily oriented towards the Lord; in communion with Him and through Him, she directs herself to the Father, in the unity of the Holy Spirit.

It continues:

> The setting up of the altar in such a way that the priest and the faithful have to face the orient – which is something of great tradition, even if not accepted by all – is a splendid application of the 'parousial' character of the Eucharist. The mystery of Christ is celebrated "until He comes from heaven" (*"donec veniat de caelis"*).

It might be expected from this that it would encourage celebration once again *ad orientem*. But as if to distract from this logical conclusion, it claims that, in the history of the liturgy, different 'symbolisms' have come to the fore or receded into the background. Vatican II rediscovered the theological status of the laity as the people of God.

> The theology of the common priesthood and that of the ministerial priesthood, are essentially distinct (*'essentia, non gradu'*) and yet related to each other (*LG* 10). This is surely better expressed through the positioning of the altar 'facing the people' (*'versus populum'*).

---

[11] *Notitiae* 322, vol 29, no 5, 245-249.

The differentiation of the 'priesthoods' is accentuated further:

> [T]he priest, as president in virtue of his ordination, is at the altar as a member of the assembly, but also, because of his sacramental character, is like Christ as Head of the Church, when he stands there facing (*gegenüber*) the Church.

Joseph Ratzinger would soundly reject this reasoning some nine years later in reply to an article in the periodical *La Maison-Dieu* by Pierre-Marie Gy, in which he wrote:

> For all together to be able to fix their gaze on him who is the Creator and causes us to enter into the liturgy of the cosmos, but who also shows us the road of history, this is what would also allow us to recover in the liturgy, in a very visible way, the profound unity of priest and faithful within their common priesthood.[12]

The editorial of the *Notitiae* article also recalls the 'meal' aspect that Ratzinger had already contradicted[13]:

> The symbolic form of the Eucharist is that of a meal, a repetition of the Lord's Supper. There is no doubt that this meal is sacrificial, memorial of the death and resurrection of Christ, which, however, in its figurative sense, has the meal as its point of reference.

The editorial comes to its concluding recommendations: the priest must have a 'greater and more sincere awareness of his ministerial role, and the altar must be held in due honour as 'the table of the mystery,

---

[12] GY 2002, here 101. See more below, in chapter 7.
[13] RATZINGER 1986, 'Form and Content in the Eucharistic Celebration', 33-60.

the point of encounter between God and men'[14]. The positioning of the altar facing the people 'is surely something desired by the liturgical legislation. Yet it is not an absolute value above all others.'

> It is necessary to explain clearly that the expression "to celebrate facing the people" does not have a theological sense but the sense of a physical positioning of the sanctuary. Every celebration of the Eucharist is "to the glory and praise of God's name, for our good, and solely for the good of all His holy Church". Therefore, theologically the Holy Mass is always turned towards God and towards the people. In the manner of celebration, it is necessary to guard against converting theology into topography, especially when the priest is at the altar. It is only in the dialogue from the altar that the priest speaks to the people. *All the rest is prayer to the Father through Christ, in the Holy Spirit. This theology must be rendered visible.*[15]

The same answer was issued by the Congregation to a *dubium* submitted to it in the year 2000: was it legitimate to celebrate Mass facing the apse? (In 1999, Bishop Foley of Birmingham, Alabama, had obliged his priests to celebrate Mass *always* facing the people.)

The Congregation replied:

> The liturgical assembly participates in the celebration in virtue of the common priesthood of the faithful which requires the ministry of the ordained priest to be exercised in the Eucharistic Synaxis. The *physical position*, especially with respect to the communication among the various members of the assembly, must be distinguished

---

[14] Cf Guardini and Schwarz in previous chapters.
[15] Author's italics.

from the interior *spiritual orientation* of all. It would be a
grave error to imagine that the principal orientation of
the sacrificial action is [toward] the community. If the
priest celebrates *versus populum,* which is legitimate and
often advisable, his spiritual attitude ought always to be
versus Deum per Jesus Christum [towards God through
Jesus Christ], as representative of the entire Church.[16]

The ruling ends thus:

> There is no need to give excessive importance to elements
> which have changed throughout the centuries. What
> always remains is *the event* celebrated in the liturgy: this
> is manifested through rites, signs, symbols and words
> which express various aspects of the mystery without,
> however, exhausting it, because it transcends them.
> Taking a rigid position and absolutizing it could become
> a rejection of some aspect of the truth which merits
> respect and acceptance.

'Legitimate and often advisable': there is more latitude regarding the
orientation of the celebration of Mass than many realise. Both decrees
make a distinction between physical and spiritual orientation. This is
inconsistent and confusing. Would it not be better if a solution was
found that 'incarnates', integrates and symbolises both? That is what
the remainder of this book will be exploring.

'Summorum Pontificum'

The election of Joseph Ratzinger as pope in 2005 put him 'on the spot'
regarding the status of the pre-conciliar Roman Missal and his criticism
of the 'new' Order of Mass. He resolved this by dint of a personal *motu*

---

[16] Communication from the Congregation of Divine Worship and the Discipline of the
Sacraments, Prot. No 2086/00/L, dated 25 September 2000.

proprio issued in 2007, known as '*Summorum Pontificum*'. This gave permission to all priests to celebrate Mass using the version of the Roman Missal immediately preceding the Vatican Council, i.e. in 1962. This was not, he claimed, a different rite, but a different form or 'usage' (*usus*) of the one Roman rite; this was to be the 'Extraordinary Form', as distinguished from the new Order of Mass, which was to be known as the 'Ordinary Form'. It was to be up to the parish priest – not the bishop – to decide whether he should 'accede to the request of the faithful' to use the Extraordinary Form. Pope Benedict did point out, in his covering letter to the bishops, that 'priests of the communities adhering to the former usage cannot, as a matter of principle, exclude celebrating according to the new books.' However, he did permit bishops to set up 'personal' parishes precisely for such exclusive celebration of the extraordinary form.

In terms of church configuration, those wishing to use the older rite universally desire Mass celebrated *versus orientem*. Where churches host celebrations in both old and new rites, this is at best confusing. In some churches an old altar is used for the Extraordinary Form and a new one for the Ordinary Form. Despite Pope Benedict's appeal for liturgical unity within the two 'forms', using two different altars for the two forms of the Eucharist in the same church is surely a sign contrary to the sacrament of unity.

Of equal concern are reports of clergy, sometimes of those more recently ordained, restoring older churches back to their pre-conciliar configuration, with or without diocesan approval. In Great Britain, the effectiveness of diocesan liturgical commissions tends to be weak, and many re-configurations of churches following *Inter Œcumenici* were architecturally or liturgically ill-advised. They merit re-assessment, but not unthinking reinstatement of the *status quo ante*.

Conclusion

The thinking behind the directive regarding Mass facing the people in *Inter Œcumenici* was confused and no rationale for it offered by the document, as should have been provided. The resultant hasty scramble to erect altars for the purpose was unforeseen: subsequent official clarifications were too little, too late.

What was the reaction in the worldwide Church to the sudden change of direction in the celebration of Mass?

Chapter 6

REACTIONS

It is generally acknowledged that article 91 of *Inter Œcumenici* resulted in a universal hurried erection of temporary altars to meet a perceived deadline of 7 March 1965.

Was this a manifestation of an unarticulated *sensus Ecclesiae*? Or was it just a reaction to the *status quo* hitherto, in which the entire Mass was celebrated by the priest with his back to the congregation? *Inter Œcumenici* had changed this situation at a stroke by directing that the Scripture readings should be read from a lectern or from the edge of the sanctuary, facing the people – and by recommending that 'a celebration facing the people can take place'.[1] The instruction also provided for a chair from which the priest is to preside, though as yet its only use was to moderate the new Prayers of the Faithful, and provide a seat for him while lay people read the non-gospel readings.[2]

The bishops of England & Wales, gathered in Rome for the third session of the Second Vatican Council, issued a hurried summary of the rubrical changes required for the celebration of Mass as from 7 March

---

[1] Inter Œcumenici, nos 49 & 91.
[2] Id, nos 56, 92.

1965.[3] It made no mention whatsoever of the final chapter of the Instruction on designing churches and altars. It must be remembered that the Instruction had been issued only in Latin; the bishops promised that an English translation would be issued by the Catholic Truth Society 'with the least possible delay'.[4]

If neither bishops on the one hand nor laity on the other were the prime movers of church reordering at this time, it can only have been the pastoral clergy, and for pastoral reasons. Certainly no one thought to challenge the change at the time: a review of Catholic worship in England between 1900 and 1980 briefly describes post-Vatican II church-building and the re-designing of sanctuaries that took place as a result of the Council, but implicitly presumes celebration *versus populum* as a standard feature of such reordering, without even mentioning it.[5] Fr James Crichton, reflecting in 1999 on its quasi-universal adoption, commented 'surely this marks the "consensus of the faithful"'.[6]

The German and Austrian episcopal conferences reacted more promptly and produced guidelines (*Richtlinien*) within months of the 1965 deadline. At the beginning of 1966, a guide to the (re-) arranging of church interiors, written by Fr Herbert Muck SJ and approved by the Austrian Liturgical Commission, was published.[7] There is much wisdom in this little book that is still relevant today.

---

[3] Pamphlet dated Rome, 20 October 1964, entitled The Sacred Liturgy: from the Hierarchy of England and Wales to the Clergy, Secular and Religious, throughout those countries.

[4] Instant translations into modern languages still lay in the future. The papal encyclical *Mediator Dei*, issued in Latin in November 1947, had still not been translated into English five months later. (From Society of Saint Gregory minute book for April 1948.)

[5] CRICHTON 1979, 89–91; see also 29–30. Crichton's seminal book, CRICHTON 1971, likewise presumes an altar facing the people.

[6] CRICHTON 1999, 67.

[7] MUCK 1966.

United, not separate

Unlike the bald directive of article 91, Fr Muck places his recommendations within broad concepts: that the church is the house of God's family, a single space for worship shared by clergy and laity, albeit hierarchically ordered. The church is 'a space for gathering into unity in Christ and a space of action'. It is more than just a functional space for executing the liturgy: there are also artistic and architectural considerations, 'the effect of which can be fully grasped only by intuition and experience'.[8]

Gathering of the people around a central altar is recommended; leaving access open on one of the four sides is not just for ritual purposes, but 'as an expression of expectation and outlook'. Schwarz, whose 'open ring' is explicitly acknowledged, would have approved.[9]

So what of the *presbyterium*, the sanctuary? He explains:

> This area is now more closely integrated into the area of the assembly of the people of God. There remains a certain contrast and a separation of this area; this is often sufficiently satisfied by the usual two or three steps, which serve to increase visibility. However, this function area does not require a separate part of the space...[10]

This is an important observation. The distinction of the sanctuary from the general shared area of the church (no longer referred to as a 'nave') should not divide the church space. Indeed, Fr Muck entitles this section: 'The formation of the altar area into a separate part of the space contradicts a fundamental wish of the liturgical reform'.

---

[8] Id, 7.
[9] Id, 8.
[10] Id, 12.

However, proximity of the altar can also be a problem. On the one hand, the demand for distance from the congregation in the name of 'transcendence' cannot be sustained, he says. Holy Communion abolishes the liturgical distance between the table of the Eucharist and the faithful who take the fullest part in it by receiving the Body of Christ and thus becoming who they are. Nonetheless,

> There should be a parable for 'transcendence' not so much in a wall or some space behind the altar, but above all the form of the space itself; this is almost a matter for our faith, in which we recognise God not only in his familiar and humble sacramental work of salvation but also at the same time in his inconceivable difference.[11]

On the other hand,

> Whoever cannot follow the events at the altar no longer feels as a participant. Only a certain distance from the altar makes everyone participants in the meal. Conversely, too great a distance makes everyone spectators, as apparently only celebrant and assistants (and in concelebrations, for example, a multitude of priests) celebrate the feast.[12]

As for the relationship of the altar to the two other principal focal points in the sanctuary, Fr Muck points out that whereas the chair and the ambo are both opposite the people, the altar is not the place for such 'confrontation' (*Gegenüberstellung*).

> The altar table is no longer in an inaccessible, alien or mysteriously distant 'sanctuary'... This table is for us the place of the greatest closeness and self-communion of

---

[11] Id, 29-30.
[12] Id, 31.

God in Christ. As the place for the communal celebration of the Mass, the altar is the centre of the assembly as the locus of its sacramental fulfilment.[13]

And he continues:

> The well-planned altar is surrounded by the Eucharistic community, without being constrained by it. At the same time, the open position of the entire altar area in the assembly shows the expectant opening of this community.[14]

Fr Muck returns to this topic later in his book when he considers what should be done in existing older churches when there is a deep space left behind the altar once it has been brought forward. Referring to such an altar:

> It is supposed to assert itself in [its] space, but it is not always also the directional goal of the space. On this point, the altarpiece is only 'threshold' (R. Schwarz) in such cases. Beyond the function centre, the view goes on to the part of the space that can be a reference to what is coming, beyond everything that has happened, the completed order of the end time, a view of the *parousia* as an end-time revelation of the Lord and his saints.[15]

Critical voice: Jungmann

In an article written in 1967, the great Austrian liturgical scholar, Josef Andreas Jungmann, reviewed the phenomenon of the 'new altar'. He is

---

[13] Id, 34.
[14] Ibid.
[15] Id, 65.

typically gentlemanly in his criticism.[16] By all means, he says, have it
for particular occasions when engendering a sense of community is a
priority, 'on a special occasion of common joy; in a celebrating youth
group; at the party in a small circle'.[17] And 'the preference for this
facility is also understandable in the early stages of the reformed
liturgy, in response to a distance [of the altar from the people] that has
been maintained for centuries'. But the prime pastoral concern is not
the altar itself, but the people who participate.

In any case, the Eucharist is an act of prayer, praise and the offering of
worship.

> Certainly one can imagine the offering also ascending
> from the middle of those gathered in a circle. But it will
> not be denied that the more obvious symbolism lies in
> suggesting an outward movement. We have Christ in our
> midst, but we look for God with him and under his
> guidance. It is He who teaches us to worship the Father
> 'in spirit and in truth'. 'Through Him' we offer prayer and
> sacrifice. The priest stands at the head of a procession that
> is on the way to God. As rich as we Christians are, we are
> still on the move, a pilgrim church. In the earthly liturgy,
> we partake of the heavenly liturgy that is celebrated in the
> holy city of Jerusalem to which we are travelling on
> pilgrimage.[18]

Critical voices: Ratzinger and Bouyer

One influential voice was particularly unhappy about Mass *versus
populum*. In 1966, Joseph Ratzinger, then professor of theology at

---

[16] JUNGMANN 1967. He had already addressed the matter of *versus populum* celebration
in his magisterial work on the Mass, published in 1951: cf JUNGMANN 1951, I, 255, fn 15,
in which he also refers to SCHWARZ 1938.

[17] JUNGMANN 1967, 379.

[18] Id, 379-380.

Tübingen, delivered a lecture at the *Katholikentag* at Bamberg, in which he said:

> We can no longer deny that exaggerations and aberrations have crept in which are both annoying and unbecoming. Must every Mass, for instance, be celebrated facing the people? Is it so absolutely important to be able to look the priest in the face, or might it be often very salutary to reflect that he also is a Christian and that he has every reason to turn to God with all his fellow-Christians of the congregation and to say together with them 'Our Father'?[19]

Another critic of universal Mass facing the people was Louis Bouyer, whose contribution to this debate is formally acknowledged by Ratzinger.[20]

Louis Bouyer (1913-2004) was a Lutheran pastor in Paris for three years before converting to Catholicism in 1939 and joining the Paris Oratory, in which he was ordained priest in 1944. He was appointed lecturer at the Catholic Institute in Paris, and wrote a number of books on liturgy and spirituality, including one on Cardinal Newman – he also read Tolkien. In 1963 he left Paris and lived in England and the United States, before returning to France in retirement.

His *Liturgy and Architecture* appeared in 1967.[21] The first five chapters trace the development of church architecture from its inheritance of the *bema* or reading desk from Jewish synagogues to its development in eastern- and western-rite churches. At the end of a chapter on Roman basilicas, he makes this point:

---

[19] RATZINGER 1967, 11-12. Quoted in LANG 2008, 28.
[20] RATZINGER 2000, 228-229.
[21] BOUYER 1967. The following quotations (except for the first) are all from chapter 6 of this book. Though Ratzinger and Lang are appreciative of Bouyer's scholarship, neither address the models he proposes in this chapter.

> [P]articipation in the celebration should not be confused
> with the mere fact of looking at it... Either we look at what
> the other person does for you, in your place, or we do it
> with him.

Of particular interest to us in this book are the proposals for church
arrangement that he makes in the sixth and final chapter, entitled
'Tradition and Renewal'.

Nowadays, we have grown used to three foci for the celebration of
Mass: the altar, the ambo and the presiding priest's chair. Bouyer's are
somewhat different:

> [There should be] three foci of celebration: the
> communication of the Word, the altar around which all
> should gather in response to the Word, and the *parousia*
> which should be the ultimate orientation; one should not
> add a fourth focus, namely the clergy or even the
> celebrant. From beginning to end the clergy should be in
> the midst of the people and with them, as yeast in the
> dough, to unite them progressively, especially by the
> Word and common prayer, then by the common offering
> and the common sacrificial meal, in view of the final
> fulfilment, when God in his Christ will be all in all.

This strongly suggests an openness for prayer in one physical direction,
liturgical east, like Schwarz's 'open ring'. And this is not just a matter
of internal church ordering:

> Having received in this present time the realities of the
> eternal world under the sacramental veil, [the faithful]
> should return to the actual world, but in such a way and
> with such a presence in them that they can pass through
> it for a final meeting with Christ, consecrating in him

everything in this passing world of their daily life, with a view to the eternal Kingdom.

This is the way of Christian worship and its dynamism... Everything in our churches, therefore, should harmonise completely with this plan and be entirely at the service of its fulfilment.

It is not surprising that he is therefore unsympathetic to Mass facing the people, where the priest fills and closes off this symbolic openness to what Fr Muck calls 'expectation and outlook'. In terms with which Ratzinger would wholeheartedly agree, Bouyer continues:

A cosmic symbolism should always be present in our sacramental celebration. The sacramental world should never become a world separated from the real world. It should give it its meaning, imprinting on it a new orientation. The whole world should rediscover, from our sacramental experience, a transparency to spiritual realities, and our renewed interior life should aim at reorganising it according to these realities. If this cannot be realised by means of the simple traditional practice of praying towards the East, it must be accomplished by other means. A building plan that leads to the altar, but does not stop there but points beyond to a cosmic and supra-cosmic perspective is therefore highly desirable. The form of the building and its decoration, as in churches of the past, should give the altar this double presence in the world, but not of the world, leading to another world, to which we should be committed.

We shall examine 'cosmic perspective' in chapter 9. As for the arrangement of the altar and ambo, Bouyer suggests that they be placed at the two foci of an ellipse – a concept that architect/theologian Muck was already working on for a church in Munich in 1966, which we will examine in chapter 11.

Bouyer recognises that there were, before the Vatican Council, three reasons for advocating Mass facing the people. The first was having the Scripture readings read facing them – now ordered by *Inter Œcumenici*. The second was to foster a better balance between the Mass as sacrifice and the Mass as 'the community meal of the People of God'; but this can only happen if the people are gathered *around* the altar table, not just on one side of it. He concedes that such an arrangement can be 'very good especially in the case of small communities, and principally when these are groups of the faithful to whom one wishes to teach the community nature of the Mass'.

But regarding Mass facing the people, 'the Instruction says nothing nor implies in any way that this should be always enforced and everywhere is the best possible form of celebration'. This is the conclusion of the previous chapter of this book. Indeed, he says:

> Far from uniting the community centred on the altar, this increases, in this case, the separation and opposition between clergy and laity: the altar becomes a barrier between two Christian castes. Far from creating greater participation of everyone, this only develops the worst heritage of the Middle Ages: the false idea that the liturgy is reserved for the clergy, as a body of privileged specialists, done for the benefit of others, but not an action done *with the people*.[22]

Even a circular gathering around the altar is not ideal as a general rule:

---

[22] Michael Kunzler notes the same from the opposite direction: having the priest on the same side of the altar as the people declericalizes him. Cf KUNZLER 1995, 152.

Once again, the ideal of a church is not that of a human
family closed in on itself. Indeed, one might ask whether
this is ever the ideal of a truly healthy family! The
Christian family should always be open: open to the
invisible Church formed by all other Christians, in this
world and the next, open to the world and, beyond the
world, to the eternal Kingdom.

Bouyer also draws attention to the symbol of the cross, preferably
suspended above the altar or mounted on the wall behind it.

The decoration of the wall behind the altar, or of the
cupola above it, with mosaics, paintings, tapestries,
windows... should always add to the cross an evocation
of this vision of faith, cosmic and supra-cosmic, which
makes the Eucharist a foretaste of the transfiguration of
the entire world, in the coming of the Kingdom.

This accords well with the report by Stefan Heid that we described in
chapter 2.

In 1969, Bouyer wrote and published a book highly critical of the post-
Vatican II liturgy.[23] Notwithstanding this, he was appointed by Pope
Paul VI, together with Ratzinger, to the International Theological
Commission, and re-appointed to it in 1974. They were also among the
founders of the theological journal *Communio*, set up in competition
with *Concilium*, both reflecting on the outcome of the Second Vatican
Council, albeit from different theological standpoints.

More from Ratzinger

In 1981, Joseph Ratzinger, then Cardinal Archbishop of Munich-
Freising, published *Das Fest des Glaubens*, a collection of previously

---

[23] BOUYER 1970.

written papers on liturgical topics. At the end of that year, Pope John Paul II appointed him Prefect of the Sacred Congregation for the Doctrine of the Faith, which greatly magnified his authority and the status of his writings. Nonetheless, it was five years before an English translation of the book appeared.[24]

His essay on orientation was actually a correction of another theologian's work, which had asserted that Mass was celebrated towards a 'holy of holies', namely, the tabernacle.

> Thus the Eucharist would be celebrated 'from' the Host 'to' the Host, which is plainly meaningless. There is only one inner direction of the Eucharist, namely, from Christ in the Holy Spirit to the Father. The only question is how this can be best expressed in liturgical form.[25]

And he continues:

> Where priest and people together face the same way, what we have is a cosmic orientation and also an interpretation of the Eucharist in terms of resurrection and trinitarian theology. Hence it is also an interpretation in terms of *parousia*, a theology of hope, in which every Mass is an approach to the return of Christ.[26]

With Bouyer, he accepts that the 'strongly felt community character of Eucharistic celebration, in which priest and people face each other in dialogue relationship... does express *one* aspect of the Eucharist'. But the danger is that it can make the congregation into a closed circle in

---

[24] RATZINGER 1986.
[25] Id, 140. The last two sentences neatly summarise the intentions of the current book, too.
[26] Id, 140-141.

dialogue with itself instead of 'engaged on a common journey toward the returning Lord'.[27]

Ratzinger returned to this theme with greater passion in his *The Spirit of the Liturgy*, published in English in 2000.[28] This time he builds up his argument from the significance of the liturgy with regard to time, history and the cosmos, and also its biblical typology. Then he comes to his chapter on 'The Altar and the Direction of Liturgical Prayer'.

He first points out that:

> Just as God assumed a body and entered the time and space of this world, so it is appropriate to prayer – at least to communal liturgical prayer – that our speaking to God should be 'incarnational', that it should be christological, turned through the incarnate Word to the triune God.[29]

He then attempts to dispel a misunderstanding that, because Jesus founded the Eucharist at the Last Supper, this 'meal' character should be reflected by gathering around the altar table. It is arguable whether this was ever envisaged by anyone for large congregations, but it leads him on to one of his more famous utterances:

> In reality what happened was that an unprecedented clericalization came on the scene. Now the priest – the 'presider', as they now prefer to call him – becomes the real point of reference for the whole liturgy. Everything depends on him. We have to see him, to respond to him, to be involved in what he is doing. His creativity sustains the whole thing... Less and less is God in the picture.[30]

---

[27] Id, 142-143.
[28] RATZINGER 2000.
[29] Id, 76.
[30] Id, 79-80.

Instead, the tradition of Christian congregations is to 'set off for the *Oriens*, for the Christ who comes to meet us'.

He concedes that 'when the altar was very remote from the faithful, it was right to move it back to the people' – in the case of cathedrals, to the crossing, being the meeting point of the nave and the *presbyterium*. The Liturgy of the Word should take place face-to-face, but 'a common turning to the east during the Eucharistic Prayer remains essential... Looking at the priest has no importance. What matters is looking together at the Lord.'[31]

Not surprisingly, this chapter of Ratzinger's book has received much attention. Too much, in his opinion. When he consented to the republication of all his literary output in his *Opera Omnia*[32], he considered omitting this chapter altogether, but eventually agreed to its inclusion. Referring to this in the Introduction to the volume of his writings on the liturgy, he says:

> [T]he idea that the priest and people should look at each other in prayer emerged only in modern Christianity, and is completely foreign to ancient Christianity. Priest and people certainly do not pray to each other, but to the same Lord. So in prayer, they look in the same direction: either toward the East as the cosmic symbol of the Lord who is to come, or, where this is not possible, toward an image of Christ in the apse, toward a cross, or simply toward the sky, as the Lord did in his priestly prayer the evening before his Passion (John 17:1).[33]

---

[31] Id, 81.
[32] RATZINGER 2014.
[33] It is to be noted that, in this Introduction, he specifically commends both LANG 2008 and HEID 2006.

This is a welcome widening of his earlier suggestion that, when Mass is celebrated facing the people, the focus of prayer should be just a cross lying on the altar.

Indeed, Pope Benedict's statements about the liturgical renewal since his election as pope have been noticeably more mellow than his earlier pronouncements. This is particularly apparent in his 2007 post-synodal apostolic exhortation, 'Sacramentum Caritatis'.[34] There is no mention there of orientation, but he counsels priests thus:

> Any attempt to make themselves the centre of the liturgical action contradicts their very identity as priests. The priest is above all a servant of others, and he must continually work at being a sign pointing to Christ.[35]

National directives: USA

Given that many churches had been hastily reconfigured in 1964/5, and the liturgical reforms to all the Church's rites were only just beginning at that time, some episcopal conferences reckoned it prudent to wait before issuing any considered statements or directives on art and architecture in relation to the new demands of the liturgical rites.

In 1977, the United States Conference of Catholic Bishops issued *Environment and Art in Catholic Worship*. It raised considerable protest, especially from the more conservative wings of the Catholic Church in that country, who felt free to ignore it when it was admitted that it had no canonical status in church law – it had not been formally approved by the entire episcopal conference. What was often overlooked was this important statement about the significance of the assembly as a liturgical symbol:

[34] Cf BALDOVIN 2008, 86-88.
[35] Sacramentum Caritatis, no. 23.

The most powerful experience of the sacred is found in
the celebrations and the persons celebrating; that is, it is
found in the action of the assembly... This was at the heart
of the earliest liturgies. Evidence of this is found in their
architectural floor plans which were designed as general
gathering spaces which allowed the whole assembly to be
part of the action.[36]

A subsequent document, *Built of Living Stones*, was published in 2000.
This time it was approved by the entire episcopal conference. In
Chapter Two it declares:

[T]he church building manifests the baptismal unity of all
who gather for the celebration of liturgy and "conveys the
image of the gathered assembly." While various places
"express a hierarchical arrangement and the diversity of
functions," those places "should at the same time form a
deep and organic unity, clearly expressive of the unity of
the entire holy people".

It then immediately continues with a paragraph entitled 'The
Congregation's Area':

The space within the church building for the faithful
other than the priest celebrant and the ministers is
sometimes called the nave.

There is no sense of a single architectural space embracing both
sanctuary and people. It goes on to talk of architectural principles about
the form and arrangement of the nave; there are then separate
paragraphs about the sanctuary area.

Regarding the visibility of the altar, it states:

---

[36] Id, nos 28-29.

During the Liturgy of the Eucharist, the altar must be
visible from all parts of the church but not so elevated
that it causes visual or symbolic division from the
liturgical assembly.

However, there are no recommendations about the possible
disposition of the people around the altar. Presumably, it is expected
that the standard configuration will see the priest facing all the people
in front of him, accommodated in traditional longitudinal pews.

National directives: England & Wales

The Bishops' Conference of England & Wales published a trilogy of
books in the early 1980s, advising best practice in liturgical celebration,
music and architecture at parish level. *The Parish Church*, published in
1984, was evidently ghost-written by an architect with a strong sense
of both liturgy and its environment. The proportionate configuration
of space and its contents are a major concern. Under the heading 'The
Place of Assembly' we read that the area allocated to the sanctuary
follows from its function 'in relationship with the assembly of
participants, the gathering which is true congregation'[37] – in other
words, the *synaxis*[38]. The sanctuary should be 'distinguished' from 'the
place of the people', without making it seem remote. 'Projection of the
sanctuary area into the people's area can help to relate the two.'[39] While
it requires the altar to be freestanding, and the celebrant as 'clearly
visible', the only mention of 'Mass facing the people' is to be found in a
quotation from GIRM relegated to an appendix.

The next authoritative statement, issued in 2006, was entitled
Consecrated for Worship. It has a quite different feel compared with its

---

[37] Id, no 55.
[38] See above, 119.
[39] Id, 162.

predecessor. There is a clear logical progression of contents under 'A Place for Celebration': the first two sub-sections are entitled 'A Place for Worship' and 'The liturgical assembly'. It sees the plan of the church as 'the image of the gathered assembly', planned specifically for the celebration of the liturgical rites.

Of the space and seating for the assembly, it says:

> The layout of the seating should be a reminder that the Christian assembly is a gathered community, celebrating together as the Body of Christ... Seating arrangements which encourage people to sit apart from their brothers and sisters in Christ or which encourages people to watch passively should be avoided. As far as possible, the members of the assembly should be able to see the faces of those others gathered with them.[40]

This presupposes a *non-longitudinal* layout of the people, but there are no suggestions as to how this is to be achieved. The document is in favour of chairs for seating, rather than pews, to enable easier reconfiguration for the needs of particular liturgies.

National directives: Germany

The German bishops were able to call on long-established and thriving academic and pastoral centres of theological and liturgical expertise. In 1985, they formed a workgroup for church architecture and sacred art (AKASK), which duly produced 'Guidelines on the building and configuration of worship spaces', first appearing in 1988[41]. It contains some significant foresights that are not found in the English-language directives we have examined.

---

[40] Id., no 135.
[41] This was the first official directive from the German bishops on this topic since Klauser's 'guidelines' in 1949.

More recently, many churches have expressed the desire
to give the liturgical celebration a spatial shape that
corresponds to today's liturgical understanding... The
search for a modern liturgy and the appropriate design
concept presupposes, at first, a dissociation from
unconsidered traditional pre-conceptions. This applies in
particular to the rigid pew arrangement in uniformly-
arranged, parallel rows. Church tradition knows quite
different forms, such as the assembly in circular form or
facing each other (e.g. choir seats). With the change of the
direction of celebrating *versus populum* (towards the
people) an attempt has been made to realize the old idea
of the *circumstantes* in existing spaces... However, this
often led to a separation between them and a real co-
existence, which could still be experienced even in the
'way' church, at least in the common orientation of priest
and congregation. Because of the loss of common
orientation, the experience of openness, and reference to
the larger community outside the congregation, was also
lost.

All space dispositions have their logic dictated by the
liturgy: the idea of the 'way' keeps the call to the
expectation of the returning Lord, the *versus populum*
corresponds to the dialogical structure of the worship,
whereas *circumstantes* suggests the celebration of the
Lord's Supper. The task would therefore be to combine
the openness of the old church with the image of the
people gathered around the altar.[42]

---

[42] Id., section 3.3.

The references to the 'way' church surely refer back to Rudolf Schwarz's models. The 'expectation of the returning Lord' is explained by the conclusion of the previous section of the document:

> The current documents do not mention an eastward orientation of the church area (apse- or entrance-eastwardness). However, the direction of prayer remains to the east, the rising of the sun, which is interpreted as a symbol of the coming Christ (see also Mt 24:27, Rev 7:2). This can also be reconciled with celebration towards the people.[43]

But how is this traditional eastward-looking attitude of prayer to be reconciled with Mass facing the people, when priest and people are praying in different directions?

The Sanctuary Stage

How does a priest celebrating the Liturgy of the Eucharist facing the people appear to them?

A deservedly popular American book on the liturgical ordering of churches is Fr Mark Boyer's *The Liturgical Environment: What the Documents Say*, now in its third edition[44]. Nearly all of the book is what its title says, a faithful reference to the official liturgical books and directives. But in a couple of early pages, the author expresses frankly his personal dissatisfaction with church configuration:

> The post-Vatican II design resembles a theatre... Even though worshippers... found themselves closer to the action, they still faced a single platform sanctuary, reminiscent of a stage, backed up against a wall. The focal

[43] Id., section 3.2.
[44] BOYER 2015.

point was essentially unchanged from a pre-Vatican II
building. Furthermore, a stage... does not foster
participation; people come to watch, to be entertained, to
be passive.

Instead, he recommends a circular or elliptical 'stadium' model, in
which no one faces a wall, and there is more communal interaction and
participation. Monastic choirs are arranged in this way, or facing each
other.

Regarding the sanctuary as a stage has only come about because the
principal 'actor' in the liturgy, the priest, is now facing the people. No
one ever thought of the sanctuary as a stage before, however
spectacular the liturgical rites that were performed in it.

The perception of the altar space as a stage is not something new. As
early as 1969, a Swiss sculptor contributing an essay to a published
symposium wandered off his subject to give a layman's view of church
configuration:

> We have put the benches horseshoe-like around the altar
> space, and from everywhere you can see the altar... In
> other words, we have a stage and an auditorium. We have
> essentially 'show' churches. We have a superbly
> illuminated marble altar construction opposite blocks of
> wooden benches. We basically have the modern cultural
> theatre, i.e. a form that suggests to the public the role of
> the spectator and obliges the celebrant to do the
> celebrating.[45]

In 2016, Cardinal Robert Sarah, prefect of the Roman Congregation for
Divine Worship and the Discipline of the Sacraments, issued an appeal
to priests to celebrate Mass facing east. Cardinal Vincent Nichols in

---

[45] SCHILLING 1969, here 187.

England and the office of the US Bishops' Conference hastily put out statements instructing priests not to change their orientation precipitately. There ensued a lively correspondence in the *Tablet*: some priests declared their satisfaction with celebrating Mass facing their congregation, but among those of a contrary opinion was one parish priest who wrote:

> Moving the altar a few yards from the back wall leaves us feeling we have abandoned the noble image of a sacred drama (which we watch) for a shopkeeper at his counter encouraging us to taste his wares. Nor has the church building of the past half century allowed us to form an architectural language for the post-Vatican II liturgy (nor, maybe, for a conciliar vision of the People of God).[46]

Close visual attention to the priest also reveals his personal idiosyncrasies, when his role at the altar, functioning *in persona Christi capitis*, is to be completely impersonal. It is not 'his' Mass, but that of the whole Church – and specifically that of the assembled people of God in this congregation at this time, whom he leads.

Conclusions

Why did *Inter Œcumenici* recommend Mass facing the people?

One reason – as we have seen in chapter 2 – was the alleged practice of the early Church, along with the predilection at the time of the Vatican Council for reviving lost rituals. Research in the past 50 years has increasingly discredited this claim.

Another factor was the experience of pioneers of the liturgical renewal, notably Romano Guardini and Pius Parsch, who had introduced a new awareness of the Mass as a celebration of the whole community, priest

---

[46] In Letters to the Editor, 9 August 2016.

and people together around the altar. But there are practical, spiritual and theological limitations to this plan. Disposition in pews around the sanctuary area is best if the arrangement is semi-circular; three separate blocks around a square, with the priest the sole occupant of the fourth side, can be divisive rather than uniting. If the format is further abbreviated, with the priest on one side and the people on the other, 'a "standing-opposite" develops' and the whole point of having the community around the altar is lost.[47]

Certainly, the celebration of liturgy 'in the round' by a small community, knit by ties of fellowship or common commitment, can be meaningful and rewarding. As we have seen, both Jungmann and Bouyer agree that such a format is *one* expression of liturgical communion. But it is not the only one. The theological limitation, as pointed out by Pope Benedict, Lang and Bouyer, is the inwardness of such celebrations. They are fine for 'retreats', precisely as such – like Rothenfels and the country retreats of Kahlefeld and Goergen. And that means limited numbers, as Guardini himself conceded.[48]

However, the symbolic relationship of liturgy to the world outside the church – and to the world-to-come beyond the church walls – also needs expression. The great challenge, as noted by the German Liturgical Commission, is to reconcile the reaching-out to the beyond with the realisation of community and communion with the Lord within.

A third reason for the recommendation of *Inter Œcumenici* that Mass should be celebrated facing the people may be this: that it was simply seen as a way of encouraging hitherto passive lay people to participate in the liturgy. Seeing the priest – and enabling the priest to see them and encourage them – may have seemed a means to that end. But the fact that no explanation at all was given for the statement of article 91

---

[47] Cf SCHWARZ 1938, 62.
[48] See above, 77.

points to the confused thinking highlighted in chapter 5. Many thought that all that was required was minimal movement of the altar to enable the priest to face the people. Despite the specific instruction, immediately following the altar-facing-the-people statement, that its 'location in the place of worship should be truly central'[49], its position in many churches is to this day no more central than it was before the liturgical reform. The objective of the reform was grossly misunderstood as a simply a matter of improving visual and oral communication between priest and people.[50]

As early as 1971, Marcel Metzger asked this question: if the purpose of Mass facing the people was to engage their participation, has not this now been achieved in practice, thanks to the reformed rites, i.e. the 1970 Order of Mass?[51] If the recommendation for Mass facing the people had been deferred until the introduction of the new Order of Mass, would it have then been more carefully integrated with it, complete with an adequate rationale?

And there is another underlying reason. Whereas the Eucharistic Prayer has always been directed to God the Father, for the last eight centuries the devotional focus has been concentrated on what is happening on the altar, specifically the conversion of the bread and wine into the Body and Blood of Christ. Priests were instructed to say the words of consecration very carefully indeed, and to this day publishers are required to print those words in capital letters and with distinct typography. Mass is seen as an encounter with Christ and his 'real presence' on the altar. The Eucharistic Prayer is regarded as just the textual shell for the words of institution. It is a particularly christological attitude – and indeed the Vatican Council's Constitution on the Liturgy is notably more christological in tone than Pius XII's *Mediator Dei*.

---

[49] Inter Œcumenici, art. 91.
[50] Cf O'LOUGHLIN 2017.
[51] Cf METZGER 1971, 138-143, here 140.

From this viewpoint, it therefore doesn't matter that the priest now stands on the opposite side of the altar: it supposedly focuses the attention on what he does at it – which is reduced to utterance of the words of consecration and the displaying to the people of the newly-consecrated elements. So whatever lies behind the altar is reduced to irrelevance – except for the 'real presence' preserved in the tabernacle, if it is situated there. It is a very stunted way of viewing liturgy.

At the time of the Vatican Council, the understanding of ritual was at a low ebb. Since then, serious study has rediscovered levels of ritual that form the basis of the liturgical rites and participation in them – which is why the opening chapter of this book is dedicated to an introduction to ritual. Participation, as Guardini stated clearly in 1964, is not about texts but about something that happens, a liturgical action *into* which the people attending should be drawn. Our Swiss sculptor expresses this well:

> We have to acquire a different attitude towards worship. It's not about seeing, it's about being. It's not about being present at the celebration (*Dabeisein*): it's about being involved within the action (*Darin-Sein*). It is not a matter of denying the priest his functional space, but, on the contrary, extending it. The point is to find a form that does not make you feel you are facing something else, but one of belonging, being involved. The altar space extends not just as far as the benches; it must reach out as far as the church walls.[52]

---

[52] SCHILLING 1969, 187-188.

PART II

REAPPRAISAL

Photo 8 – Los Angeles Cathedral, USA

Photo 9 – Oakland Cathedral, USA

Photo 10 – Clifton Cathedral, Bristol, England

Photo 11 – Our Lady & St Vincent's, Potters Bar, England

Photo 12 – St François-de-Molitor, Paris, France

Photo 13 – Pallottine Church, Vallendar, Germany

Photo 14 – St Barbara's, Moers, Germany

Chapter 7

ONE PRIESTLY PEOPLE

> But you are a chosen race, a royal priesthood, a holy
> nation, God's own people. (1 Pet 2:9)

In chapter 1 I questioned the symbolism of the priest standing on the
other side of the altar.[1] Rudolf Schwarz asked the same question,
deliberately refraining from answering it.[2] Is the priest a leader of his
people in their worship of God from their side of the altar, or an 'angel
from God' from beyond the altar threshold, exercising a priesthood
inherently different from them?

What do we mean by 'priest'? There exists an unfortunate confusion
caused by linguistic usage. The New Testament uses two distinct Greek
words, *hiereus* and *presbyteros*, translated into Latin as *sacerdos* and
presbyter. In English we have only the one word, 'priest'. This is
etymologically derived from 'presbyter' – and we still have 'presbytery'

---

[1] See above, 22.
[2] See above, 112.

as a priest's dwelling[3] – but in French and Italian both original words have survived, even though they have come to mean almost the same, someone formally ordained to priestly ministry. In the New Testament, however, the two original Greek words have quite distinct meanings.[4]

Christ the High Priest

'We have a great high priest (*archiereus*) who has passed through the heavens, Jesus, the Son of God' (Heb 4:14). He was able to mediate for the human race because he took on our humanity for the very purpose of restoring it to its Creator. Through his self-sacrificial death he accomplished his Father's will, and so 'became the source of eternal salvation for all who obey him' (Heb 5:9). He is now 'seated at the right hand of the throne of the Majesty in the heavens, a minister (*leitourgos*) in the sanctuary and the true tent that the Lord, and not any mortal, has set up' (Heb 8:1-2). He is the mediator of the new covenant between God and humanity who has entered 'into heaven itself, now to appear in the presence of God on our behalf' (Heb 9:24).

> Therefore, my friends, since we have confidence to enter the sanctuary by the blood of Jesus, by the new and living way that he opened for us through the curtain (that is, through his flesh), and since we have a great priest (*hiereus*) over the house of God, let us approach with a true heart in full assurance of faith, with our hearts sprinkled clean from an evil conscience and our bodies washed with pure water. (Heb 10:19-22)

The whole of Jesus' life consisted of worship of his Father in loving obedience to his will, as well as in loving service of those he had come

---

[3] But Latin *presbyterium* is the part of the church that is known in English as the sanctuary.
[4] This chapter owes much to RICHARDS 1995 and O'COLLINS 2010. See also GALOT 1985, DODD 1967, KWASNIEWSKI 2006. For an ecumenical viewpoint, see TORRANCE 1996.

to save, for whom he gave his life as a supreme act of propitiation. Read chapter 17 of St John's gospel – known justifiably as 'the priestly prayer' although the word 'priest' does not occur in it: Jesus is praying to his Father for himself and his disciples, 'that they may all be one'.

And he continues that prayer for ever, since 'he eternally intercedes for the world,... offers himself through the Holy Spirit to the Father,... acts on earth as primary minister in all the Church's preaching and sacramental life, and in heaven remains for ever the Mediator through whom the blessed enjoy the vision of God and the risen life of glory'[5].

And who are those who are invited to associate themselves with him, their bodies "washed with pure water"?

Co-heirs with Christ

These are all Christians who have been washed with the waters of baptism – the ones to whom the author of the first Epistle of St Peter addressed his letter:

> Come to him [Jesus], a living stone, though rejected by mortals yet chosen and precious in God's sight, and like living stones, let yourselves be built into a spiritual house, to be a holy priesthood, to offer spiritual sacrifices acceptable to God through Jesus Christ. (1 Pet 2:4-5)

The word used here for 'priesthood' is *hierateuma*, derived from *hiereus* – and here it is neatly defined as the anabatic, 'upward' offering of 'spiritual sacrifices acceptable to God through Jesus Christ', the great High Priest. Christians are corporately united with Christ in his priestly worship of his Father.[6]

---

[5] O'COLLINS 2010, 265.
[6] The terms 'priests', 'kings' and 'saints' are only used in the New Testament of the whole membership of the Church collectively. The only singular priest is Jesus himself.

And we read in book of Revelation how the Lamb of God has ransomed people 'from every tribe and language and people and nation; you have made them to be a kingdom and priests (*hiereis*) serving our God' (Rev 5:9-10).

The Second Vatican Council, in its Dogmatic Constitution on the Church, *Lumen Gentium* (*LG*), combined the theology of the letter to the Hebrews with that of 1 Peter and Revelation:

> Christ the Lord, High Priest (*Pontifex*[7]) taken from among men, made the new people "a kingdom and priests (*sacerdotes*) to God the Father". The baptized, by regeneration and the anointing of the Holy Spirit, are consecrated as a spiritual house and a holy priesthood (*sacerdotium*), in order that through all those works which are those of the Christian man they may offer spiritual sacrifices and proclaim the power of Him who has called them out of darkness into His marvellous light. Therefore all the disciples of Christ, persevering in prayer and praising God, should present themselves as a living sacrifice, holy and pleasing to God. (*LG* 10)

Ordained for ministry

If this sacerdotal character is common to all Christian people, how is the ordained ministry related to it?

Lumen Gentium immediately continues from the previous excerpt:

---

[7] A 'pontifex' was a member of the council of high priests in ancient Rome. Subsequently it became a title given to a bishop in the early Church, and this usage continued in the Church as an alternative title for a bishop. The Pope is often referred to as *Pontifex Maximus*. Literally a 'bridge-builder', therefore metaphorically one who builds bridges between gods/God and human beings.

> Though they differ from one another in essence and not
> only in degree, the common priesthood of the faithful
> and the ministerial or hierarchical priesthood are
> nonetheless interrelated: each of them in its own special
> way is a participation in the one priesthood of Christ.

It is indeed clear that there can only be one priesthood, that of Jesus
Christ, which his whole people share. And indeed, we read further in 1
Peter: 'You are a chosen race, a royal priesthood, a holy nation, God's
own people' (1 Pet 2:9).

The word used for people is *laos*, which gives us the English word 'laity'.
Ordained clergy still remain members of 'God's own people' after
ordination, and therefore still technically laity, albeit with a special
ministry, rather than a separate caste of 'clergy'.[8]

Fr Jean Galot expresses the dignity of the universal priesthood thus:

> The universal priesthood expresses... the fullness of the
> holiness which Christ bestowed on his Church and on all
> her members. This holiness entails a divinization of
> human life. It represents the highest mode of
> consecration that can ever be granted to a human being.[9]

The difference between ordained and non-ordained must be sought
elsewhere. When we turn to Scripture and look for some description of
the practice of Church authority in the early Church, we find that it is
exercised by *episkopoi, presbyteroi* and *diakonoi* – bishops, presbyters
and deacons.[10] Here are some illustrative excerpts:

---

[8] Cf KUNZLER 1995, 57. Cp Code of Canon Law, no 207, 1.
[9] GALOT 1985, in chapter 6C3a. But in the following section he says 'Christ requires of
the Twelve a more complete consecration, more like his own', and proposes this as the
model for the ministerial priesthood.
[10] Galot advises that, in sub-apostolic times, these terms did not have the precise
definitions of function and scope that we now ascribe to them. In particular, deacons

Paul, addressing the presbyters at Ephesus on leaving them, says:

> Keep watch over yourselves and over all the flock, of which the Holy Spirit has made you overseers (*episkopoi*), to shepherd the church of God that he obtained with the blood of his own Son. (Acts 20:28)

In 1 Peter we read (5:1-4):

> Now as an elder (*presbyteros*) myself and a witness of the sufferings of Christ, as well as one who shares in the glory to be revealed, I exhort the elders among you to tend the flock of God that is in your charge, exercising the oversight (*episkopountes*), not under compulsion but willingly, as God would have you do it—not for sordid gain but eagerly. Do not lord it over those in your charge[11], but be examples to the flock. And when the chief shepherd appears, you will win the crown of glory that never fades away.

What is clear in these two passages are the references to shepherding and pastoral care (from Latin *pastor*, a shepherd). It is taking the image of Jesus the Good Shepherd in John chapter 10 as the ideal for ministry in the Church.[12]

---

performed much more than 'serve at tables' (Acts 6:2-4). There is no biblical evidence for the role of leaders in baptizing, celebrating the Eucharist, or instituting others in their leadership roles, though commissioning for mission involved the imposition of hands and invocation of the Holy Spirit (Acts 13:3; 14:23; 1 Tim 4:14; 2 Tim 1:6).

[11] 'Those in your charge' is a translarion oi *tōn klerōn*. It is an ironic quirk of etymological history that its derivatives, *clerus*, Italian *clero*, English cleric and clergy, now means those *taking* charge. See also Acts 1:17, where it means a share in ministry. For the origin of these words, cf 'cleric' in Wikipedia.

[12] Galot (chapter 7B) describes the essence of priestly ministry under the title of 'shepherd'.

And indeed, the apostles by their very name have a mission, a job for which they are sent – from Greek *apostolos*, one who is sent out. That is a share in the mission of Jesus himself, 'the *apostle* and high priest of our confession' (Heb 3:1), who was sent by the Father on his mission to reconcile humanity to Him. Jesus sent out the apostles to preach and minister the Good News of the Kingdom. Bishops are described frequently as 'successors to the apostles'[13].

Nowhere in the New Testament are the apostles described as *hiereis*, priests, but by the early second century the understanding of the bishop's role and status as representative of Christ, and even 'image of the Father' is attested by St Ignatius of Antioch. It is the bishop who makes the celebration of the Eucharist lawful – and St Ignatius calls him a 'priest', even a 'high-priest'[14].

Not so St Augustine. 'The one and only priest is the mediator himself, the sinless head of the Church'[15] – Jesus Christ. 'The reason, though, why all of us bishops are called priests (*sacerdotes*) is that we are the people in charge.[16] However, it is the whole universal Church which is the body of that one priest. To the priest belongs his body. That, after all, is why the apostle Peter says to the Church itself, "A holy people, a royal priesthood" (1 Pet 2:9).'[17]

Priesthood and presbyterate

There are, then, two distinct profiles: on the one hand, the 'common priesthood' shared by all God's people, and, on the other hand, the apostolic ministry of preaching, mission and pastoral care exercised by

---

[13] Cf e.g. *LG* 20.
[14] Ignatius of Antioch, *Letter to the Smyrnaeans*, 8,2 and 9,2.
[15] Augustine, *Sermon 198*, 51 – HILL 1997, 220.
[16] In *De Civitate Dei*, 20, 10, Augustine says that both *episcopi* and *presbyteri* are called *sacerdotes*, but so are all Christians because they are members of a single *sacerdos*.
[17] Augustine, *Sermon 198*, 49 – HILL 1997, 218. Augustine makes no mention of presbyters in this sermon.

bishops, presbyters and deacons. 1 Peter makes no explicit connection between the priesthood of Christ and the ministry of presbyters. The priesthood of the Church is to be found not in their ministry but in Christ alone, in his Paschal mystery.[18]

The Vatican Council's Decree on the Ministry and Life of Presbyters (*PO*) is specifically aimed at those ordained ministers who are neither bishops nor deacons. In the original Latin of this decree the word *sacerdos* is used only of Christ himself and his priesthood; ordained priests are described throughout as *presbyteri*. But English translations have failed to maintain this careful distinction and use the word 'priest' to translate both 'priest' and 'presbyter' indifferently, confusing them.

Whatever the linguistic difficulty with which we are saddled, it is clear that the office of presbyter, or indeed of bishop, is not some super-priesthood. The sharing of Christ's priesthood endowed by baptism is not affected or changed by ordination. The hierarchy of bishops, presbyters and deacons is a graded sharing in the mission of Jesus, passed on to his apostles and through them to today's ministers of his word and of his pastoral care. It is thus a constitutive structure of the Church, overlying and distinct from the priesthood common to all God's people, laity and clergy alike.

It is indeed a *ministry* different in essence, as *Lumen Gentium* stated, because bishops, presbyters and deacons have a particular responsibility for continuing the mission of Jesus conferred on them by the laying on of hands at their ordination, which is a consecration to *ministry*.[19] Hence its description as 'ministerial priesthood', as in this paragraph from the General Instruction of the Roman Missal:

---

[18] VANHOYE 1980, 266.
[19] *PO* 2 makes clear that the difference between the priesthood of the laity and the 'priestly office' (*officium sacerdotalis*) is one of ministry. St Paul describes his calling 'to be a minister (*leitourgon*) of Christ Jesus', but immediately refers to his 'priestly service (*hierourgounta*) of the gospel of God' (Rom 15:16).

> [T]he nature of the ministerial priesthood also puts into its
> proper light another reality, which must indeed be highly
> regarded, namely, the royal priesthood of the faithful,
> whose spiritual sacrifice is brought to completeness
> through the ministry of the Bishop and the priests in union
> with the Sacrifice of Christ, the one and only Mediator.[20]

The function of ministerial priesthood is 'to be the sacrament of Christ's
mediation, [to] manifest the presence of Christ-Mediator... Apart from
Christ's priesthood, it has no value or content; apart from the common
priesthood [of the people of God], is has no meaning or use'.[21]

Attempts at clarification

In 1992, the newly-published Catholic Catechism described the
ministerial priesthood as being 'at the service of the common
priesthood'.[22] It went on to state that it 'differs in essence from the
common priesthood of the faithful because it confers a sacred power for
the service of the faithful'.[23] This 'sacred power' or authority conferred
by priestly ordination is nowhere defined, but may perhaps be
understood by analogy with the *exousia*, the power of the Holy Spirit to
heal, to reconcile and to sanctify – and the authority to do so – as
exemplified by Jesus when he cured the sick paralytic in Mk 2:10, and
shared with his disciples in Mk 6:7 when he gave them *exousia* over
unclean spirits.

In 1997, a Vatican Instruction appeared, stating that 'the essential
difference between the common priesthood of the faithful and the
ministerial priesthood is not found in the priesthood of Christ, which
remains forever one and indivisible... The diversity exists at the *mode* of

---

[20] GIRM, no. 5.
[21] VANHOYE 1977, 160.
[22] Catechism of the Catholic Church, no 1547. See also no 1581.
[23] Id, no 1592.

participation in the priesthood of Christ'.[24] Ordination to the ministerial priesthood is 'rooted in the Apostolic Succession' and 'renders its sacred ministers servants of Christ and of the Church by means of authoritative proclamation of the Word of God, the administration of the sacraments and the pastoral direction of the faithful'.[25] In 2002, Pope John Paul II described the ministerial priesthood as a special 'form of participation in Christ's mission', thus in terms of ministry.[26] But this fails to explain how this is a difference *of priesthood*. Indeed, the emphasis is on the interdependence of ordained and common priesthood: 'between both there is an effective unity since the Holy Spirit makes the Church one in communion, in service and in the outpouring of the diverse hierarchical and charismatic gifts.'[27]

Lay people also share in the apostolate.[28] 'In the Church there is a diversity of service but unity of purpose.'[29] Not only do the laity share in the priestly, prophetic and royal office of Christ; they are to proclaim and give witness to God's glory by their lives and share in the mission of the Church. According to the Decree on the Apostolate of the Laity, this is to be done under the leadership of their 'priests'.[30] But even its original Latin unhelpfully describes them here as *sacerdotes* rather than *presbyteri*.

In persona Christi capitis

In the liturgical assembly we have the community of Christian faithful, ordained and 'lay', exercising their common priesthood of worship of God and intercession for the world. The bishop or presbyter is entitled

---

[24] Inter-Dicasterial Instruction *'Ecclesiae de mysterio'*, dated 15 August 1997, article 1.
[25] Ibid.
[26] Address by Pope John Paul II to Brazilian bishops, 21 September 2002.
[27] *'Ecclesiae de mysterio'*, article 1, and see *LG* 4.
[28] The title of the first chapter of the Council's Decree on the Apostolate of the Laity (henceforward *AA*).
[29] *AA* 2.
[30] *AA* 10.

to lead the community in the liturgy by virtue of the authority of leadership conferred on him by ordination. He is entrusted with the pastoral ministry of 'gathering the sheep' to hear the word of God and to be fed by it. By doing so he is continuing the mission of Christ himself.

> In the ecclesial service of the ordained minister, it is Christ himself who is present to his Church as Head of his Body, Shepherd of his flock, high priest of the redemptive sacrifice, Teacher of Truth. This is what the Church means by saying that the priest, by virtue of the sacrament of Holy Orders, acts *in persona Christi Capitis...*[31]

...in the *persona* of Christ the Head. This is a direct reference to Col 1:18 ('He is the head of the body, the church') and to Eph 4:15-16:

> We are to grow up in every way into him who is the head, into Christ, from whom the whole body... makes bodily growth and upbuilds itself in love.

This use of the Pauline image of head and body is very helpful in clarifying the relationship of bishop/presbyter both to Christ the High Priest[32], and to the priestly people whom he leads in worship, and who worship with him as a single community. It also makes clear that the offering of every Eucharist is always that of the whole Church, head and body.[33] 'The head cannot be separated from the members, nor can

---

[31] *Catechism*, no 1548. The description of the action of the ordained priest as being *in persona Christi* goes back to St Thomas Aquinas (STh, III, q.22, 4c and elsewhere), and has a long history. The addition of the attributive *capitis* is found in *PO* no. 2 and later documents (see further in DANTAS 2020). Note how the images of 'head' and 'shepherd' are conjoined here, as also in *PO* no. 6.

[32] Cf id., no 1545. This quotes St Thomas Aquinas as stating that 'Christ alone is the true priest, but others are His ministers' (*Ad Hebr.,* 7-4 – reference corrected). The identity with Christ is sacramental, for 'no human being, as such, participates in the unique, personal and incommunicable priesthood of Christ' – KILMARTIN 1998, 377.

[33] Dodd (DODD 1967, 686) describes the mystery of (ministerial) priesthood as 'the sacrament of the universal Headship of Christ drawing all... to the unity of His Body'.

the members from the head.'[34] Before any distinction of ministry, the Church is one holy people of God.

Therefore, continuing *LG* 10:

> The ministerial priest, by the sacred power he enjoys, teaches and rules the priestly people; acting in the person of Christ, he makes present the Eucharistic sacrifice, and offers it to God in the name of all the people. But the faithful, in virtue of their royal priesthood, join in the offering of the Eucharist.

'Acting in the person of Christ' – indeed, the *exousia* or 'character' the priest receives at ordination authorizes and enables him, in celebrating the Eucharist, to so identify with Christ the High Priest that he becomes his instrument, so that what Christ performed at the Last Supper – "This is my Body... This is my Blood" – takes place at the Eucharist: 'he has been enabled to function transparently as Christ's own voice and hands'[35].

'We worship and pray to the Father in such a way that it is Christ himself who is the real content of our worship and prayer.' And 'in the Spirit the prayer that ascends from us to the Father is a form of the self-offering of Christ himself'.[36]

---

[34] Pope St Leo the Great, *Sermon 12 on the Passion*, 3.

[35] KWASNIEWSKI 2006, 321. 'He is both speaking and doing *ex persona Christi*, at once distancing himself—"he said to his disciples..."—and daring to quote and to act in the first person: "Take this, all of you, and eat it: This is my Body...." (id, 325). Gerhards counsels caution: 'But [note] the primacy of the epicletical before the assertive: priestly ministry (and priestly spirituality) culminates in the ministry of intercession which God is fulfilling in His saving action here and now - the epiclesis of the Holy Spirit. The primacy of the epicletic prevents a one-sided power mentality in relation to the priestly action "in persona Christi". The presence of Christ is not decreed, but solicited: "Send your spirit upon these gifts of bread and wine, that they may become for us the body and blood of our Lord Jesus Christ" (GERHARDS 2011b, 279).

[36] TORRANCE 1996, 209, quoted in O'COLLINS 2010, 227 and 266.

Thus in offering sacrifice to God in the role of Christ as both head of the community he serves, and as an image of Christ the High Priest, the presbyter's direction of prayer and worship is – like the people offering with him – essentially anabatic, towards God the Father. Jesus addressed his High Priestly prayer to Him; now the bishop/presbyter, *in persona Christi capitis*, is addressing the Father with his prayers and offering, those of the community who surround him, and those of the whole body that is the Church.

> Because in Christian worship everything takes place by means of signs perceptible to the senses, there is a need of a representation, a making visible of the one who mysteriously presides over and sustains the liturgical celebration. The one who presides fulfils this task [of representation]... He, as it were, goes ahead of the procession, which is on its way to God.[37]

Is it not therefore preferable that this united offering of praise and prayer to the unseen God be symbolised by a united gesture of direction?[38] Yes, Christ is present sacramentally in the Eucharistic species, and is symbolised by the altar on which they are located. But the sacrificial action of Christ's self-offering and ours points beyond it, to 'where' the glorified Christ is now with the Father.[39]

> For here we have no lasting city, but we are looking for the city which is to come. Through him, then, let us continually offer a sacrifice of praise to God, that is, the fruit of lips that confess his name. (Heb 13:14-15)

---

[37] KUNZLER 1995, 58.
[38] See above, 126, for Pope Benedict's statement on this.
[39] See Rudolf Schwarz in chapter 4 above. Reinhard Messner talks of the 'eccentric centre of the community', meaning a 'centre' or focus beyond it. Cf MESSNER 2003.

Chapter 8

THE ALTAR-TABLE

The altar is the focal point of a Catholic church. Its history has already been sketched in chapter 2, where its orientation and location were reviewed. However, it is necessary to consider further its liturgical and theological significance.

The meal that makes community

The Last Supper was held at one or more low dining tables arranged in a U-shaped profile, with Jesus and the apostles reclining round them: Jesus, the host, would have taken his place at one end.[1] Whether or not it was a Passover meal[2], breaking a loaf of bread and sharing the pieces among the guests was notable and noticed: indeed, it was significant enough for the Emmaus disciples, reclining with Jesus for supper, to

---

[1] BRADSHAW 2012, 2. Cf HEID 2019, 417 & 419 for sixth-century depictions of the Last Supper in mosaic in the nave of Sant' Apollinare Nuovo, Ravenna and in the diocesan museum of Rossano. Compare with traditional 16th-century depictions based on Leonardo da Vinci's painting in Santa Maria delle Grazie in Milan, with everyone seated (instead of reclining) and Jesus at the centre.

[2] The synoptic gospels have it as a Passover meal, John as a meal on the eve of the Passover. One theory is that two different calendars were in use.

recognise him 'in the breaking of bread' (Lk 24:30,35)[3]. The Pentecost converts 'devoted themselves to the apostles' teaching and fellowship, to the breaking of bread and the prayers' (Acts 2:42), and indeed the early Christian community was 'day by day attending the temple together and breaking bread in their homes' (Acts 2:46). Historically, 'breaking (of) bread' has been generally reckoned as referring to early celebrations of the Eucharist[4], but recent scholarship has cast doubt on the assumption that the term as used by Luke in Acts should be univocally identified with a sacramental celebration.[5]

Jesus' sharing of the Last Supper with his disciples must be understood in the context of the many other meals that he shared with them, and indeed shared with many people of all social strata – including sinners – as the gospels witness. 'Commensality', table-fellowship, sharing food around a common table, is an important, even essential facet of Jesus' teaching about valuing the ordinary things of life and sharing them generously.[6] Moreover, Jesus' lessons about human equality and service are encapsulated by the imagery of community meals, in which the exalted will be humbled and the humble exalted (Lk 14:7-11), where there is no distinction of class or race – in contradiction to the prevailing culture of the time, where the order of seating at meals was *intended* to demonstrate and confirm social strata.

Note, too, how St John records the Last Supper not by the incipient Eucharistic ritual described in the synoptic gospels (Mk 14:22-25, Mt 26:26-29, Lk 22:14-20), and in 1 Cor (11:23-26), but by the common

---

[3] LIGIER 1966, 18 reckons that the disciples would have also recognised him by the words of the blessing he pronounced over the bread, which would have been distinctively his own.

[4] E.g. GIRM 83.

[5] BRADSHAW 2012, 12-14. In Acts 27:35-36 Paul 'took bread (*arton*), and giving thanks to God in the presence of all he broke it and began to eat. Then they [the whole ship's company] were all encouraged and ate some food (*trophēs*).' See also MCGOWAN 2015.

[6] O'LOUGHLIN 2015a appeals for a serious rethink of understanding about the Eucharist in these terms. Cf also BRADSHAW 2010, 41-45; BRADSHAW 2012, 21; O'COLLINS 2010, 21-23.

menial service of foot-washing, about which he records Jesus' words: "for I have given you an example, that you also should do as I have done to you" (Jn 13:15) – a different kind of "do this in memory of me", one surely not intended to be restricted to an optional annual ritual performance, at the Mandatum on Maundy Thursday, nor limited to meal-times.

Indeed, it is the lack of community service that makes St Paul so angry with the Corinthians: 'when you meet together, it is not the Lord's supper that you eat. For in eating, each one goes ahead with his own meal... Shall I commend you for this? No, I will not!' (1 Cor 11:20-22). *Koinōnia*, communion-fellowship, is essential, even a criterion, for participation in the Lord's supper, which Paul then goes on to describe (1 Cor 11:23-26).

It must be noted that the Jewish tradition out of which the Eucharist developed, especially as exemplified in the *seder*, the Passover rite, saw solemn meals as both thanksgiving-sacrifice and communion-sacrifice, for Jewish prayer always begins with blessing God for his beneficence.[7] It is the *todah*, the thanksgiving-sacrifice, that is prized more highly than any other form of sacrifice: see especially Psalm 50 (LXX 49). This feature of thanksgiving as an essential preface to communion is precisely the structure of the Liturgy of the Eucharist.

Paul refers to 'the table of the Lord' (1 Cor 10:21), as distinct from 'the table of demons' – pagan altars. The writer of the letter to the Hebrews, writing some decades later, distinguished Christians from Jews: 'We have an altar from which those who officiate in the tent have no right to eat' (Heb 13:10). The implication is that Christians have their own *altars*, from which they eat their own communion-sacrifice.[8] And indeed the Jewish passover was precisely this type of sacrifice – an offering to God in which the eating of prescribed food was not only a

---

[7] BRADSHAW 2012, 5-8.
[8] BRADSHAW 2010, 42.

memorial of a past event (in a strong, anamnetic sense) but also an act of worship.[9]

The two terms, 'table of the Lord' and 'altar' are found interchangeably in early descriptions of the Eucharist.[10] Indeed, the connection between the two terms goes back to the prophet Malachi, who refers to 'altar' and 'table of the Lord' in the same verse (Mal 1:7), and to 'a pure offering' or sacrifice (Mal 1:11).

Holy bread, blood and the temple

There are other Old-Testament connections: one is between the old covenant, sealed with animal blood cast against an altar (Ex 24:6-8), and the 'new covenant in my blood' (1 Cor 11:25); another is between the shewbread or 'bread of the presence', the twelve loaves set out in the temple beside the altar of incense 'before the Lord' (Ex 25:30, Lev 24:7-9, cf Mk 2:26), and the Christian use of bread for the Eucharist.[11]

There is indeed another approach to the theology of the Eucharist, developed by Margaret Barker.[12] She has studied the Jewish literature of the time and related it especially to the Letter to the Hebrews. She proposes that the origin of the Eucharistic rite is to be found in the liturgy of the Jewish temple, particularly in the ritual of the Day of Atonement (Yom Kippur).

---

[9] BRADSHAW 2010, 62.

[10] HEID 2019, 27-68; POCKNEE 1963, 13.

[11] See BARBER 2013, 119, who claims that 'Luke's presentation of the Eucharistic rite seems to evoke three particular offerings: the bread of the presence, the Passover and the *todah*'.

[12] See BARKER 2003, especially chapter 5 'Temple Roots of the Christian Liturgy', also the papers available on her website (www.margaretbarker.com) : 'Temple and Liturgy' (2009) and 'Our Great High Priest. The Church as the New Temple' (2012). Methodist by tradition, Barker freely admits that her thinking has been strongly influenced by her experience of Eastern Orthodox liturgy.

In the first Temple (before its destruction in 587 BCE), the anointed High Priest entered the Holy of Holies on that day, offered goat's blood for the remission of sins, and, together with his fellow-priests, even drank some of it mixed with vinegar.[13] Jesus 'took a cup, and when he had given thanks he gave it to them, saying, "Drink of it, all of you; for this is my blood of the covenant, which is poured out for many for the forgiveness of sins"'(Mt 26:27-28). This is the definitive Day of Atonement, the renewal of the original covenant of God with mankind, broken by Adam's sin and now restored once-for-all in Jesus. He, the anointed Messiah, the Christ, is the new and everlasting high priest 'according to the order of Melchizedek' (Heb 6:20).

Melchizedek brought out bread and wine for Abram (Gen 14:18). Jesus was not of the priestly tribe of Levi – in fact, the Passover was the one event of the Jewish calendar that was *not* led by a priest. The new priesthood is not a matter of tribal inheritance. In the temple the shewbread, the bread of the presence, was sacred to God and expressed His presence – it could only be consumed by the temple priests. In Matthew's account of the Last Supper, 'Jesus took bread, and blessed, and broke it, and gave it to his disciples, and said, "Take, eat; this is my body"'(Mt 26:26). He had himself become the new Bread of the Presence, to be shared by all his disciples.

In the Temple, the Holy of Holies was the place where God's presence was accomplished, His Kingdom and reign fulfilled. It therefore had an eschatological significance. The invocation *maranatha*, 'come, Lord Jesus', occurs both as the final words of St Paul's First Letter to the Corinthians, and as the final words of the first recorded *anaphora*, in the *Didache*, which, like the Letter to the Hebrews, dates from the final decades of the first century CE.[14] This text instructs members of the Sunday assembly to 'give thanksgiving after having confessed your

---

[13] Cf Lev 4:8-10. All the gospels record that Jesus drank some vinegar as he was dying.
[14] Caution should be exercised in naming the rite described in the *Didache*. 'More recently... there has emerged a growing consensus that it was one of the forms of early Christian meal out of which the later Eucharist developed' (BRADSHAW 2012, 16).

transgressions, that your sacrifice may be pure' – see the reference to Mal 1:11 noted above. But it contains no reference to the Last Supper or to the redemptive effects of Christ's sacrifice.[15] Nor does Justin's description of an early Eucharist, nor the Strasbourg Papyrus, an early (third century?) *anaphora*.[16] Scholars conjecture that the origins of the Eucharistic Prayer are to be found in the Jewish *birkat-ha-mazon*, or formal thanksgiving after meals.[17]

The narrative of the Last Supper only appears in Eucharistic Prayers from the middle of the fourth century, notably in the text that dates from that time and has become the Roman Canon (Eucharistic Prayer I).[18] The redemptive theme has come to be expressed in the *anamnesis* which immediately follows. The Roman Canon then also refers to 'the offering of your high priest Melchizedek' which is described as 'a holy sacrifice, a spotless victim' by forward reference to Christ.[19]

Obviously, the physical configuration of temple worship, with a distinctive Holy of Holies, could not be carried over into Christian worship while it still had no buildings dedicated to this purpose. The Eastern liturgical tradition later developed a ritual and architectural tradition that reserves the east-end sanctuary of its churches to clergy, who perform behind a richly decorated iconostasis which closes them off from the laity. Maximus the Confessor (580-662) sees the altar as the throne of God, the sanctuary as heaven, the nave as earth. For him the Eucharist is 'the eschatological sacrament *par excellence*, collapsing sacred past, present and future, and also merging heaven and earth in the glorious celebration of the paschal mystery of Jesus Christ'.[20]

---

[15] Paul's term 'the Lord's supper' (1 Cor 11:20) is not repeated in Patristic literature. Tertullian comes nearest to it with *convivium dominicum* and *cena Dei* (*Ad uxorem* II, 4, 2; II, 8, 8; *De spectaculis* 13, 4).
[16] BRADSHAW 2010, 52-53.
[17] BRADSHAW 2012, 6-7, 16; MAZZA 1986, 16-21.
[18] BRADSHAW 2010, 54; MAZZA 1986, 57-59.
[19] MAZZA 1986, 80.
[20] BLOWERS 2016, 166-195, here 175.

Western liturgy and architecture developed differently. Nonetheless, St Augustine paints a two-layer picture of Eucharistic celebration. He describes how, when the high priest alone used to enter the Holy of Holies, all the people stood outside. But now, while the bishops stand at the altar, the people are inside, 'hearing and attesting and receiving' – standing about the altar, taking part in the liturgy. But there is also an eschatological level. 'Just once in the whole course of time our one and only priest rising from the dead, our Lord Jesus Christ, entered the true, not the figurative, holy of holies, beyond the veils of heaven, offering himself for us. He entered, and there he now is.[21] But the people, together with us bishops, are still standing outside; we haven't yet risen "to go to meet Christ and remain with him for ever" (1 Thess 4:17) inside.'[22] The Eucharist is a celebration today of a mystery to be fulfilled tomorrow.

From table to altar

Early accounts of the Eucharist in the first-century *Didache*, and in the second-century writings of Justin martyr, do not specify altar or table. St Ignatius of Antioch, writing at some time in the second century, encourages the Christians of Philadelphia in Asia Minor to take part in the Eucharist zealously, for there is 'one flesh of our Lord Jesus Christ, one chalice for union with his blood, on one *altar* under one bishop with his presbyters and deacons'.[23]

Like the apostle Paul, the third-century North African fathers, Tertullian and Cyprian of Carthage, distinguished the pagan altar (*ara*) from the Christian (*altare*).[24] As we saw earlier, Tertullian describes not only an evening *convivium* at which the guests reclined, but also a morning celebration at which *eucharistiae sacramentum* is consumed,

---

[21] Heb 9:11-12,24.
[22] Augustine, *Sermon 198*, 53 – HILL 1997, 221.
[23] Ignatius of Antioch, *Epistle to the Philadelphians*, 4, quoted in HEID 2019, 49.
[24] JENSEN 2019, 40.

presumably around a wooden table.[25] By Cyprian's time some decades later, morning celebrations had become the norm, not least because it was only then that the entire community could assemble[26]. So they must have gathered in a building large enough to accommodate them.

Once permanent buildings for Christian worship became possible under Emperor Constantine and developed thereafter, fixed stone altars became the norm, albeit with regional variations.[27] Altars came to be identified with what took place on them, such that fixed altars came to seen as signifying Christ, the living stone (1 Pet 2:4; cf Eph 2:20-21)[28]. So the designation 'table' receded into the background, although Latin *mensa* (table) came to be adopted as the technical description of the flat top of the altar, as distinct from the *stipes*, or supports beneath it.

In Rome, the supreme sacrifice of martyrs was seen as witness and symbol of Christ's sacrifice, and honoured by incorporating their sarcophagi into the *stipes* of altars, or beneath them. This has a scriptural foundation in Rev 6:9: 'I saw under the altar the souls of those who had been slaughtered for the word of God and for the testimony they had given'. The observance of this tradition is particularly evident in the 'confessions' underneath the main altar of St Peter's basilica and elsewhere, and also in the incorporation of relics into new altars even to this day. In the absence of sarcophagi, however, altars were of modest dimensions, perhaps little more than a metre square – there was no room for candles, missals or other decorations.[29]

---

[25] Tertullian, *Ad uxorem* II, 4, 2; II, 8, 8; *De corona,* 3, 3.
[26] Cyprian, *Epistolae* 63, 16 – 'ut sacramenti veritatem fraternitate omni praesente celebremus'.
[27] There were some wooden altars in England as late as the 15th century (POCKNEE 1963, 37).
[28] GIRM 298.
[29] JUNGMANN 1951, I, 109, note 37.

The public recognition of Christianity in the fourth century led to a huge number of new converts, with great crowds at liturgical celebrations in the vast new churches being built. More people attended, but with less appreciation of why. At the end of the century, St John Chrysostom complained about their poor behaviour and warned them not to receive Holy Communion if they were not properly prepared for it – so they didn't.[30] It was the beginning of communion-less attendance of the laity at Mass – and to its celebration becoming an entirely clerical affair.[31] In 1215, the fourth Lateran Council had to compel lay people to receive Communion at least once a year. The norm of rare reception of Communion lasted until the reign of Pope Pius X[32], but his measures to encourage daily reception of Holy Communion failed to reintegrate it with the Eucharistic participation that his 1903 letter *Tra le sollecitudini* had promoted, with the result that Communion was distributed frequently, even principally, outside of Mass, and therefore perforce from the tabernacle. This practice of 'tabernacle Communion' continues to this day even within Mass, despite official contrary recommendations.[33]

By medieval times, the original Jewish source of thanksgiving- and communion-sacrifice had become transmuted into 'the sacrifice of the Mass' understood as a sacramental offering of Calvary, and as an occasion for the miracle of transsubstantiation. Neither of the original concepts of thanksgiving and communion featured in popular devotional understanding of the Mass. The revived use of the word 'Eucharist' is entirely due to the Liturgical Renewal, but even now its meaning as 'thanksgiving' is opaque to many people.

---

[30] BRADSHAW 2012, 63-67.
[31] Chauvet calls it 'the confiscation of the baptismal priesthood of the entire people of God by the priests' – CHAUVET 1994, 309.
[32] His decree *Quam singulari* of 1910 reinstated the reception of Communion by children 'from the age of reason', but there had been an earlier decree in 1905 encouraging daily reception of Holy Communion by the faithful.
[33] *SC* 55.

Earthly and heavenly altar

The principal celebrant of the Eucharistic sacrifice is Jesus Christ himself, the one and only High Priest, offering himself eternally to the Father: he is 'the priest, the altar and the lamb of sacrifice'[34], 'through whom alone the divine work for many (*leitourgia*) can take place, lifting up humankind – and through him the whole of creation – into the fullness of life in the Trinity'[35].

The bishop or presbyter who leads the local church in praying the Eucharistic prayer does so '*in persona Christi capitis*', as we have seen. In the Preface he prays in union with the whole heavenly host, acknowledging 'Holy, holy, holy' – and indeed the altar, though materially on earth, is symbolically a heavenly altar.

> With Christ the heavenly liturgy of the Trinity had appeared on earth... [It] has its home on earth in the Son of God made man. His body is the temple of this liturgy (Mark 14:58), and its gates stand open inviting to participation in the divine life.[36]

Therefore, in response to this invitation to divine communion, the Church prays, as the Roman Canon (Eucharistic Prayer I) says:

> In humble prayer we ask you, almighty God:
> command that these gifts be borne
> by the hands of your holy Angel
> to your altar on high,
> so that all of us, who through this participation at the altar
> receive the most holy Body and Blood of your Son,
> may be filled with every grace and heavenly blessing.

---

[34] *Roman Missal*, Preface V of Easter.
[35] KUNZLER 1995, 45.
[36] KUNZLER 1995, 41.

Thus Joseph Ratzinger claims: 'we become contemporaries with Jesus Christ's own act of worship, into which, through his Body, he takes up worldly time and straightway leads it beyond itself... [and] into the communion of saints of all times and places...' And he continues: 'The altar is the place where heaven is torn apart. It does not close off the church, but opens it up – and leads it into the eternal liturgy.'[37] Guardini speaks of a 'divine remoteness' beyond the church altar[38], represented symbolically by the traditional east-end apse image or stained-glass window behind the altar. In the incarnation, God crossed over to our side in order to draw us to His side: 'His descent draws us upward... so that we might become "partakers of the divine nature"'[39].

The altar is thus the place of God-human communication, a threshold, as Guardini and Schwarz describe it. A threshold defines a boundary. Schwarz, in particular, sought to express this in his 'plans' – even in his *Ringkirche*, with people around three sides of the altar. The fourth side was to be empty, expressive of a divine presence that is also an absence.

We can meet God at this symbolic altar, but cannot tread over into His side, at least until he takes us to Himself in death. Instead He crosses over to our side of the altar in order to give us Himself sacramentally in Holy Communion, as an anticipation of the banquet meal at the heavenly altar: 'Blessed are those called to the supper of the Lamb' (cf Rev 19:9, now used as the liturgical invitation to Holy Communion).

Both sacrifice and meal

This encounter with God is activated especially by the priest exercising his ordained ministry as he prays the Eucharistic Prayer on behalf of

---

[37] RATZINGER 2000, 70-71, translation amended. Original: '...Ort des aufgerissenen Himmels...' Cf also HEID 2019, 355.
[38] GUARDINI 2014, 43.
[39] Id, 44, 46. The reference to "partakers of the divine nature" is to one of prayers at the Offertory in the older Roman rite, in turn drawn from the Collect for the Christmas Mass of the Day.

the assembled community. In doing so, he is associating himself and the worshipping congregation with the sacrifice of Christ himself, once in time but continued in eternity – Christ the mediator between God and Man because God and man himself, and therefore high priest of mankind, presenting his sacrificial offering to his Father (Heb 4:14; 9:11-12). Christ is both he who offers and that which is offered, priest and victim. His people are invited to offer themselves to God similarly, and thus enter into his self-offering.[40] St Paul says to the Roman faithful: 'I appeal to you, therefore, brothers and sisters, by the mercies of God, to present your bodies as a living sacrifice, holy and acceptable to God, which is your spiritual worship (*logikē latreia*)' (Rom 12:1).

The sacrifice of the Mass is the *anamnesis* – the formal remembrance of a past event which actualises it in the present – of the total self-giving of Jesus Christ to his Father, in loving obedience to his will. It is an entering into his sacrifice, which is a *tōdah*, a thanksgiving-sacrifice offered by Jesus to his Father[41]; Christians unite themselves with his sacrifice by a celebration that is both thanksgiving and communion.

When we say "we offer the sacrifice of the Mass", it is not primarily our offering, but his, in which we are privileged to participate.[42] This cannot be done fruitfully, however, without the willingness of the participants to enter into the spirit of his self-offering – by offering themselves and all that is dear to them to the will of God, as Jesus did. That will was the salvation of humankind, for which purpose the Son of God became incarnate as a human being. His saving sacrifice was for our benefit. In giving himself wholly to his Father, he also gave himself to us as our food and drink, as the sacrament of his Body and Blood.

---

[40] SC 48.
[41] RATZINGER 1986, 51-60.
[42] Better precision and understanding of what is meant by 'sacrifice' in relationship to the Eucharist is overdue. See, for instance, KIRWAN 2007; KILMARTIN 1998, 337-383. Presbyterian Professor Torrance calls earthly liturgy 'an echo of the sacrifice of Christ made on our behalf' (TORRANCE 1993, 96).

Sacrifice and communion are therefore not two separate things, but one and the same act of Christ's self-giving, to his Father and to his Church. For sacramental communion, all its members have to do materially is to provide bread and wine, food and drink as the basis and symbol of human life, so that by the *epiclesis* or invocation of the Holy Spirit, these gifts may become Christ's Body and Blood for our sustenance and union with him.[43]

The ritual consumption of the sanctified bread and wine is an integral part of the Eucharist, and indeed its most visible and readily discernible sacramental sign. 'For as often as you eat this bread and drink this cup, you proclaim the Lord's death until he comes' (1 Cor 11:26): 'in this way, these sacramental actions alone – for Paul excludes the paschal context – form the memorial of the Lord Jesus'.[44] This gives added importance to the symbolism of eating and drinking as the most universal social nature of the human meal as a means of sharing table-fellowship with members of one's own community, and strangers too.[45]

Altar-table

Bread and wine are brought to the altar in preparation for the communion-meal. And it is from the altar that, having been sanctified by epiclesis, in anamnesis of the Paschal mystery, they are served to the people who are present for them to eat and drink. Does this make the

---

[43] Thus the *Catechism* (no 1353), which, however, then goes on to say that 'in the *institution narrative*, the power of the words and the action of Christ, and the power of the Holy Spirit, make sacramentally present under the species of bread and wine Christ's body and blood'. What about the eastern-rite Liturgy of Addai and Mari, which does not contain the gospel words of the institution narrative? This apparent difficulty was eventually decided by a decree of the Holy See in 2001, which stated: 'The words of Eucharistic Institution are indeed present in the Anaphora of Addai and Mari, not in a coherent narrative way and *ad litteram*, but rather in a dispersed euchological way, that is, integrated in successive prayers of thanksgiving, praise and intercession'. Cf also BRADSHAW 2012, esp. 314-315, and KWASNIEWSKI 2006.
[44] LIGIER 1966, 22.
[45] O'LOUGHLIN 2015a *passim*.

altar an earthly or celestial 'dining table'? Is the Eucharistic Prayer a rather elaborate 'grace before meals'?[46]

From the late 4th to the early 20th century the Mass was not seen as the occasion for the sharing of Communion among those attending it. At a 1932 Eucharistic Congress Mass in Dublin attended by thousands of priests as well as lay people, the bishop-celebrant was the only one to receive Holy Communion.[47] But now, after the Liturgy Constitution's still lukewarm recommendation that Communion under both kinds may be conceded to the laity[48], we have the sacramental signs of a sacred meal – indeed, *the* sacred meal – in 'a fuller form'[49] shared by as many as possible of those attending and participating in the liturgy. Blessed indeed are those called to the supper of the Lamb, who now celebrate its anticipation in the Eucharistic sacrifice-meal. As the second preface of the Holy Eucharist says:

> And so we approach the table of this wondrous Sacrament,
> so that, bathed in the sweetness of your grace,
> we may pass over to the heavenly realities here
>   foreshadowed.[50]

One should not therefore shirk the symbolic and liturgical connection between altar and dining-table. Catholic theology has traditionally resisted the term 'communion-table' as being too redolent of some Protestant theology's denial of the sacrificial significance of the Mass. But indeed the altar is the 'table of the Lord' from which his people are fed and enter into communion with him and fellowship with their co-communicants, one Body in Christ.

---

[46] RATZINGER 1986, 38 writes: '*Eucharistia* is *also* (but not solely) the grace said before the sacred meal. But the meal symbolism is subordinated to a larger whole and integrated into it.' (Original italics)
[47] O'LOUGHLIN 2015a, 36-37.
[48] SC 55.
[49] GIRM 281.
[50] Original: '...ad caelestis formae imaginem transeamus'.

In pastoral practice there is much that militates against that perception of a sacred meal. The Eucharist is fulfilled in a special way when all its participants both eat and drink the Holy Communion, as the Lord directed. But Communion under both kinds is generally rare, though more common in Anglophone countries than elsewhere.[51] 'Because there is one bread [-loaf], we who are many are one body' (1 Cor 10:17), but the use of individual round hosts denies the important symbol of sharing a single broken bread.[52] Despite repeated recommendations that people should receive Communion from hosts consecrated at the same sacrifice in which they have been participating, the use of hosts consecrated at a previous Mass and fetched from a tabernacle denies the symbolism of sharing the same meal.[53] And although Eucharistic ministers – and sometimes altar servers – may actually consume the hosts all at the same time, Communion is otherwise distributed to individuals, albeit united in a single procession, or is it just a queue?[54] The congregational singing of a Communion Song, intended to show the 'communitarian' nature of the rite[55], is well-intentioned but generally unpopular, because perceived as a distraction from personal devotion.

Direction

We have then 'in play' an earthly altar and a heavenly one, an earthly 'table of the Lord' and a heavenly banquet. The earthly pair are visible,

---

[51] O'LOUGHLIN 2015a, 173, also O'LOUGHLIN 2015b, 276-278. The practice is locally dependent on the whim of the local parish priest.

[52] 'It is... expedient that the Eucharistic bread... be made in such a way that the priest at Mass with a congregation is able in practice to break it into parts for distribution to at least some of the faithful... The action of the fraction... will bring out more clearly the force and importance of the sign of unity of all in the one bread, and of the sign of charity by the fact that the one bread is distributed among the brothers and sisters' (GIRM 321). People readily perceive and appreciate the significance of receiving a piece of broken host at Communion.

[53] SC 55. There has never been any rubric even mentioning the fetching of hosts from a tabernacle for use during Mass. See O'LOUGHLIN 2015b, 270-272.

[54] Reinhard Messner describes this as a 'deficit' of liturgical reform: cf MESSNER 2013. But practical alternatives for all but the smallest assemblies are difficult to visualise.

[55] GIRM 86.

sacramental and symbolic of the heavenly pair. Is not the altar the focal point of the entire Liturgy of the Eucharist, one might ask?

Even though the altar might be identified with Jesus Christ, as we have seen, it is with him as 'priest' and 'lamb of sacrifice', making his offering. We make our offering with him and through him – to whom? to God his Father and ours. Despite the symbolism of solidity conveyed by many altars, it represents a threshold, a transitional boundary-point between two domains, the earthly and the heavenly. To see it as an all-embracing and exclusive focal point, a 'black hole', is to espouse a christological rather than a trinitarian focus for liturgy – a mistake, as Guardini and Schwarz pointed out.[56]

It may be true that 'the altar... is the place where it is truly the centre toward which the attention of the whole congregation of the faithful naturally turns.'[57] However, good church architecture places the altar within a much broader context, expressive of a worship that may focus on it according to ritual requirement, but which extends far beyond it.

The form of the Liturgy of the Eucharist is first anabatic, from worshipping to worshipped, from the assembly to the unseen Father, *through* Jesus Christ, in the power of the Holy Spirit. That is the movement forward, 'eastward', from the Procession of Gifts through the Eucharistic Prayer to the praying of the Lord's Prayer, *over and beyond the physical altar,* waiting 'until he comes again' (Memorial Acclamation) 'like the daystar from the east' (Lk 1:78).

The altar of thanksgiving-sacrifice is both heavenly and earthly; it is also integral with the communion-sacrifice. 'The altar is not only the

---

[56] See above, 91 – and Pius XII's definition of liturgy on page 4. Cf also Torrance, as reported in O'COLLINS 2010, 224-229.
[57] GIRM 299.

place of transubstantiation, but also that of the transformation of the
faithful that receive the Eucharist from it.'[58]

For the action *then* becomes katabatic. God in his beneficence feeds
those who have worshipped Him from the altar-table in the form of His
communion-food, consumable as bread and wine but sanctified as the
sacrament of the Body and Blood of his Son. Communicants become
the Body they receive, and are committed by the Blood of the New
Covenant they drink to live by that sacred covenant. That Holy
Communion is also the sacrament and anticipation of 'the supper of the
Lamb' hereafter, when 'the Lord of hosts will make for all peoples a
feast of rich food' (Is 25:6), the divine banquet of fulfilment.

The altar-table should be physically and symbolically located among
the people who are privileged to be guests at the Lord's Supper. But it
should also represent the threshold where the human meets the
divine.[59] For the host of our liturgical celebration and festive event is
not the local priest but Jesus himself, sacramentally here and also not
here, because glorified. It is Him that we recognise, as his disciples did
at the here and not-here of Emmaus, in the breaking of bread.

---

[58] GERHARDS 2004, 225. Cf Eucharistic Prayer III: 'Look, we pray, upon the oblation of
your Church and, recognising the sacrificial Victim (*agnoscens Hostiam*)... grant that we,
who are nourished (*reficimur*) by the Body and Blood of your Son and filled with his Holy
Spirit, may become one body, one spirit in Christ.' Thus there is a close connection
between the offering of the sacrifice by the whole assembly and their subsequent Holy
Communion. See MAZZA 1986, 137-142.
[59] 'The Altar – Centre or Threshold?': see GERHARDS 2011a, 134-141.

Chapter 9

COSMIC VISION

Every Eucharist is inescapably a celebration of the whole Church. To be a celebration of a local church community and, at the same time, of a worldwide Church of all ages in union with the communion of saints – and indeed with the choirs of heaven (cf the Preface and 'Holy, holy') – this is a mystery. The Christ who is present sacramentally and spiritually in the liturgical celebration is also the Christ who is beyond location, glorified, 'seated at the right hand of the Father'.

Every celebration of the Eucharist has cosmic significance, extending way beyond the particular parameters of space and time within which individual celebrations in churches take place. The careful preparation of liturgical celebrations by local communities, each with their own cultural and historical traditions, is both laudable and necessary. But it can sometimes result in a parochial narrow-mindedness, as if the celebration of the liturgy was a purely local affair. While this may express local community, it is counter-symbolic of the wider scope and outreach of the liturgy.

The destiny of creation

Every liturgical celebration is also an event in salvation history. It is an integral part of the great movement forward of the whole world towards the heavenly destiny that is the plan of God the Creator, encompassing all creation. 'We know that the whole creation has been groaning in labour pains until now; and not only creation, but we ourselves... groan inwardly while we wait for adoption, the redemption of our bodies. For in hope we were saved.' (Rom 8:22-24)

Teilhard de Chardin (1881-1955), the Jesuit palaeontologist and theologian, saw evolution as the movement of creation towards its God-appointed destiny, 'according to His purpose which he set forth in Christ as a plan for the fullness of time, to unite all things in him, things in heaven and things on earth' (Eph 1:9-10). That fullness (*plerōma*) of time (*kairos*) is the 'omega point' when God will be 'all in all'.[1] Christ is the Logos, 'the eternal Word, the eternal Meaning of the universe dwelling in the Son'.[2]

In the meantime, God has set humankind to be stewards of His creation, and responsible to Him for it. The increasing awareness of this ecological responsibility in the last decades is timely. Pope Francis has spelled out humankind's relationship with nature in his encyclical *Laudato Si'*. For 'nature as a whole not only manifests God but is also a *locus* of his presence. The Spirit of life dwells in every living creature and calls us to enter into relationship with Him'[3]. Creation in all its wonder is not only a motive for worship but also the means by which worship can be exercised.

The sacraments: signs of creation's fulfilment

The Sacraments are a privileged way in which nature is taken up by God to become a means of mediating

---

[1] Note that Greek has two words for time: *chronos*, the quantitative measure, and (as here) *kairos*, the proper or opportune time for action, having a qualitative, permanent nature. For de Chardin's 'omega point', cf his *The Phenomenon of Man* (Harper Perennial, original 1959) and *The Future of Man* (Image, original 1964).

[2] RATZINGER 2000, 34.

[3] *Laudato Si'*, no. 88.

supernatural life. Through our worship of God, we are invited to embrace the world on a different plane. Water, oil, fire and colours are taken up in all their symbolic power and incorporated in our act of praise... For Christians, all the creatures of the material universe find their true meaning in the incarnate Word, for the Son of God has incorporated in his person part of the material world, planting in it a seed of definitive transformation.[4]

It is in the Eucharist that all that has been created finds its greatest exaltation. Grace, which tends to manifest itself tangibly, found unsurpassable expression when God himself became man and gave himself as food for his creatures. The Lord, in the culmination of the mystery of the Incarnation, chose to reach our intimate depths through a fragment of matter. He comes not from above, but from within, he comes that we might find him in this world of ours.[5]

For Teilhard de Chardin, the change wrought on the elements of bread and wine in the Eucharist is a privileged *locus* of the growth and destiny of the universe. 'The central mystery of transubstantiation is haloed by a divinization, real though attenuated, of all the universe.'[6] From the cosmic element into which he has entered through his incarnation and in which he dwells eucharistically, 'the Word acts upon everything else to subdue and assimilate it to himself.'[7]

Pope Benedict XVI, writing earlier as Joseph Ratzinger, reported that for Teilhard 'the transubstantiated Host is the anticipation of the transformation and divinization of matter in christological "fullness".

---

[4] Id, no. 235. Romano Guardini also saw this connection between liturgy and nature: see above, 68.
[5] Id, no. 236.
[6] Excerpt from DE CHARDIN 1918.
[7] Ibid.

In his [Teilhard's] view, the Eucharist provides the movement of the cosmos with its direction; it anticipates its goal and at the same time urges it on.'[8] As Pope, Ratzinger went on to say this more explicitly in a homily in 2009:

> The role of the priesthood is to consecrate the world so that it may become a living host, a liturgy: so that the liturgy may not be something alongside the reality of the world, but that the world itself shall become a living host, a liturgy. This is also the great vision of Teilhard de Chardin: in the end we shall achieve a true cosmic liturgy, where the cosmos becomes a living host. And let us pray the Lord to help us become priests in this sense, to aid in the transformation of the world, in adoration of God, beginning with ourselves, that our lives may speak of God, that our lives may be a true liturgy, an announcement of God, a door through which the distant God may become the present God, and a true giving of ourselves to God.[9]

'Priests in this sense' must refer to the priesthood of the laity, as we examined in a previous chapter. For Alexander Schmemann[10],

> [T]he basic definition of man is that he is *the priest*. He stands in the centre of the world and unifies it in his act of blessing God, of both receiving the world from God and offering it to God – and by filling the world with this eucharist, he transforms his life, the one that he receives

---

[8] RATZINGER 2000, 29.

[9] Homily at Vespers at Aosta Cathedral, 24 July 2009: https://w2.vatican.va/ content/ benedict-xvi/en/homilies/2009/documents/hf_ben-xvi_hom_20090724_vespri-aosta.html.

[10] Alexander Schmemann (1921-1981) was an Orthodox priest and dean of Saint Vladimir's Orthodox Theological Seminary, New York. His deeply spiritual writings on the liturgy have been a major influence in the thought of Catholic liturgical scholars Aidan Kavanagh (1929-2006) and more recently David Fagerberg.

from the world, into life in God, into communion. The
world was created as the 'matter', the material of one all-
embracing eucharist, and man was created as the priest of
this cosmic sacrament.[11]

In his final book[12], Schmemann clarifies his understanding of
sacraments: 'a sacrament is primarily the revelation of the
sacramentality of creation itself, for the world was created and given to
man for conversion of creaturely life into participation in divine life.'
He continues:

> A sacrament is both cosmic and eschatological... It is
> cosmic in that embraces all of creation, it returns it to God
> as God's own... and in and by itself it manifests the
> victory of Christ. But it is to the same degree
> eschatological, oriented towards the *kingdom which is to
> come*.[13]

Eucharist, epiphany of the kingdom

And the Eucharist is *the* symbol of the kingdom – not only in its future
fulfilment, but even now, because it makes present the reality of the
kingdom, as the epiphany of what is to come[14]. Schmemann is insistent
that the Christian understanding of symbol – and therefore of
sacrament – should see it not as something illustrating some feature of
Christian doctrine or practice, but as *manifesting* the reality it
symbolises. Louis-Marie Chauvet defines a symbol as pointing to a
distinct, *absent* reality. Schmemann will not countenance such an idea.

---

[11] SCHMEMANN 1966, 16. Italics original.
[12] Acknowledged as his 'crowning achievement', this was *The Eucharist: Sacrament of the Kingdom* - SCHMEMANN 1987, here 33-34.
[13] Id, 34.
[14] Cf Fagerberg's commentary on Schmemann's work: FAGERBERG 2004, 73-105. 'Liturgy is God's act of cosmic sanctification, and the Christian cult is where this divine activity breaks surface: therein lies liturgy's eschatological significance, and the reason why it is a "Divine Liturgy" and not a human ritual' (*id*, 87).

For him the original meaning of symbol (from Greek *sym-ballō*) is 'what is joined together'. Indeed, 'it is the manifestation and presence of the *other* reality – but precisely as *other*, which... cannot be manifested and made present in any other way than as a symbol'.[15]

Icons will come to mind. 'For the icon does not "illustrate" – it *manifests*, and does so only to the degree that it is itself a *participant* in what it manifests, inasmuch as it is both presence and communion.'[16]

But Schmemann is less concerned with static objects than with the liturgical *synaxis* or assembly, especially on the Lord's day, which he sees as a symbol of the kingdom *already realized*: 'the Church epiphanizes the kingdom, as a handshake epiphanizes friendship or a kiss manifests love'.[17] In the Eucharist, we meet and share communion with him 'at his table in his kingdom'.

However, it is still work in progress. The *reditus*, the return to God from a fallen world, is being made not only for ourselves, but on behalf of those whom we left behind outside the church doors. We are baptised as a priestly people, and the task of all priests, both ordained and lay – including also Christ the High Priest – is to intercede for others.

> For we are flesh of the flesh, and blood of the blood of this world. We are part of it, and only by us and through us does it ascend to its Creator, Saviour and Lord, to its goal and fulfilment. We separate ourselves from the world in order to bring it, in order to lift it up to the kingdom, to make it once again the way to God and participation in his eternal kingdom... For this [the Church] was left in the

---

[15] Id, 38. This definition might be applied to the reserved Sacrament.
[16] Id, 45.
[17] FAGERBERG 2004, 192.

world, as part of it, as a symbol of its salvation. And this symbol we fulfil, we 'make real' in the Eucharist.[18]

In Orthodox liturgy, the bread and wine to be used at the Eucharist are set aside and have the ritual of *proskomidē* performed over them before the liturgy proper begins. Schmemann interprets this preparation as 'referring the bread and wine, i.e. our very selves and our whole life, to the sacrifice of Christ, their conversion precisely into *gift* and *offering*'[19]. Only then 'can we begin the liturgy – the eternal offering of him who offered himself, and in himself all that exists to God, the ascent of our life to that place, the altar of the kingdom'[20].

Such symbolism could very properly be transferred to the offertory procession of the Roman rite, *mutatis mutandis*. Already the *berakah*-type prayers said by the priest refer to 'work of human hands', symbols of all creation and humankind's role in its flowering. What is needed is the perception that the bread and wine being brought forward, 'taken up' in procession as a symbol of offering are but symbols of the self-gift and self-offering of and by all the members of the gathered assembly. The procession movement itself is one in which all the participants can take part symbolically, even if vicariously. So when the bread and wine are subsequently transformed, divinized by calling on the Holy Spirit in the Eucharistic Prayer, the whole assembled community is, by association with the act of offering, transformed, divinized, made one with the sacrifice of Christ.

Participating in the heavenly liturgy

'Lift up your hearts.' The symbol of ascent, of being united with the heavenly altar, continues. At every Mass, the Preface concludes by uniting the assembly with the choirs of heaven: 'Holy, holy, holy Lord

---

[18] Schmemann, id, 53; quoted in Fagerberg, 193.
[19] Schmemann, id, 110.
[20] Id, 111.

God of hosts...' When the congregation sings it, they join the heavenly chorus of praise. 'Earthly and heavenly liturgy harmonize.'[21] 'Like St John in the Spirit on the Lord's Day, we lift up our hearts above and beyond the liturgy of earth and in breath-taking wonder and indescribable joy echo the heavenly Song of the Lamb.'[22]

As we have seen in chapter 7, this is all possible because of Jesus Christ, our Mediator and Great High Priest (Heb 4:14). Through him 'we have confidence to enter the sanctuary by the blood of Jesus, by the new and living way that he opened for us through the curtain (that is, through his flesh)' (Heb. 10:19-20).

> You have not come to something that can be touched...
> But you have come to Mount Zion and to the city of the
> living God, the heavenly Jerusalem, and to innumerable
> angels in festal gathering, and to the assembly of the
> firstborn who are enrolled in heaven, and to God the
> judge of all, and to the spirits of the righteous made
> perfect, and to Jesus, the mediator of a new covenant, and
> to the sprinkled blood that speaks a better word than the
> blood of Abel. (Heb. 12:18, 22-24)

'You *have* come' – already! Perforce we remain earthbound, but heaven-bound.

In the Orthodox tradition of architecture, church interiors are designed to represent a vision of heaven, and are closely linked to the celebration of the liturgies that take place within them. 'Just as in the earliest Christian era, so also today, in its best Byzantine or Russian incarnation, the temple is experienced and perceived as *sobor*, as the gathering together of heaven and earth and all creation in Christ.'[23]

---

[21] GERHARDS 2017, 227. Cf SC 8.
[22] Torrance 1993, 96.
[23] SCHMEMANN 1987, 19.

Pope St John Paul II had a great respect for Eastern spirituality. 'Beauty, which in the East is one of the best loved names expressing the divine harmony and the model of humanity transfigured, appears everywhere: in the shape of a church, in the sounds, in the colours, in the lights, in the scents.'[24]

The Western tradition of church architecture lost that integrated liturgical symbolism at the end of the Romanesque period, as we saw in chapter 2. Clearly it cannot be simply revived in the same artistic and architectural form. A principal challenge for the ongoing renewal of the Roman rite is to develop new architectural forms and configurations which will better express the liturgies that take place in them, for the glory of God, using the manifold forms of creation with which He has endowed humankind.

> Then I saw a new heaven and a new earth; for the first heaven and the first earth had passed away, and the sea was no more. And I saw the holy city, the new Jerusalem, coming down out of heaven from God, prepared as a bride adorned for her husband. (Rev. 21:1-2)

Denis McNamara challenges churches planning building or refurbishment to ask their prospective architects the question 'How will you make our church a sacramental image of the heavenly Jerusalem?'[25]

How indeed can both churches and the liturgies take place in them reflect both immanent presence within, and cosmic and supra-cosmic scope beyond? In the next chapter, we will examine how our perception of the significance of our church buildings might be developed.

---

[24] John Paul II, Apostolic Letter *Orientale Lumen* (2 May 1995), 11: *AAS* 87 (1995), 757. Quoted in *Laudato Si'*, no. 235.
[25] MCNAMARA 2009, 219. See the whole of chapter 5 of this book, 71-81.

Chapter 10

SPACE FOR ENCOUNTER

A church is a privileged place for encounter with God. Its architecture and art should be sacramental – symbolic of the reality of the mystery of God and enabling that reality to be perceived as 'present'. Or, more precisely, both present and absent, for this God is immanent, dwelling among us right now, but also transcendent, beyond our reach. This is a God who is both *mysterium tremendum et fascinans*, the awesome, fascinating mystery[1], and at the same time *intimior intimo meo*, closer to me than I am to myself[2].

A church is – or should be – 'a dramatic setting for the interplay of transcendence and immanence...'[3] Transcendence is by definition beyond measurable time and space. Man can only conceive of it and perceive it because s/he has the innate ability to do so. 'Within a church, at least in the classic sacramental tradition, the ascending curve of human self-transcendence and the descending curve of divine immanence intersect.'[4]

---

[1] OTTO 1923.
[2] St Augustine, *Confessions*, 3, 6, 11.
[3] KIECKHEFER 2004, 102.
[4] Ibid.

Fundamental to the aesthetic of the classic sacramental church is a sense of participation in a reality greater than any individual and greater than any particular community – a dramatic evocation of a sense of being caught up in something greater than oneself, and greater than the experience of any one place or time, requiring a keenness of presence and conviction. But more specifically, the classic sacramental church is characteristically marked by a sense of aspiration, of mystery, and of timelessness.[5]

A church that 'breathes' the Mystery becomes a fitting location for the sacred liturgies that take place in it. But it also becomes an integral part of the worship, both public and private, of all who enter it. They worship both in the church and with the church ('church' here both with and without capital letters). Its architecture, its history of prayer extending over many years, its sense of being lived in by the local community – all these are elements of the ambience that fosters and enables the prayer of those who cross the threshold of the building and experience the spirit of God dwelling in it.

The Presence of God

In the Bible we see how God's chosen people attempt to describe their sense of God's presence with them in spatial terms. We may use the three models proposed by Bert Daelemans in his excellent book, *Spiritus Loci*[6].

As a prelude, we can start with Jacob's dream (Gen 28:11). He sees a ladder reaching up to heaven. It's a spatial image, and he gives the place a name: Bethel, house of God. House of God indeed, and house of His people.

---

[5] Id, 103.
[6] DAELEMANS 2015, here 19-27.

The first model is that of a tent. God is present to his people as an occasional visitor to their tent of meeting (Ex 29:45-46), but their situation is one of exile, soothed only by the prospect of a future in God's Promised Land. The Ark of the Covenant is a 'place' for God, but it is continually on the move – anywhere can be a resting place for encounter with God. His people are a pilgrim people: what matters is God's continual guarding and guiding presence with them rather than the arbitrary and temporary locations of the Ark and of the tent of meeting.

The image of tent continues in the New Testament. 'The Word was made flesh and dwelt among us' (Jn 1:14): a more literal translation is 'the Word was made flesh and *pitched his tent* among us'. Jesus' life on earth was limited in earthly time. Paul, maker of tents, could illustrate a tent's temporary nature: 'For we know that if the earthly tent we live in is destroyed, we have a building from God, a house not made with human hands, eternal in the heavens' (2 Cor 5:1). A tent is at best the image of a provisional or temporary dwelling-place.

The second model, by contrast, is that of a temple. Despite Samuel's veto on David's plan to build a temple (2 Sam 7), his son Solomon built one (1 Kings 6-8). Here at last was a permanent dwelling-place: God was to inhabit the Holy of Holies with his *shekinah*, his divine presence. The danger was always that this presence of God was to be considered as Israel's exclusive possession.

The God of Israel, who deigned to be experienced occasionally in a tent, but only by Moses and those He has chosen, was a transcendent, awesome God. The same God, worshipped in the temple, was an immanent God, and Israel too easily forgot that this God was also transcendent, beyond the bounds of the temple.

The third model is the New Testament *ecclesia*, the assembly of people. Jesus is present wherever two or three are gathered in his name (Mt 18:20). Here there is no specified location at all, neither tent nor temple. True worshippers will not worship God the Father in a temple in Jerusalem or in any other fixed location, but 'in spirit and truth' (Jn 4:21-24). Nonetheless, it is evidently important that Christians should gather in places that symbolise their faith in a God who is at the same time both present and absent. Present, as he promised, in every gathering of his people in the name of Jesus, and especially in sacramental communion in his Body. Absent because that communion in Jesus Christ, for all the doctrine of the Real Presence, is still a sacrament, still a sign of a fulfilment yet to come, when 'we shall see him as he is' (1 Jn 3:2).

That tension between immanence and transcendence, between presence and absence, between the now and the hereafter, is crucial to Christian spirituality – and to its architecture. If its history from the thirteenth to the twentieth centuries was skewed towards exaltation of the transcendent – mighty buildings sometimes more tributes to human endeavour than divine glory – its sequel over the last fifty years has seen the pendulum swing to an 'architecture of immanence' which emphasises the presence of Christ in the local assembly and its liturgical celebrations, but has too often been inward-looking and uninspiringly functional.[7]

At this point, we need to consider the matter of sociological scale. For what size of stable community was a particular church built? Is that the scale of its current community?

Scale and community

One may distinguish three 'sizes' – chapel, parish church, cathedral – and two types – public and monastic.

---

[7] Cf TORGERSON 2007 – and Daelemans' critique of Torgerson in DAELEMANS 2015, 89-91.

A chapel speaks of a small, intimate community, a 'house church', of up to 50 or 100 members. They know each other by name, and this social interaction easily finds expression in communal worship. Close participation in the Eucharist is facilitated. Holy Communion is both the expression and the spiritual reinforcement of this natural community. The sense of the presence of Christ can be very immediate, even intimate, in such gatherings. It is particularly appropriate for religious communities and for retreat houses. But there is a danger of an inward-looking, sect-type self-sufficiency – a sense of the immanent presence of God to the exclusion of any sense of transcendence.

We have seen this model at Rothenfels. Guardini and his successors Kahlefeld and Goergen, to whom we may add Frédéric Debuyst[8] and also Richard Giles[9], see this 'house church' model as optimal almost exclusively. As we have seen, Guardini regretted that it could not be so in practice[10]. Schwarz knew that the Rothenfels model could not be transplanted elsewhere[11] – he realised that it was principally a matter of size: the sociology and sense of community among an assembly of 100 or so committed young people at Rothenfels was very different to vast congregations of 2000 in his church at Aachen.

That is also the sociological difference between a community in a chapel and one in an average-sized parish church. Members of congregations of more than 100 are unlikely to know all other members personally.[12] The larger the numbers, the greater is the danger of the church being regarded as a divine 'service station' to which attendees arrive as individuals, receive the sacraments as individuals, and depart without

---

[8] DEBUYST 1968.
[9] GILES 2004.
[10] See above, 77.
[11] See above, 92.
[12] Thomas O'Loughlin comments that 'except in most unusual situations, gatherings larger than a hundred people are virtually unknown before modern times'. O'LOUGHLIN 2015a, 96, fn 6. This cannot apply to the huge churches built from the early 20th century onwards, as we shall see in the next chapter.

speaking or relating to anyone; even the Sign of Peace is likely exchanged with strangers.

A large urban parish obliged to celebrate many Masses every weekend in order to satisfy the numbers attending has the greater problem of coalescing several distinct (and variable) congregations into a viable parish community. Where possible, a single Eucharist each Sunday as a gathering of the whole community is highly symbolic as well as good sociology.

Then there is the cathedral. On the one hand its size may constitute an impressive statement of Christian witness. Its regular participants may come from a wide area, and its congregations may include a large proportion of visitors, even curious tourists. It may be able to support musical resources out of the reach of parishes. Its liturgies may be splendid spectacles, but the participation of those attending them may well be of a quite different order to what might be expected in a parish church – and, *a fortiori*, in a chapel. The sheer size of a cathedral may be eloquent of a transcendent God, at the expense of the immanent. And a sense of community may be completely absent. In fact, many cathedrals hold weekday Masses in side-chapels, rightly allocating space appropriate for the relevant congregation sizes.

In contrast, a monastic foundation will have a very close sense of community – nearest to the chapel model in terms of the close identity of community and communion, but often using a larger scale of building as an expression of the centrality of worship in the monks' vocation. If the abbey church is shared with a local parish community, there may be particular distinctions and relationships to be established between the two communities.

Sacred Emptiness

What is the first feature to strike a visitor as he or she enters the doors of a church? Is it quantities of chairs in serried ranks, filling every available space, all facing a stage? Is not this the plan of a playhouse or lecture theatre, expecting a presenter and an audience? Many American evangelical churches give this impression. At least traditional pews immediately distinguish a church from a theatre. The presence of kneelers may even encourage a visitor to drop to his or her knees and say a prayer.

Hopefully and intentionally, the church space will grasp the beholder as expressive of something incommensurable. It is well to be speechless and spend some moments allowing oneself to be taken in by the experience. There are reports that young people, who may profess no faith, find immense cathedrals and their choral liturgies expressive of a spiritual dimension not experienced elsewhere.

Daelemans suggests three ways in which a 'sacred emptiness' can be a symbol for transcendence, for an encounter with the God one cannot see.[13]

The first is 'leeway' – a spaciousness that gives 'breathing space', that expresses, in its volume and freedom from constriction, room for a God who is beyond all space. The traditional loftiness of churches, and their light-filled interiors, are signs in this direction. Reducing the number of benches and chairs can also be beneficial: 'the more pews you have, the more you give the impression that [liturgy] is about teaching and learning and not about celebrating'[14].

The second is a sense of inaccessibility – a sense that the most important Person or object of encounter is present but invisible, here and not-here, even significantly absent, a 'vacant throne for the divine Majesty'. Schwarz's Fronleichnamskirche in Aachen, with its enormous blank white wall behind the altar, has been criticised for being too abstract.

---

[13] DAELEMANS 2015, 205-213.
[14] SPICHTIG 2017, 43.

He wanted to symbolise the inaccessibility of God the Father beyond the 'threshold' of the altar, and his friend Guardini supported him.[15]

The new Cistercian monastic church of Nový Dvůr in the Czech Republic is, following their tradition, completely white. Behind the altar and invisible from the nave, downward steps lead to the cemetery, symbolising death as the passover from life with the immanent God experienced in earthly liturgies on this side of the altar to life with the transcendent God beyond it.

The third symbol of transcendence is orientation – does the church point towards or lead into the Mystery of God that the walls cannot contain? In particular, is the far end of the church that faces the entrant and participant – the nominal 'east' end of the church – adorned with windows or artwork that lead one to a sense of a measureless 'beyond'?

Directedness

The human body is directional. Our eyes naturally look forward. We have to crane out necks to look up, or turn our heads to look sideways. The phrase 'looking forward' has a derived meaning as an aspiration for something yet to come.

There is a long tradition in many religions of directing one's prayer in a particular direction. This can be towards a visible icon or representation of the divine or revered person to whom one prays. The histories of Christian art and devotion include not only mosaics adorning apses but also icons and statues for more close-up veneration. In Catholic churches the statue or image of the Virgin Mary, and other statues, are greatly valued and frequented for private and devotional prayer in front of them. The practice of prayer before the Blessed Sacrament,

---

[15] See above, 92. The installation in Fronleichnamskirche, after the Second Vatican Council, of an additional altar facing the people – with the priest inevitably standing behind it – has compromised Schwarz's intended symbolism, even though bis original altar is still *in situ*.

especially when exposed in a monstrance, expresses a desire for a physical but symbolic location towards which one can address prayer. The prayer services at Taizé, which draw young people from all over the world, are always directional.

The required or recommended direction of prayer can also be indicated by a sign on a wall of the worship space indicating a focal point external to the building. We saw in chapter 2 how from early centuries it was customary to place a cross in churches and even in Christian homes to denote the east, the traditional direction for prayer. The *qibla* for Muslims and the *mizrah* for orthodox Jews are of great importance to their adherents. Eastward orientation of Christian churches bears witness to the same tradition.

We have also seen how western Christian architecture from the fourth century Roman basilicas to the end of the Romanesque era in the twelfth century enjoyed decorated apses expressing a heavenly kingdom beyond the walls of the church. And we referred to east-end stained-glass windows, many in Anglican churches, in which the pictorial content progresses thematically upwards and heavenwards. In chapter 4 we examined how Schwarz's plans have a strong directional element that is both theologically and liturgically significant.

The Second Vatican Council encouraged a revived sense of eschatology – the understanding that, in terms of salvation history, we stand in the period between the founding of the kingdom of God by Jesus Christ 2000 years ago and its final fulfilment at the end of time. There is a future beyond time. Moreover, 'in the earthly liturgy, by way of foretaste, we share in that heavenly liturgy which is celebrated in the holy city of Jerusalem toward which we journey as pilgrims'[16] – as those apse mosaics endeavoured to illustrate.

---

[16] SC 7.

It is ironic and unfortunate, therefore, that the change to celebration of Mass facing the people resulted in an 'architecture of immanence' in which the altar and the priest immediately behind it became the unique central focus of church architecture, to the exclusion of any sense of a 'God of the beyond'. As Pope Benedict bewailed, the Mass can give the impression of an encounter with the priest as he continually faces the congregation, rather than an encounter with the God one cannot see.

An encounter with God *as Other* is the very essence of worship. In chapter 1[17], we cited a priest who felt it necessary to point out that the words of consecration are not addressed to the people, even though the priest is facing them as he says them.

Conceiving the beyond

Architects have long been challenged with the question "what do you propose to do with the 'east' wall, so that it expresses symbolically the God whom we worship, the God who is beyond the walls of the church?"

One might at this point object that, to obey the architect's axiom that form should follow function, we should define first how we use the church building – specifically for celebrating the liturgies (of baptism and other rites, as well as of the Eucharist), but also for devotions and for private prayer. This can become a circular argument. We are taking it as read that a Christian church is both a *locus* and an enabling symbol of encounter with God who is both immanent to it and transcendent beyond it, therefore suitable for the celebration of liturgies that are both current salvation events and foretastes and pledges of the heavenly Jerusalem.

---

[17] See page 21.

A brief review of some contemporary solutions to 'east' ends may be classified under three headings: windows, light, images. Windows can be sub-classified as transparent, opaque and symbolic.

The 'east' wall of the church of St François-de-Molitor in Paris is made entirely of transparent glass, with a plain slender golden 'cross of glory' in the centre (see photo 12). It actually faces north and looks out onto a garden; the south opens directly onto a city street. The architect (Jean-Marie Duthilleul) continues:

> To the north, then, the beginning of history, the garden where Man lived blessed by God on the side of the knowledge of good and evil, and to the south, the city on the way to the heavenly Jerusalem, the ultimate destiny of humanity.[18]

The eschatological direction is therefore, paradoxically, away from the window, not towards it. This interpretation has an allegorical feel about it. We shall examine the implications for the orientation of the liturgy there in the next chapter.

Large 'east'-facing windows with crosses against them outside or inside were in vogue in the 1980s, especially by Irish architects. Examples are to be found at St Joseph's Church in Redhill, Surrey, and St Edward the Confessor, San Clemente, California. One drawback is that the priest, when celebrating at the altar in front of a bright window, can only be seen in silhouette. In reply, one might suggest that his role as the assembly's worship-leader is to be symbolic and impersonal, *in persona Christi capitis* – and not pitched as the central focus. We examined this in chapter 7.

A window similar to the one at St François-de-Molitor is to be found in the Lutheran church of the university at Otaniemi in Finland. Here the

---

[18] DUTHILLEUL 2014, here 42.

cross stands outside the window, and therefore doubles as both an external cross of missionary witness and an interior symbol of worship, challenging the worshipper to bring the cross of Christ to the world after the service. Inevitably, in Finland, it looks out onto a forest.

Another very similar example is Tadao Ando's church at Tomamu in Japan, where the external cross stands some distance from the window, in the middle of a lake. The problem with this and the cross at Otaniemi is that it may be perceived as giving nature a salvific significance that it does not have.

At Heilig Kreuz church at Dülmen in Germany, there is also a wide window and outline cross. This time the window closes off an open area which stands no less than 14 steps above the main area of the church (there is a crypt beneath it). Being so elevated, it looks out onto the sky.

Very different in scale, but with a profiled cross against an alabaster window, is that of the cathedral church of Our Lady of the Angels in Los Angeles (see photo 8). The designer, José Rafael Moneo, intended it to be exteriorly significant as a representational sign, but on the interior expressing the unreachable mystery as symbol.[19] However, the cross-shape may not be readily perceptible as such from the interior, and there is also a large cross standing on the sanctuary floor, away from the back wall.

As an example of opaque glass one may take the church of St Florian in Munich. Here the glass sculptress Hella Santarossa designed three windows, incorporating blue for the Marian chapel, red for the baptistery and sunlight yellow for the main celebration space, where it dominates – even overpowers – the sanctuary area. What is remarkable is the three-dimensional effect she has obtained. This non-figurative

---

[19] Daelemans, 226.

composition opens up another, virtual, imaginative space, a space for the "eschatological imagination"'.[20]

Then there is the remarkable symbolic glass of Tadao Ando in his Church of Light at Ibaraki. An entirely dark sanctuary wall has a plain cross in glass excised over the entire height and width (8 x 6 metres) of the 'east' wall. Daelemans comments:

> What do we look at? The wall or the cross – which is not really there. This cross is present as *absence*, because it is cut out of the wall. As Christian symbol it is there and not there, that is, not less, but *more* than there. For a Christian, this could be a magnificent symbol of death and resurrection.[21]

This art may be more suited to contemplation than liturgy. Of more immediate liturgical interest is the abstract glass design that constitutes the focus of the Pallottine church at Vallendar in Germany (see photo 13). The space in front of the clear 'east' window is the former raised sanctuary area, which is open as 'an expression of man's inability to express God in a picture. God is not "tangible", not to be taken hold of'[22]. What one actually sees is a designed glass 'curtain' in front of the natural window behind it. 'It is a "window to heaven" to keep open, so that no one loses hope.'

The Nicene Creed speaks of Jesus Christ as being 'light from light': there is potential here for symbolic representations of the intra-trinitarian procession of the Son from the Father. Indeed, the symbol of light shines throughout the Church's biblical and liturgical tradition.[23] 'Manipulation of light is a classic way to create an aura of

---

[20] Id, 236.
[21] Id, 152. Original italics.
[22] From this church's website at http://www.haus-wasserburg.de/haus-wasserburg/pallotti-kirche.html, accessed 17 January 2018.
[23] Cf GERHARDS 2011a, 56-62.

mystery... In various ways, light calls attention to itself and to a presence beyond itself.'[24] It fills space, but it is non-spatial: 'the sacramentality of light bathes both subject and space in reality that renders architecture nonexistent'[25].

Schwarz's churches have wraparound clerestory-level windows illuminating the entire church. Sometimes, as at Bottrop, the windows overlooking the sanctuary are deeper – and the one there also has an 'eye', which in Schwarz's imagery would be a symbol of God the Father (see photo 5).

Natural light, playing directly or indirectly onto the wall behind the altar in an otherwise darker sanctuary area, can give it an undefined luminescence. The light source may be at the side of the sanctuary, illuminating the wall behind the altar, as at the Lutheran Christ Church at Minneapolis and St Engelbert's in Cologne. When the entire sanctuary is lit indiscriminately, the effect of 'back illumination' is lost.

At Notre Dame de l'Arche de l'Alliance in Paris, a simple Latin cross is ingeniously projected upon the curved sanctuary wall, suggesting an ungraspable or spiritualized Cross of Glory.[26]

There are also churches with a complex interplay of light and architectural form that defy simple description. The chapel of the new Stanbrook Abbey at Wass in North Yorkshire falls into this category. There are multiple axes for the entry of the nuns and of the laity, and of the Word and the Eucharist – the latter leading to a distinct Blessed Sacrament chapel lying behind and beyond the apse of the main church space.

---

[24] KIECKHEFER 2004, 107.
[25] WEDIG 2015, 136.
[26] Daelemans, 247.

Images can be representational or abstract. If they are too realistically figurative, they can have the same effect as many second-rate statues do – not conveying a sense of the beyond at all. Images of the risen and glorified Christ, appropriate thematically, need to have both a present and an absent aura to them. The style and medium of the icon is more appropriate than realistic imaging.

A successful example can be found at the small church of St Barbara at Moers, in the German Ruhr (see photo 14). The typical chapel layout of nave and raised chancel has been completely reordered. The altar has been relocated to the middle of the nave. The end wall of the former sanctuary area has a large mosaic image of the risen Christ displayed on it, overlooking the baptismal font.

The huge figure of Christ the Light that dominates the cathedral of that name in Oakland, California is in a class of its own (see photo 9). The image, which towers above the sanctuary, is actually made of aluminium panels pierced with 94,000 perforations, which let light through it into the interior, and (in the dark) let the interior lights project the figure out into the city. Thus it lives up to its name: 'the architecture transfigures ordinary light into the transcendent Light of Christ'.[27] But whereas the monumentality of most cathedrals expresses transcendence, the proportions of this huge image in relation to the rest of the church give an impression of overpowering immanence: your final judgement is taking place right now!

Western iconography

The liturgical movement has inspired little new artistry. In default, recourse has been made to inspiration from the historic Romanesque tradition and from the still-living Eastern icon tradition. But this has not been easy. Church communities cling to their traditional devotional plaster statues and 'suffering' crucifixes, which are near-

---

[27] Daelemans, 216.

impossible to integrate with an entirely different artistic tradition unseen in Roman-rite churches since the thirteenth century.

To adorn an existing or new apse with painting or mosaic is an exceedingly costly exercise, even after parishioners have been persuaded of its justification on liturgical grounds. Besides churches in the Eastern Orthodox tradition, there are modern Roman-rite examples to be found in the United States – for example, at St Monica & St George church in Cincinnati and the cathedral of St Joseph, Wheeling, West Virginia[28].

Smaller-scale iconography is easier to harmonise within a church built with a different concept of statuary or pictorial imagery. Hanging crucifixes above the altar, being a standalone feature in a church, may portray the crucified in a symbolic, quasi-exalted state, with golden crown and priestly garments signifying the aeviternal Christ, Redeemer and High Priest in time and beyond time.

Sacraments: events for meeting God

In this chapter, we have been looking at churches, their spaciousness and their orientation, from the point of view of an individual observer. But they are built to enable a community to worship there and meet God as His *ecclesia*, as His people called by God to be holy, to be in communion with Him.

The liturgy is the privileged place of encounter between God's immanent presence in the world and His transcendence beyond the world. Ideally, it should be celebrated in a church that artistically and architecturally reflects both. 'The most successful forms of religiously adequate architecture are those that try to balance precisely those two aspects in the overall expression that the building seeks to achieve.'[29]

---

[28] McNamara 2009, 157, 182-3, 211.
[29] Daelemans, 131, quoting Brown 2004, 84.

For 'architecture enters intrinsically into the action of the liturgy. Material place symbolically amplifies the liturgical action, and the liturgy, in turn, draws into itself the spatial and the material.'[30]

As the visible symbol of invisible inhabitation, the most intimate union with God, a church is mystagogic space. The Rite of Christian Initiation of Adults sees mystagogy as the final stage of initiation of new members of the Church, taking place ideally during the Easter season, enabling the newly initiated to 'savour the mystery' of the sacraments they have received and of the encounter with God that they have experienced. But this encounter in mystery should not be restricted to them: it should be experienced by all worshippers. The liturgy should be an 'epiphany', a manifestation of God in mystery that should touch and grasp all who celebrate it.[31]

That requires 'space for God'. It is certainly appropriate for a church to be thought of as the *domus ecclesiae*, the home of God's people in that place. But 'however good and supportive they are to one another, Christians are fed ultimately by something more invisible, namely Christ himself, and so there is a need of foci that can carry the eye and other senses beyond the immediate human presence...'[32] The people, even when facing the priest across the altar, must be enabled to perceive the presence of the Mystery around and beyond him. The church is also the *domus Dei*, the house of God whom the house cannot contain. 'When a contemporary church succeeds in creating the right *expansion*, *expression* and *expectation* of the Mystery, it is a valuable specimen of *mystagogic space.*'[33]

Of these attributes, it is 'expectation' that is our current topic of interest – expectation of the realisation of the Mystery that is both immanently within and transcendentally without the church walls. 'Liturgy

---

[30] MANNION 2004, 145.
[31] See quote from Guardini above, 11.
[32] Daelemans, 134, quoting BROWN 2004, 346.
[33] Daelemans, 317. Italics his.

suggests a redefinition of place: no longer is it to be thought of as a being-there but as a being-toward.'[34] Whatever geographical direction the church faces, the significance of the 'beyond' beyond the nominal 'east' wall is therefore very important. We have seen in this chapter how modern architects have expressed this directedness in the design of churches. But it must also be expressed in the celebration of the liturgy that takes place in them. How?

---

[34] Id, 41, quoting LACOSTE 2004, 25.

Chapter 11

ONE ASSEMBLY, ONE SPACE

Ever since the 1920s, architects have been developing church designs comprising a single overall space, instead of a distinct chancel and sanctuary area separated from the nave by steps and Communion rails.

The *première* of these churches was Notre Dame de Raincy near Paris, built in 1921-23 by Auguste and Guillaume Perret. Its construction marked a huge step forward in constructional techniques: thin concrete pillars supporting a high overall roof, leaving the walls light with glass in concrete frames. In the sides of the church the glass is clear: only the east wall/window behind the sanctuary, shaped as a shallow apse, is a brilliant blue. What is most significant is that the altar space is elevated but otherwise not separated from the rest of the space.[1]

German architects took the cue, and until the outbreak of the Second World War many churches of similar construction were built. What is significant is that all their architects worked with liturgical scholars. We have seen how Rudolf Schwarz worked with Romano Guardini. Similar partnerships were to be found in Dominikus Böhm and Martin

---

[1] MUCK 1961, 33.

Weber with Abbot Ildefons Herwegen of Beuron, and Robert Kramreiter with Pius Parsch of Klosterneuburg in Austria.[2] And in the 1950s two of Guardini's disciples, Heinrich Kahlefeld and Aloys Goergen, worked with Emil Steffann and Sep Ruf respectively to design two significant churches in Munich, as we have seen.[3]

Church authorities and architects in Britain were totally oblivious to such forward thinking, and new churches there continued to be built, even in the 1950s, with sanctuaries structurally distinct from naves. The unique British example of a church constructed at that time with an altar facing the people – and with them accommodated on three sides of it – is that of Fr James Crichton at Holy Redeemer, Pershore, Worcestershire, consecrated in 1959. As with the German churches just mentioned, here there was a liturgy scholar working with his architect.

Sir Frederic Gibbard's circular design for Liverpool's Metropolitan Cathedral was accepted in 1959 and the church eventually opened in 1967. Whatever problems arise from a circular church plan with a central altar, the benefits of including everyone within a single worship space with a single focus cannot be gainsaid.[4]

Gibbard confessed to having no understanding of the liturgical movement. He was not alone. An author summarising British Catholic church design in the 1970s reported how Lanner, a building construction company specialising in template 'wigwam' churches, offered designs '*even* influenced by the liturgical movement'[5] – which had influenced European church design a full 50 years earlier! In any case, such influence was scarcely visible inside these churches – Lanner only ever provided a shell and was not concerned with internal configuration, a classic case of form having little to do with function. It was simply presumed that, after the example of Liverpool Cathedral,

---

[2] PACIK 2010, VII–XXVII. See above, 56.
[3] See above, 86.
[4] Another example is the underground basilica at Lourdes, capacity 25,000 people.
[5] PROCTOR 2014, 102. Italics mine.

designed before the Vatican Council, churches of circular or polygonal shape were to be the new preferred standard.

Clifton Cathedral (Bristol), opened in 1973, was the first British cathedral to be designed and built after the end of the Second Vatican Council (see photo 10). Polygonal churches were still in vogue, but commendably the church was designed functionally, from the inside outwards: the design brief specified the liturgical rites to be celebrated within it. The leading architect did his homework and discovered that European church authorities were 'more attuned to the reorganisation of church planning than was the case in England'[6]. At an early planning meeting between the architects and their church clients, the sanctuary, nave, baptistery and Blessed Sacrament chapel were defined as distinct areas. So the architects came up with a design consisting of contingent hexagonal spaces, of which the principal one rises 90 metres into a fleche. But this does not span the whole worship space: it rises only above the sanctuary. This space is raised three steps above the nave space for the laity, which has a lower ceiling. The sanctuary and nave are quite distinct spaces.

The same distinction can be seen in the American bishops' *Built of Living Stones*, with its section entitled 'Congregation's Area', whereas the General Instruction of the Roman Missal, to its credit, simply emphasises the need to 'bring about a close and coherent unity that is expressive of the unity of the entire holy people'[7]: there is no reference in this Instruction to a nave or 'congregation area'. The sanctuary is described functionally, and is to be marked off from the body of the church 'either by its being somewhat elevated or by a particular structure and ornamentation'[8].

---

[6] http://www.cliftoncathedral.org/history/architect, accessed on 25 November 2017.
[7] GIRM, no. 294.
[8] Id., no. 295.

Altar and ambo: bipolar design

The structure of the Mass had been clarified by the Liturgy Constitution as consisting of the Liturgy of the Word and the Liturgy of the Eucharist, two 'parts' or 'tables' that make a single act of worship.[9] The traditional church layout had made provision for only one focal point: the high altar. Now there was a requirement for at least two foci – or, following *Inter Œcumenici*, three including the priest's presidential chair. The Scripture readings were now to be read from an ambo lectern, not by the priest standing at the altar. How then, was Mass 'in the round', with people all around the altar, to be celebrated when the focus of the Liturgy of the Word was elsewhere? And, given the Liturgy Constitution's emphasis on due attention to the Word of God, is its status adequately symbolised by simply adding a lectern at the side of the existing sanctuary?

The form and content of the two liturgies is quite different. The Liturgy of the Word is a time for listening to a reader, deacon or priest. It is naturally directional, and requires provision of seating. The Liturgy of the Eucharist is one of prayer and participation in Holy Communion. If space permits it, therefore, it is best to have two distinct purpose-designed adjacent areas, with everyone taking part in the Procession of Gifts between them. That is precisely what takes place regularly at St Gregory of Nyssa Episcopal Church in San Francisco. There, the space for the Liturgy of the Word is elongated, with people sitting facing each other, the reader at one end, the presider at the other. They then process to the open space under the octagonal dome, where they surround the altar for the Liturgy of the Eucharist.[10]

---

[9] SC 56; Dogmatic Constitution on Revelation, no 21.

[10] Cf KIECKHEFER 2004, 37-41. They actually *dance* in procession. There have also been proposals to use two entirely separate buildings linked by a corridor for the liturgies of the Word and Eucharist. There were experiments to implement this configuration in Ireland in the 1970s.

This principle is practised on weekdays at St Benedict's Abbey, Atchison, Kansas, USA, and at Douai Abbey, England, where lay participants are invited to sit in the monastic choir for the Liturgy of the Word and process with the monks to surround the altar for the Liturgy of the Eucharist.[11]

There are obvious limitations of space and on numbers of participants for such a celebration to take place in two distinct locations. What can be done to present two balanced foci to an assembly of static participants?

Monastic choirs, with seats in two banks facing each other, have from time immemorial used large lecterns in the centre of the choir, or at one end, from which to read scriptural and patristic readings as part of their *opus Dei*, the Divine Office. A simple extension of this scheme, with the altar at the opposite end of the choir, made it suitable for the celebration of Mass. A balance between the two 'tables' of the liturgy was thus achieved. But the priest's chair was then outside this closed quadrilateral space. One solution was to make the space between the two 'sides' wide enough to accommodate the altar between them, and have the priest's chair at the opposite end to the ambo.

This is the plan of Brentwood Cathedral in England, where the axis is transverse across the rectangular floor space, and the bishop's *cathedra* balances the ambo on the other side. The downside of this plan is that it divides the congregation into two distinct blocks at some distance from each other.[12]

Maintaining the axis longitudinally, as in monastic choir stalls, can lead to craned necks to see the other end of the space, and undue concentration on whoever happens to be sitting opposite one. The solution appears to be simple for anyone acquainted with a little

---

[11] McCARTHY 2014, 85, 105-106.
[12] Other reservations about this design have been expressed: cf SEASOLTZ 2005, 264f.

geometry. A circle has only one focus, at the centre. An ellipse has two, one at each end: it is naturally bipolar. There is also a midpoint at the centre.

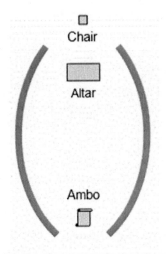

So one solution is to place the altar at one focus, the ambo at the other; the people are arranged at the circumference of the ellipse, with the priest's chair completing the ellipse at one end of its major axis.

The chapel at the former Pastoral Liturgy Institute at Carlow in Ireland was reordered in rectangular form in 1980, with the altar in the centre. The institute was closed in 1996 and transferred to Maynooth. However, it may well have influenced the design of one of the rare elliptical bipolar-design parish churches in Ireland, the Irish Martyrs' church at Ballycane, Naas, opened in 1997. This church in turn was the inspiration for the design of the church of Our Lady and St Vincent, Potters Bar, England, opened in 2006 (see photo 11).

There are a number of similar bipolar-design parish churches in the United States: St Julie Billiart at Tinley Park, Illinois and Corpus Christi, Round Lake, New York state, are good examples. The size of the congregations requires the altar and ambo to be raised on steps for good visibility.

In Germany, there have been several new bipolar churches of elliptical design. The one at Westerland on the North Sea island of Sylt is a particular example. The elliptical floor plan and high brick walls with high windows are redolent of some of Rudolf Schwarz's designs. The church has been sized for the very large tourist influx in the summer; in the winter the assemblies are quite small. The configuration has been

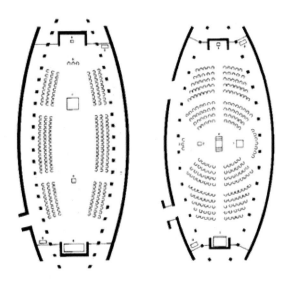

Westerland – two options for configuration

a matter of discussion. At first, the plan was for seating around the perimeter of the ellipse, leaving a wide and empty central space between the altar and ambo. It was then thought to turn the axis through 90° in order to bring the seats closer to one another in the centre of the church and create a more intimate milieu.[13] Whether this was ever implemented is unclear; the original plan is the one currently in use.

Converting existing churches to such a layout has been more demanding – and not always successful. Imposing an elliptical format onto a rectangular floor plan can be untidy and wasteful of space. In England, Plymouth Cathedral was reconfigured to a bipolar design in the 1990s but has now reverted to a longitudinal 'way' model.

---

[13] GERHARDS 1999, 44-47.

In all these bipolar examples there is no distinct sanctuary as such. The whole space is what German-speakers have come to term '*Communio-Raum*' – a space for fellowship and communion shared by the entire assembly. There are designated locations for the altar and ambo at the focal points of the space, and for the priest's chair, at its 'head'. But there is no separated *presbyterium* reserved for the clergy and vested servers: instead, the area in which the visual liturgical action takes place is defined by the ring of people, and perhaps by flooring design, but not by a step.

There is no place for a tabernacle within the ellipse.[14] This is technically correct, inasmuch as it is not an integral feature of the Liturgy of the Eucharist. Moreover, as part of the distribution of Holy Communion, the taking of hosts for the Communion of the Sick to a tabernacle outside the ellipse is symbolic of the fact that there are other members of the community who are not present but are joined in communion with those who are. At Potters Bar church, there is a secondary transverse axis to the church with transept extensions to the building; one is a beautiful Blessed Sacrament chapel for private devotion (with access when the main church is closed), the other a *catechumeneon*, a room for the instruction of catechumens.

Bipolar ordering: an assessment

There are many advantages of this layout compared with the traditional longitudinal arrangement. It obliges the congregants to be conscious of other members of their community standing opposite them, which some people with a more private sense of a me-and-my-God relationship find intrusive.

The distinctive status of altar and ambo as the focal points of the two liturgy 'tables' is clearly symbolised – a feature that is lacking in circular

---

[14] At Westerland, the location of the tabernacle behind the president's chair is curious.

configurations. There is an obvious and effective place for the president's chair on the perimeter, behind the altar.

There is an empty space in the centre of the church between the altar and ambo. This is a good location for an event where an additional object needs to be accommodated and made central for the occasion – the coffin at a funeral, the couple at a wedding. It is not the right place for a third permanent liturgical focus, such as the baptismal font – and indeed the location of this as the symbol of initial entry into the eucharistic community is problematic in relation to the closed ellipse that this layout presents.

There has been a natural tendency for altars to gravitate towards the mid-point of the space, where there is maximum room for it – see photos 11 and 12. This makes the altar-table the central focus, which may be seen as indicative of communion. But it destroys the balance with the ambo. The priest's chair then assumes a greater significance as balancing the ambo on the opposite end of the ellipse's major axis.

Apart from special uses, this emptiness can be counter-productive, especially in a large church like Westerland, where it can dominate the excessive distance between ambo and altar. Perhaps this was the reason for the proposed alternative configuration in this church.

It has been argued that the emptiness of this space can symbolise the waiting for the coming of the Lord at the end of time.[15]

> The freed centre becomes the eschatological sign that the assembled church is always directed to something overwhelmingly greater, in whose expectation it celebrates liturgy. However, the real thing has to happen in this free space. The assembly, together with the leader, must be understood as a community that is in waiting...

---

[15] GERHARDS 1999, 26.

The free centre articulates the community expectation "of a completely different self-giving" and is "at the same time a reference to it". The basic reference to God is thus incorporated into the spatial form of the church.[16]

But this is more effectively symbolised spatially by a reference point outside the ellipse and beyond it.

The elliptical shape is 'enclosing', which is symbolically ambiguous. On the one hand, the sense of community and mutual responsibility for one's neighbour is clear. On the other hand, it is entirely inward-looking. Bouyer's comment is relevant:

> [I]t is essential that the local assembly of the Church of Christ should remain open: open naturally to the invisible gathering of the saints in heaven, but also to other Christian communities, and finally open to the world in which the People of God are to accomplish the ministry of their royal priesthood.[17]

The need to symbolise openness to a transcendent beyond has led to a re-evaluation of the bipolar plan at the beginning of the 21st century. Professor Gerhards wrote in 2011:

> The liturgical reform after the Second Vatican Council, in the sense of the Liturgical Movement, emphasized the assembly aspect over that of worship... More recently, the cosmic dimension has regained greater importance over the sociological: the oriented assembly. This term expresses the polarity of each liturgical assembly, which on the one hand is related like any communication community, but on the other hand, is based on a

---

[16] WEISER 2002.
[17] BOUYER 1967, chapter 6.

counterpart that lies outside itself. The spatial anomaly of centring and orientation, which is also present in the Jewish synagogue, can be considered an essential feature of liturgical spirituality. Each celebration transcends the concrete assembly.[18]

---

[18] GERHARDS 2011b, 276-277.

Chapter 12

DIRECTION RESTORED

The liturgy is a dynamic *action* – that of 'Christ the priest and his Body, the Church', in which 'all who are made children of God by faith and baptism... come together to praise God in the midst of his Church, to take part in her sacrifice, and to eat the Lord's supper'[1].

The importance lies therefore in *what* is done, rather than *where*. The Eucharist can be celebrated in a battlefield with a reader holding a battered Bible and the priest celebrating at a camp table. The direction of worship needs to be based on the significance of what is done, rather than the furniture to be used. The Liturgy Constitution and subsequent documents have rightly relegated the requirements for the space needed for the liturgy to the end of their respective treatments. Form follows function – and, because the function here is ritual in nature, the form should reflect its symbolism and significance.

In the light of what has been written above, we can nominate three distinct key actions in a Eucharistic celebration[2]:

---

[1] *SC* 7, 10.
[2] Cf MESSNER 2003, 27-36. Cf also METZGER 1971, 143.

- the proclamation of the Word
- the rendering of Eucharistic thanksgiving in praise and prayer to God the Father through his Son, Jesus Christ, in the power of the Holy Spirit
- the communal sharing in Communion in the Body and Blood of the Lord

How is the gathered assembly best configured to enable them to participate in these three actions, according to their different natures – and their different 'communication vectors'[3]?

Proclamation

God speaks to his assembled people through the deacon (or priest in default) and reader proclaiming His Word from the ambo.

In many churches, the Word of God is proclaimed from a simple lectern, often – alas! – of no greater visual importance than a similar lectern erected for the convenience of the priest at his chair.

As already noted, an earlier tradition, with roots extending back to Jewish antecedents, was to build one or two high stone ambones in an enclosed area in the nave space, to illustrate the importance of the readings of the Word of God and to ensure that they were audible.[4] High pulpits attached to pillars or walls of Renaissance-age churches were intended to enable preachers to be heard, but had lost all relationship with the altar space.

The proclamation of the Word is an event: it is always Good News, as if announced for the first time. It is the self-donation and self-revelation of God, for which the Eucharist gives thanks. 'Faith comes from what

---

[3] Cf SPICHTIG 2017, 35-36.
[4] Cf BOUYER 1967. See the churches of San Clemente and Santa Sabina in Rome.

is heard' (Rom 10:17), which is why its proclamation precedes the sacramental celebration.[5]

There is one Word of God, which is why a single ambo is now preferred. It should reflect its importance by its construction and location. Its design should complement that of the altar, and be of the same or similar material. Consideration should also be given to a place of reservation for the Gospel book or Bible, analogous to that of the Eucharistic breads in the tabernacle.

In the Byzantine liturgy, the procession corresponding to our Gospel procession (the 'little entrance') takes place at the beginning of the Liturgy of the Word, not before the Gospel. In the full execution of the Roman rite, there is the complication of having one ambo but two books of readings, the Lectionary and the Gospel book.[6]

The ambo should be used exclusively for the proclamation of the Word of God. The homily should be delivered preferably from the priest's chair[7], its distinctiveness and position expressing the priest's kerygmatic and teaching ministry as distinct from the ministry of proclamation of the deacon or reader. The ambo should certainly not be used to announce the intentions of the Prayers of the Faithful, despite the option provided by the Missal.[8]

---

[5] GERHARDS 2017, 332.

[6] This is compounded by the anomaly whereby, in the Entrance Procession, the reader may carry the Gospel book (which he may not read from unless he is a deacon), but not the Lectionary, from which he/she will be reading. Some joined-up thinking is required here.

[7] GIRM 136 says 'chair or ambo', thus giving first preference to the chair. The homily may be more effectively delivered from elsewhere in the church, depending on its layout.

[8] GIRM 71, which states that the intentions may be announced 'from the ambo or another suitable place'. The latter should be preferred. As in common Anglican practice, this can be done by one or more lay people from within the assembly space, with the aid of a portable microphone. This symbolises better the 'Prayer of the Faithful'. However, the first-named announcer of the intentions is the deacon, then a cantor (musicians take note), then a lector, then 'one of the lay faithful'. (*ibid.*)

The reader's ministry as spokesman for God is thus important and privileged. A cantor who sings the Responsorial Psalm is properly called a psalmist, and is similarly privileged. The congregation stands for the reading of the Gospel, reserved to deacon or priest and embellished with candles and incense.

It is obvious that the people (including the priest) should face the reader addressing them with God's Word. They respond by acclamations ('Thanks be to God', 'Praise to you, Lord Jesus Christ') and also in the Responsorial Psalm. This will have established a two-way axis in the church, normally longitudinal, even when the ambo is not central on this axis but displaced to one side – as occurs frequently in order to preserve the altar as the prime static focal point of attention in the church.

The Liturgy of the Word should always conclude with the Prayers of the Faithful.[9] Which way should both priest and people face for these? Surely in the direction from which the readings have been proclaimed, for the prayers are a reply to the God who has just spoken to them through the minister of the Word.

Prayer and praise

As we saw in chapter 2, the outflowing of prayer and praise by priest and people has historically been directed not to the altar but over and beyond it. The assimilation of the altar to Christ the High Priest in his sacrifice is undoubtedly correct, but, as we explained earlier, his salvific offering and sacrifice was to his unseen Father.

---

[9] GIRM 69 says that in Masses with the people, the Prayer of the Faithful *'de more habeatur'* – should *normally* be held. Restricting it to Sundays is thus unwarranted. Each part of the Mass consists of or concludes with prayer: the Introductory Rites with the Collect, the Liturgy of the Word with the Prayer of the Faithful, the Preparation of the Gifts with the prayer over them and the Communion Rite with its concluding prayer.

The Rite of Dedication of a Church makes this clear:

> The anointing with chrism makes the altar a symbol of
> Christ, who, before all others, is and is called 'The
> Anointed One'; for the Father anointed him with the
> Holy Spirit and constituted him the High Priest so that
> on the altar of his body he might offer the sacrifice of his
> life for the salvation of all.[10]

Because it is the physical location of the gifts of bread and wine and
their sanctification into the sacramental Body and Blood of Christ, the
altar is a sublime point of 'holy exchange', of divine-human
communication. We have seen in previous chapters how it is seen as a
threshold – a meeting point between the holiness of God and his holy
but pilgrim people.

But this symbolism of God and Man on opposite sides of the altar is
spatially incompatible with Guardini's liturgical ideal of Mass with the
congregation gathered all around the altar – and totally at odds with
'Mass facing the people', when the priest stands on one side of the altar,
and the people on the other side.

Schwarz perceived the symbolism of threshold more thoroughly – his
last book is entitled 'Church Building: World before the Threshold'[11].
He sees it in both general terms as the interface between Creator and
creature – 'where God and world meet each other'[12] – and more
specifically as a concept to be represented architecturally in church
design. We have examined Schwarz's templates in detail in chapter 4.
The boundary of the threshold is the altar.

---

[10] Rite of Dedication of a Church, article 16.
[11] *Kirchenbau: Welt vor der Schwelle* (SCHWARZ 1960).
[12] The title of a book by Albert Gerhards, GERHARDS 2011a.

The insights of Guardini and Schwarz regarding the significance of 'threshold' in configuring church spaces, ignored after Vatican II, have been re-evaluated in recent years, such that they have been jointly acclaimed as 'pre-conciliar critics of post-conciliar church spaces'.[13]

It will be evident from the foregoing that prayers addressed to God the Father by priest and people together are best symbolised as such when the entire body that is praying them faces in the same direction – towards the nominal east. For the Eucharistic Prayer, this is particularly appropriate.

> In its first section, the Eucharistic Prayer is, above all in its oriental expressions (but also in the more recently created Fourth Eucharistic Prayer of the Missal) an offering of praise (Greek *logikē latreia* – Rom 12:1), praise of the divine name, which culminates in the Quedusha, the Sanctus. The fulfilment of the world is already apparent: the Church, together with the angels, stands before God and anticipates the eschatological praise of liberated creation.[14]

How to symbolise this two-way holy intercommunication whose 'outer' focal point lies ineffably and invisibly beyond the altar? From the fourth to eleventh centuries and later, great apse mosaics endeavoured to depict a heavenly paradise with a glorious Christ. Occasionally, triumphal arches at the entrance to sanctuaries would culminate with a hand pointing downwards, the 'hand of God'. High east-end stained glass windows showed a rising narrative of Christ's earthly life, with his kingship at the apex.

The Eucharistic Prayer comes to its conclusion with the raising of the sanctified gifts and the trinitarian doxology addressed to the Father:

---

[13] GERHARDS 2013, 234.
[14] GERHARDS 2011a, 137.

'Through him [Christ], and with him, and in him,
O God, almighty Father,
in the unity of the Holy Spirit,
all glory and honour is yours,
for ever and ever.'

And immediately after the people have acclaimed the Great Amen, they continue with Jesus' prayer to his Father and ours, the 'Our Father'.

Holy Communion

But then there comes an important change of attention and direction. The gifts have been 'eucharistized' – offered to God and sanctified by Him. Now it is time to celebrate His gracious return of the gifts to their givers, the sanctified to those to be sanctified by them.

The Lord's Prayer is traditionally a pre-Communion prayer in all rites.[15] But after the embolism prayer that concludes it, the subsequent prayers are all addressed to Jesus Christ and focussed on the communion of priest and people in Him to be effected sacramentally. Instead of the directional focus of prayer used hitherto, now, quite suddenly, we have a centripetal focus centred on the sacramental elements.[16]

---

[15] 'Give us today our daily bread' has, in this context, obvious Communion overtones. 'Daily' is the traditional translation of the rare Greek adjective *epiousios*, which can also be translated 'needful' or (ESV alternative, and Jerome) 'for tomorrow'. Jerome also renders it as 'supersubstantial'. See JUNGMANN 1951, II, 280; BARKER 2003, 101.

[16] 'The Eucharistic Prayer, as prayer of the liturgical assembly, has the orientation from us to the Father... On the other hand, the rite of Communion has the orientation of the Father to us' – KILMARTIN 1998, 381. Lang concedes that 'parts of the Communion Rite' should be conducted, like the Liturgy of the Word, facing the people, but does not specify precisely which parts (LANG 2009, 19, 136).

First peace is shared as a prelude, then the bread (preferably a single bread for smaller assemblies) is broken as a sign of sharing.[17] In the Roman rite, the priest remains silent and the 'Lamb of God' chant is sung during the fraction. In the Anglican Rite of Communion, the community is drawn into the event of the fraction by these words, drawn from 1 Cor 10:16-17:

> *Priest:* We break this bread
> to share in the body of Christ.
> *All:* Though we are many, we are one body,
> because we all share in one bread.

The priest's prayers of preparation are then addressed to the Christ present in the sacramental species. There follows the 'Lord, I am not worthy' and the communion of priest and people. All receive the Body of Christ in order to become the Body of Christ – and in the early Church, the priest-celebrant (even the pope) received the sacrament from deacons, like everyone else.

There is union in so many senses: with Christ, in Christ, with each other as members of the same Body. That can be symbolised by the gathering of the community around the common dining-table for the sharing of the food and drink that is communion in the Lord.

The Ordained Priest as Leader of Worship

All three principal liturgical functions that we have delineated are performed by the entire gathered assembly. But the Liturgy of the

---

[17] GIRM 321 specifies that the Eucharistic bread 'be made in such a way that the priest at Mass with a congregation is able in practice to break it into parts for distribution to at least some of the faithful'. Small, individual round breads are in fact counter-symbols of unbrokenness, of lack of sharing. Large breads up to 23 cm (9 inches) in diameter are easily available. People readily perceive and appreciate the symbolism of bread that is shared when they are offered a broken piece at Communion. See my article 'The Breaking of Bread' in *Music and Liturgy*, 26/1 (2000), 30-35.

Eucharist evidently requires an ordained priest to lead that offering of prayer and praise, one who by his pastoral ministry calls the people (*ekklēsia*), gathers them into the unity of congregation (a word that means literally 'a flocking-together'), and leads them – directs them! – in worship. This is a richer and more active concept than just 'presiding' over them.

Since Vatican II, the chair for the priest celebrant has been seen as an important item of sanctuary furniture. In fact he only sits in it when he is *not* actively leading – when he is listening to the readings and at the time of silence after the people's Communion. The *locus* of presidency must enable him to greet the assembly in dialogue and address them in his homily, but especially to lead their shared prayers at the Collect and after Communion, and that is towards the God who is the addressee of these and all other liturgical prayers – an act of worship best symbolised if he leads everyone to face the same direction.

GIRM recommends that the best place for the chair is at the head of the sanctuary, facing the people, 'unless the design of the building or other circumstance impede this'[18]. This is the legacy of Theodor Klauser (see chapter 2). But the priest's presidency should in no way compete with the principal axes of the *exitus* of God's Word in proclamation, and of the responding *reditus* of prayer and praise. The priest is subject to the Word just as much as the other members of the assembly, and might well take his place among them to hear it proclaimed, facing the ambo. The location of the chair should be off-centre: the ministry of the priest-leader, too, is one of service of both God and his people, and should be symbolised as such.[19]

---

[18] GIRM 310. The 1984 *Caeremoniale Episcoporum*, which might have been expected to recommend the traditional placement of the *cathedra* centrally behind the altar, in fact merely states (art. 47) that 'its placement should make it clear that the bishop is presiding over the whole community of the faithful'.

[19] See Louis Bouyer's statement above, 138.

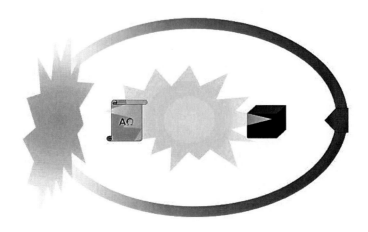

Oriented assembly

In summary, therefore, we have a threefold focus for the Eucharistic liturgy: that of proclamation, of prayer and praise, and of shared communion. This is illustrated in a PowerPoint presentation prepared by Peter Spichtig OP for the Swiss Liturgical Institute (see diagram above).[20]

Although he comments that the conflicting directional and centripetal requirements can never be fully resolved, he proposes the above conceptual plan, in which the priest is located at the right-hand apex of the ellipse, the altar at the focus near him, the ambo at the other focus. But unlike the elliptical plans examined in the previous chapter, it is open-ended. The wall at the left-hand end 'would be better if not decorated, but it could be slightly shaped'[21] – a very Schwarz-inspired

---

[20] Entitled 'Der angemessene Gottesdienstraum' and available (as at May 2020) on https://www.liturgie.ch/praxis/kunst-und-kirchenbau/kirchenbau. The full title reads 'The right space for worship: being Church in a ritually and spatially expressive form'. The diagram is reproduced by kind permission of Peter Spichtig. His commentary on it can be found in SPICHTIG 2017.

[21] SPICHTIG 2017, 44.

solution! Nonetheless he sees the focus of prayer being 'towards the epiphanic centre', where the processional cross, ambo and altar are situated.

An article by the architect Johannes Krämer appeared in the periodical *Gottesdienst* in 2001. It was entitled 'Open and Oriented Assembly'.[22] The first part of his article is on the need for the right space for worship – open, uncluttered, 'an invitation for people to become empty to God' and to wait, ready for encounter with Him. Church spaces 'do not end in themselves, but in accordance with what happens in them, beyond themselves'.

By the time that a would-be participant in the Mass has arrived and taken his seat, the spaces around him are already having a good or bad effect on his preparedness for the liturgy (see above, chapter 10). That is why the environment within the church is so important.

Krämer writes:

> The altar and ambo are arranged on an axis (preferably the main axis of the space) with the centre in between. While the worshippers gather on three sides around the altar, the ambo stands on the fourth, open side. Behind the ambo there should be an 'opening, liberating image of God' with a cross flanking the axis in front of it. White or abstract surfaces of a wall or apse are well suited for such an 'image of God'.

The influence of Schwarz is evident! Krämer continues:

> The priest no longer faces the congregation during the celebration of the Eucharist, but stands in the midst of the congregation facing the open side with the cross. If the

---

[22] KRÄMER 2001. See commentary also in GERHARDS 2001, 216-217.

church faces east, the orientation is even literally understood and the experience increased by the orientation towards the rising sun. With such a concept, even the direction in which the texts and prayers are spoken might make their meaning and content more clearly experienced.

For the 'end-point' behind the ambo, he specifies (with cited reference to Schwarz):

An 'opening, liberating image' (e.g. the empty white wall) stands for the indescribable God. Before that, the cross stands at the point of transition to the actual church space as the active space of the Holy Spirit.

The place of the priest's chair is not described, but is shown in an accompanying sketch as the central seat in the front row of the block facing the altar and ambo. The author suggests that the tabernacle be placed in its own side chapel.

Also shown in Krämer's sketches are the contrasting directions of proclamation (ambo to assembly) and prayer (assembly to end-point beyond the ambo), compared with the centripetal direction of 'Eucharist'. But there is no commentary on this in the text, nor suggestions as to how this might be realised in practice.

Rothenfels revisited

In 2005, a conference was held at Rothenfels castle on the topic 'Dimension and Form. Perspectives for Liturgy and Architecture'. The concluding Eucharist was held in the old chapel (see photo 3), which had been configured especially for the occasion (see plan below). Burkhard Cramer, church architect from Frankfurt, commented on the celebration.[23] 'The congregation formed, as it were, a chalice which awaits its filling in three parallel rows.' The priest 'takes its place at the apex of the community, at the same time both part of the community and the priest of the celebration'. There is no ambo lectern: 'the ambo is the human being himself, who puts himself at the service of the Word of God. The hidden God faces us and speaks to us.'

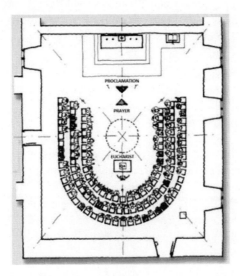

With the preparation of the gifts, the table-fellowship of the Lord begins. Representatives of the congregation bring to the altar a bowl of hosts, chalice, wine and water. Bread and wine - symbols of the self-giving of the community. The priest comes out of the round of the community to the altar, looking out over the circle of the community. The external direction of prayer is a reflection of the inner orientation toward God.[24]

---

[23] CRAMER 2006.
[24] Cp above, 127.

In the Eucharistic Prayer 'the small gathering is connected with the fellowship of heaven and the faithful of all time - the whole Holy Church' in earth and heaven, symbolised by the silver *corona lucis* shining above them.

> The reception of Communion takes place under both kinds. Communion helpers and priests stand opposite the assembly in the open part of the ring, thus closing the circle... The community becomes what it receives – the Body of Christ.

Oriented examples

— *St François-de-Molitor, Paris*

See photo 12. The 'east' window with its slender cross was described in the previous chapter. The pew arrangement is ellipsoid (with a gallery level), with a somewhat narrow gap between the enclosing front pews in which to accommodate the movement of priest and ministers. The ambo faces into the space from the ellipse focus nearest the window. The font is at the other ellipse focus, very close to the door into the street. One of the front seats is slightly distinctive and is intended to include the priest's chair.

The altar is at the midpoint of the space. And here is the surprise. It is built on a platform designed for the priest to celebrate the Liturgy of the Eucharist *facing the door*, with his back to the window.

The architect, Jean-Marie Duthilleul, explains that the axis of the church is between a garden and the city.[25] The ambo is placed near the window as a reminder of the time when God spoke to Man in the garden of Eden: it faces not only the altar but, through the doors into the street, the city beyond, to which the Good News is addressed. The

---

[25] DUTHILLEUL 2014.

altar constitutes a central rock, around which the faithful gather and become the Body of Christ. 'The community takes flesh and is at one and the same time always opened by Christ to other people, to other different people.' And immediately he adds the following, without explanation. 'The priest himself celebrates facing the city, facing the three big doors.'

In fact, the Penitential Act takes place with the priest and ministers standing between the font and the altar, facing the window.[26] Daelemans comments:

> In theory [the priest] could stand on the other side, facing the light. In that way, light, cross and garden would be given more theological and eschatological weight, as an architectural expression of the *parousia,* holding open a ring tempted to close in on itself.[27]

And the footnote to this paragraph notes that others have found Duthilleul's solution 'weak, antinomical and disoriented... Indeed, it counters the *ad orientem* during the Eucharistic Prayer.' But Daelemans adds: 'The contrast with the communal gathering around the altar as Christocentric focus also has *theotopical* value, which must not be overlooked.' He is at least implicitly aware of the tension between the directional and the centripetal in the Liturgy of the Eucharist.

Duthilleul says that, at the beginning of the project to build the new church, Cardinal Lustiger pressed into his hands a copy of Bouyer's *Liturgy and Architecture.* And indeed, in the frontispiece of the issue of the review, *Communio,* in which the architect's article is printed, there is a quote from Bouyer:

---

[26] DAELEMANS 2015, 275.
[27] Id, 273.

> [T]he Christian Church, like the synagogue before it, should be orientated along a common axis, so that the celebration can realise the passage from one focus to the next, especially the call of the Word of God, then the ascent towards the altar, and, beyond the visible altar, our journey pursued in this world until our arrival in the world to come.[28]

This explains Duthilleul's axis of ambo-altar-world, but the context of Bouyer's text refers to the 'pilgrimage towards the eternal city', 'towards the eternal Kingdom, the eschatological presence of the living God'.

— *St Barbara, Moers, Germany*

After destruction in the Second World War, a new chapel for this community was built in a simple brick-built traditional style and opened in 1950. The installation of a new organ and central heating in the late 1990s presented the opportunity for a second liturgical reordering. See photo 14.

The former 'east'-end raised sanctuary became the location for the baptismal font. The terminal wall was decorated with a full-height image in plaster mosaic of the 'resurrected and returning Christ' – somewhat similar in effect to that of Oakland Cathedral.

The former 'way' church arrangement of pews was transformed into a spacious rectangular altar space surrounded by pews on three sides. The ambo is slightly forward of the sanctuary steps, the small square altar slightly backward of the centre of the space. The priest's chair is in front of the sanctuary steps and practically invisible. The tabernacle is located in a small Blessed Sacrament chapel situated at the side of the entrance foyer under the organ gallery: it is thus distinct from the liturgical space, but easily accessible from it.

---

[28] BOUYER 1967, chapter 6.

One might question the position of the baptismal font between the ambo and the terminal wall. On the other hand, the overpowering figure of the risen Christ is highly symbolic of the meaning of baptism, and the space would be a highly effective location for the Liturgy of Baptism at the Easter Vigil. However, the raised sanctuary area is also in practice assigned to the choir (the organ completely fills its gallery); their presence facing down the church completely negates the significance of the 'open fourth side'.

— *Pallottine Church, Vallendar, Germany*

This church, on a site with roots in the 12th century and now a pilgrimage venue, was refurbished in 2001. See photo 13. Like Moers, but on a larger scale, the altar/ambo space is surrounded on three sides by seating. It is raised on a two-step platform. The fourth side is nominally free, and features on the terminal wall the glass curtain described in chapter 11. However, pilgrimage numbers evidently oblige this space to be used occasionally as a fourth side of seating.

The priest may stand either side of the altar, and it appears that in common usage he stands with his back to the window, thus closing the fourth side.

There is no apparent priest's chair. The tabernacle is located in a separate Blessed Sacrament chapel.

Oriented assembly: assessment

The *directional* element has certainly been restored in all three of the churches examined – and for the special occasion in 2005 at Rothenfels – even if implemented unexpectedly in the Paris church. The focus point at Vallendar may be too abstract, especially in view of the status of the church as a pilgrimage venue welcoming groups of visitors unused to such symbols. Krämer's suggestion of installing a plain, slender cross at or near the terminal focus works well at St François-de-Molitor – and similar configurations of cross and window listed in the previous chapter could also be integrated liturgically. The historical precedents for a plain cross beyond the altar were examined in chapter 2.

Images depicted on the end wall, being the focus of prayer, would have to be chosen very carefully and executed to the highest standards of artistry. The mosaic of the risen Christ at Moers is very effective. It is important that the fourth side be strictly and permanently reserved as a 'Holy of Holies' area, not used for overflow seating or as a stage for choir or concerts, as it appears to be used occasionally.

The *centripetal* element is less well realised. The priest, facing 'east', while standing in the midst of the people, has most of the congregation behind him. The priest may be able to show them the host and chalice at the elevation and at the doxology of the Eucharistic Prayer by raising the elements high enough. But the fraction can only be seen by those level with or in front of the altar, and similarly at 'Behold the Lamb of God' before Communion. At the Rothenfels event, all the ministers of Communion left the altar and administered the sacrament facing the assembly from the 'fourth side'.

And a central altar cannot readily also symbolise a threshold, as Schwarz would have wanted.[29]

Conclusions

The Liturgy of the Word is naturally directional. God speaks to us from beyond the ambo, through the reader. We reply to Him in praise and prayer.

The two configurations for the Liturgy of the Eucharist, directional and centripetal, appear to be mutually exclusive, even contradictory. But they are in fact ritually sequential.

---

[29] Cf GERHARDS 2011a, 134-141.

The Eucharistic Prayer, together with the Lord's Prayer and its embolism, are addressed to the unseen Father. It is centrifugal. It is important to underline this, because for many priests and people the climax of the Mass is the consecration of the bread and wine through the words of institution. The elevations make this an intensely *centripetal* point, at least devotionally. But the words of institution are actually a parenthesis in the Eucharistic Prayer. Textually (in Latin), they are a long relative or dependent clause between the first epiclesis and the anamnesis.[30] They are a recollection *before God the Father* of the saving work of Jesus Christ. The addressee of the entire Eucharistic Prayer remains God the Father.[31]

Commentators are surprisingly inconsistent about the direction in which the Eucharistic Prayer should be prayed. Graham Hughes states, on the one hand:

> Ambiguity about 'direction', in fact, wholly vitiates the notion of the worship service as a 'dialogue' [with God]. It is to generate a semiosis in which all the action (communication) is effectively contained within the room itself: there is no semiosis of 'other', of 'beyond', of 'frontier', of 'engagement'.[32]

---

[30] In Eucharistic Prayers I & II beginning with 'Qui', in III & IV with 'Ipse enim', in each case referring back to the preceding epiclesis. In all four Prayers, the words of institution are followed by the Eucharistic Acclamation (addressed to Christ, strangely), then the anamnesis '(Unde et) memores' or 'Unde... recolimus'.

[31] Regarding the genuflections after the elevations, Mazza comments (MAZZA 1986, 9): 'If, then, a gesture is directed to the sacrament itself, it ought to be part of a larger plan in which the words are also addressed to the sacrament. This, if the anaphora were addressed to the Son, there would be no difficulty in explaining the genuflections during and after the account of institution. In fact, however, the anaphora is addressed to the Father; it is to him that we relate what Jesus did at the Last Supper.'

[32] HUGHES 2003, 163. 'Semiosis' is the analysis of a (potentially) 'meaningful' situation or circumstance. Hughes advocates facing the sanctuary with the people to address God, and turning around to bless the people, as from God.

And on the other (on the next page):

> [T]hough the Prayer of Thanksgiving over the eucharistic gifts... is obviously addressed to God, none of us, I imagine, is going to relinquish the 'basilican' position in which the leader stands behind the table.[33]

Professor Albert Gerhards, similarly:

> Wherever possible, one should carry out common orientation. The different language roles of addressing the community, proclamation, prayer must be directed, e.g. by changing location or turning to the altar or to the cross at the prayers. At the Eucharistic Prayer, the Eucharistic gifts should form the observed reference point, behind which the priest steps back.[34]

It is true that the epicleses *refer to* the elements[35], but the Eucharistic Prayer is not addressed *at* them: even the words of institution are a recounting *before the Father* of the action of His Son at the Last Supper. But here the liturgical and devotional understandings clash. For centuries now, the 'miracle of the Mass' has been concentrated on the words of consecration: bells are rung at this moment[36] and incensations take place.[37] Such a tradition has to be taken into account, at least for pastoral reasons. But the words of institution form part of the great 'forward' act of thanksgiving that unites this offering to the Father with that of Christ the High Priest.

---

[33] Id, 164.
[34] GERHARDS 2000, 68. '...Beim Hochgebet sollen die eucharistischen Gaben den erfahrbaren Bezugspunkt bilden, hinter den der Priester zurücktreten hat.'
[35] The second (Communion) epiclesis could be enhanced by appropriate gestures, just as the priest is instructed to 'extend his hands over the *oblata*' for the first epiclesis.
[36] They were intended to alert the faithful when the Eucharistic Prayer was said by the priest silently – now no longer. See also O'LOUGHLIN 1995a, 182.
[37] GIRM 150.

The focus is different when it comes to the Communion Rite (after the Lord's Prayer). As explained above[38], there is then a strong case for directing attention and prayer centripetally to the Eucharistic elements. Nonetheless, 'blessed are those called to the supper of the Lamb' – there is an outward, eschatological focus as well as an inward, sacramental one.

Is it possible to represent this distinction of focus, oriented and centripetal, ritually? If so, how should such a liturgy be configured?

Before proposing an answer to these questions, it is appropriate to consider an unmistakable feature of Catholic churches: the tabernacle.

---

[38] See above, page 172.

Chapter 13

ALTAR AND TABERNACLE

We sketched the history of the reservation of the Eucharist in chapter 2. As the Liturgical Renewal developed in the first half of the twentieth century, the question arose as to how the altar could be reinstated in its own right as the centre of the Eucharistic celebration, while maintaining due reverence to the presence of the Blessed Sacrament reserved in the tabernacle, then still attached to the altar. We have seen how Rudolf Schwarz wrestled with the conflict of the two competing foci, and eventually saw the Mass as 'the throbbing heart' and the reserved sacrament as 'the resting head'.[1]

Purpose and Usage

The principal purpose of reservation of the Eucharist is, of course, to provide Holy Communion for the sick, and, as *viaticum*, for the dying. The reverence due to it has developed into the cult of worship of the Blessed Sacrament outside Mass, both privately and in public devotions, sometimes for extended periods of time.

This raises the question of the relationship of reservation of Holy Communion to the Eucharist that provides it. A hundred years ago,

---

[1] See above, 115.

Communion was distributed often and even principally outside the celebration of Mass and therefore perforce from the reserved Sacrament in the tabernacle. Even though Communion is now distributed almost exclusively within Mass (except to the sick), the habit of 'tabernacle Communion' is still universally common and even considered as the norm – despite the Vatican Council's clear recommendation that the faithful should 'receive the Lord's body under elements consecrated at that very sacrifice' in which they have just taken part.[2] In the 'Offertory Procession' they have brought forward the gifts of bread and wine to be sanctified at the Mass and to be returned to them to sanctify them. They have a right to be so fed.

Of course it may be occasionally necessary to regulate the number of hosts in the tabernacle by distributing some at Mass. But regular 'tabernacle Communion' of the faithful present at Mass is a counter-symbol that their Communion is separate from and unconnected to the Mass that they have just been (and still are) celebrating.[3]

This is particularly noticeable when the tabernacle is at some distance from the altar, and the priest or minister goes to fetch the ciborium and bring it to the altar before the people's Communion. The same disjunction is less visually intrusive but still noticeable when the tabernacle is situated directly and closely behind the altar.[4] At the beginning of Mass the priest will have genuflected towards it, but he then conducts the entire Liturgy of the Eucharist with his back to it, as if it was not there – something that some sensitive priests find uncomfortable[5]. Come Communion, he communicates himself from the elements he has just consecrated (as he is obliged to do), then turns his back on the altar to retrieve a ciborium from the tabernacle, from

---

[2] *SC* 55, GIRM 85. There has never been any provision in the rubrics for fetching a ciborium from the tabernacle before Communion.

[3] Cf O'LOUGHLIN 2015b, 270-272.

[4] Contrary to Roman regulations: see above, 122.

[5] Some have been known to draw a curtain in front of the tabernacle before Mass.

which the faithful are provided, as if their Communion was something quite different from his.

The reservation of the Eucharist is better seen as a *prolongation* of the Mass from which it is derived, rather than the setting and context for it. It is from that prolongation that Communion is brought to sick members of the community, and through which they are united to the Mass that has just been celebrated, and to the community who have celebrated it.

Location

We have seen earlier how, historically, the tabernacle 'took over' and superseded the altar on which it was placed.[6] When the entire church is directed towards the tabernacle in prime position at the centre of the 'east' end, the danger arises that all prayer – and even the Mass itself – is perceived as an offering *towards the tabernacle*. This is a theological nonsense, as Joseph Ratzinger made plain.[7]

Writing some two decades later, he included in his *The Spirit of the Liturgy* a chapter on 'The Reservation of the Blessed Sacrament'.[8] One might cavil at his assertion that the Eucharistic presence in the tabernacle signifies the 'complete fulfilment' of the 'Eucharistic celebration'[9] – the Eucharist does not require anything additional to complete it, at least this side of heaven. But he continues: 'A church without the Eucharistic Presence is somehow dead, even when it invites people to pray'. This emotion is keenly felt in many places.

In fact, one comes to church for worship with two quite different motives or intentions. One is to take part in Mass or public devotions with other members of one's community: an event and ritual

---

[6] See above, 50.
[7] See above, 142.
[8] RATZINGER 2000, 85-91.
[9] Id, 90.

celebration. The other is for private prayer. Ideally they should be accommodated in different spaces configured for their distinct uses. The one is liturgically structured with altar and ambo, and appropriate accommodation for a Sunday congregation – the greater part of the entire church space. The other is ideally a smaller quiet area suitable for silent prayer and contemplation.[10] The first speaks action – the liturgy of the 'passover' of the Paschal mystery, an event in salvation history every time it is celebrated. The other speaks stasis, permanence: the Lord has indeed passed over but is still and always here.[11]

In 1967, the Sacred Congregation of Rites issued the Instruction on Eucharistic worship, *Eucharisticum Mysterium*. It recommended the placing of the tabernacle 'as far as possible... in a chapel distinct from the middle or central part of the church' and 'suitable for private prayer so that the faithful may easily and fruitfully, by private devotion also, continue to honour our Lord in this sacrament'.[12]

The first edition of the General Instruction of the Roman Missal in 1970 quoted this recommendation, preferring the separate chapel.[13] However, in the 2002 revision it was considerably watered down:

> It is more in keeping with the meaning of the sign that the tabernacle in which the Most Holy Eucharist is reserved not be on an altar on which Mass is celebrated. Consequently, it is preferable that the tabernacle be located, according to the judgment of the diocesan Bishop:

[10] For public devotions such as Exposition of the Blessed Sacrament, It can be brought to the altar from which it was derived.
[11] Cf SCHWARZ 1938, 202 f.
[12] *Eucharisticum Mysterium*, no. 53; cf also the 1973 Decree of the Sacred Congregation of Rites on Holy Communion and Worship of the Eucharist outside Mass (HCWE), no. 9.
[13] GIRM (1970), no. 276.

a. Either in the sanctuary, apart from the altar of celebration, in a form and place more appropriate, not excluding on an old altar no longer used for celebration;

b. Or even in some chapel suitable for the faithful's private adoration and prayer and organically connected to the church and readily visible to the Christian faithful.[14]

One other paragraph of *Eucharisticum Mysterium* – now largely forgotten – deserves our attention. It reads:

In the celebration of Mass the principal modes of worship by which Christ is present to His Church are gradually revealed. First of all, Christ is seen to be present among the faithful gathered in His name; then in his Word, as the Scriptures are read and explained; in the person of the minister; finally and in a unique way (*modo singulari*) under the species of the Eucharist. Consequently, because of the sign, it is more in keeping with the nature of the celebration that the Eucharistic presence of Christ, which is the fruit of the consecration and should be seen as such, should not be on the altar from the very beginning of Mass through the reservation of the sacred species in the tabernacle.[15]

Although the tabernacle is no longer housed on the altar on which the Eucharist is celebrated, its presence in close proximity to the altar from the beginning of Mass makes this gradual unfolding of the presence of Christ in the course of a Eucharistic celebration impossible to realise.

---

[14] GIRM, no. 315.
[15] Eucharisticum Mysterium, no. 55, HCWE no. 6.

Where, as recommended after the Vatican Council, small chapels have been set up as distinct spaces for private prayer before the Blessed Sacrament, they have been greatly appreciated. This has always been the case in larger churches and cathedrals, where Blessed Sacrament chapels have acquired their own aura and distinctive art: see the Blessed Sacrament chapel at Buckfast Abbey with its splendid modern stained-glass window.

The most recent advice from the Congregation for Divine Worship and Discipline of the Sacraments is to be found in the 2004 Instruction, *Redemptionis Sacramentum*:

> According to the structure of each church building and in accordance with legitimate local customs, the Most Holy Sacrament is to be reserved in a tabernacle in a part of the church that is noble, prominent, readily visible, and adorned in a dignified manner and furthermore suitable for prayer by reason of the quietness of the location, the space available in front of the tabernacle, and also the supply of benches or seats and kneelers.[16]

If located near the entrance to the church, such Blessed Sacrament chapels have the advantage of being noticed and noticeable to all before they enter the main liturgical area. Security considerations also favour such a location: they can remain open when the rest of the church is locked. In some churches this chapel is also used for weekday Masses. But distance from the main altar can be not only a logistical problem; there can also arise the perception that there is little logical connection between the two worship spaces.

Locating the tabernacle in a side chapel within a single-nave church may bring it near the altar but give the impression of 'sidelining' the Blessed Sacrament. There have been many cases of such experiments

---

[16] Art. 130.

being overturned and the tabernacle restored to the former high altar. Where the church consists of a single indivisible space, this may well be the only option available. However, where the old sanctuary is deep, it may be possible – having brought the altar 'down' to the nave – to close it off with a transparent or fretwork screen and furnish it as recommended above.

In new and rebuilt churches, this difficult visual relationship of altar and tabernacle can be addressed more thoroughly. Some bipolar churches have a transverse axis with a transept chapel situated in a clear spatial relationship with the central midpoint. We have seen successful examples at Our Lady and St Vincent, Potters Bar, and at St François-de-Molitor in Paris. The fact that these chapels lie outside the main area of the liturgical assembly can even remind parishioners that their absent sick fellow-members, for whom the tabernacle contents are intended, are physically outside their church space but still members of their Eucharistic community.

Liturgy and Devotion

Tradition dies hard, but in different ways in different cultures. Catholics in some countries continue to expect a tabernacle, rather than the altar, to be the distinctive central feature of their churches – and indeed as a statement of Catholic identity in comparison with churches of other Christian traditions. Many dioceses in the United States favour the central, east-end location of the tabernacle – Bishop Robert Morlino of Madison, Wisconsin, decreed in 2016 that in all churches of his diocese the tabernacle should be placed in the centre of the church, behind the altar. By contrast, the guidelines produced by the German bishops in 1988 (6th edition, 2002) advised that siting the tabernacle on the central axis of the church is 'less appropriate to the present understanding of the liturgy and should be avoided if possible'.

One may ask whether the apparent enthusiasm for restoring the tabernacle to a central position in the church, particularly noticeable in the United States, is partly due to the loss of a sense of 'the beyond' in the reformed liturgy when celebrated with the priest continually facing the people – a purely human dialogue replacing a God-human dialogue. People feel the need for a God-oriented directional focus for their worship.

There is a problem when the tabernacle becomes the overriding focus of orientation and of the church itself. It then constitutes a devotional envelope within which the liturgy is celebrated, to which the liturgy can appear as subservient. But the Directory on Popular Piety and the Liturgy, issued by the Congregation for Divine Worship in 2001, makes it clear that the liturgy has primacy over devotions.[17] In particular, it states:

> [A]ll forms of Eucharistic devotion must have an intrinsic reference to the Eucharistic Sacrifice, or dispose the faithful for its celebration, or prolong the worship which is essential to that Sacrifice.[18]

The tabernacle is not an integral feature of the liturgy itself, and should therefore not have such an overbearing presence as a visual focus in the main area for liturgical celebration that it distracts participants during the celebration of the Eucharist. As we have noted before, 'The altar... is the place where it is truly the centre toward which the attention of the whole congregation of the faithful naturally turns.'[19] Indeed, in the Rite of Dedication of a Church the altar is consecrated with chrism, but the rite does not include even a blessing of the tabernacle before the Blessed Sacrament is placed in it.

A balanced theology of eucharistic adoration in relation to the liturgy is hard to find. Because it is a devotion, manuals of liturgy tend to

---

[17] Congregation for Divine Worship and the Discipline of the Sacraments, Directory on Popular Piety and the Liturgy: Principles and Guidelines, December 2001, nos. 11-13.
[18] Id, no. 161.
[19] GIRM 299.

ignore it. Pope John Paul II, in his 2001 encyclical *Ecclesia de Eucharistia* ('Church from the Eucharist') describes worship of the Eucharist outside Mass as 'of inestimable value for the life of the Church', but 'strictly linked to the celebration of the Eucharistic Sacrifice' from which it is derived[20]. And 80 years ago, Pius Parsch explained:

> The Mass is not a 'devotion'; it is not the adoration of the Eucharist; it is the sacrifice offered by Christ, and in this offering we are actually participating since it is also our sacrifice. We come to Mass, we celebrate Mass, not so much to adore Christ in his Divinity as to offer Him, the Divine Lamb, to our heavenly Father.[21]

The question for liturgists and architects is how to make both this connection and the distinction between Mass and Eucharistic devotion apparent.

Sacrament awaiting fulfilment

Back in 1925, Abbot Anscar Vonier was at pains to explain how the key to the doctrine of the Eucharist was precisely that it was a sacrament, a sign of a reality that is not constricted to time or place, and is indeed not of this world[22]. There is indeed Real Presence, but it is also a sign of absence, of a fulfilment still in the future, still to be realised eschatologically in the heavenly liturgy. 'For now we see in a mirror, dimly, but then we will see face to face' (1 Cor 13:12). A simple symbol of this would be to install permanently closed curtains *behind* the tabernacle, symbolising 'the inner shrine behind the curtain, where Jesus, a forerunner on our behalf, has entered' (Heb 6:19; cf 10:19-22).

---

[20] Directory, no. 25.

[21] PARSCH 1939, 237.

[22] VONIER 1925, 122. Vonier bases his exposition on the writings of St Thomas Aquinas, here *Summa Theologica*, III, q. 75, a. 1 ad 3.

Can a tabernacle therefore substitute for the eschatological 'east'-end focus that we have outlined in the previous chapters?

Joseph Ratzinger, in *The Spirit of the Liturgy*, sees the tabernacle as the 'Holy of Holies', 'the tent of God, his throne'. And he continues: 'The New Jerusalem is anticipated in the humble species of bread'.[23] Yes, indeed. The Eucharist points beyond itself, to an eschatological fulfilment 'when sacraments shall cease'[24] – and therefore beyond both altar and tabernacle. As we have seen earlier, our worship is not just christological, it is trinitarian.[25] We offer the sacrifice of Christ to his Father, as he did. The reserved sacrament in the tabernacle, like the altar, points beyond itself, to the higher reality it signifies. It is the locational *means* of our prolonged eucharistic worship, not its final *end*.

The highly respected liturgist, Josef Andreas Jungmann, wrote a fine article on Eucharistic piety in 1960 – after the summoning of the Vatican Council but before it formally started.[26] He compared traditional devotion to the Blessed Sacrament to the renewed understanding of the Eucharist revived by the liturgical movement.

> Perhaps the difference can be formulated as follows: Eucharistic piety, which in the last centuries has brought to the fore the cult of the Eucharist, fixed its gaze on the Blessed Sacrament and said: here is the Saviour, here is the centre of all Christianity, God is present here. Of course, the Eucharistic piety born of the liturgical movement, in which the early Christian attitude of the Eucharist is revived, affirms the real presence, affirms worship of the Lord in the sacrament, but adds: the presence of the Lord in the sacrament is not the final

---

[23] RATZINGER 2000, 89-90.
[24] Cf the hymn (of Anglican origin) 'O thou, who at thy Eucharist didst pray', the last verse of which begins 'So Lord at length, when sacraments shall cease'.
[25] See above, 4, 91; and Directory on Popular Piety, nos. 76-80.
[26] JUNGMANN 1960.

word, is not its only mode of being. The presence of the Lord in the Sacred Host in thousands upon thousands of places is indeed a real but secondary presence, a kind of reflection of the primary presence. The primary presence, the primary mode of being of the Lord, is the one in which, by virtue of his resurrection with his transfigured humanity, he is at the right hand of the Father. The Eucharist, therefore, must be viewed transparently, as it were, towards the transfigured Christ, where he lives in the glory of the Father. The prayer of the Church, therefore, where it appears in its full classical form, is addressed to God the Father, through Christ the Lord, *per Christum dominum nostrum.*[27]

If, in the refurbishment of an existing church, it is necessary to retain or restore a tabernacle at its 'east' end, then let that 'end' not be a cul-de-sac, as if there was nothing beyond it. Instead, let there be a window or image behind and above it – as suggested in the previous two chapters – to indicate that the Lord is risen and gone before us in fulfilment of his Paschal Mystery, from which he will one day return to claim us as his own.

---

[27] Id., 186-187.

Chapter 14

ORIENTED ASSEMBLY

In the Foreword of this book, the intention was expressed to propose a forward-looking solution to address the shortcomings of the current standard configuration in Catholic churches.

As already suggested, in small communities the best solution may well be the use of separate spaces for the Liturgies of the Word and of the Eucharist, furnished appropriately for their distinctive rituals. A long longitudinal church could also be configured likewise. The offertory procession then becomes the ritual movement of the entire gathered assembly between the two spaces.

The proposal outlined in this chapter requires not only an updated architectural concept but ideally also some adjustments to the current ritual. This may not be possible in practice: Schwarz says about his 'plans' that it may be necessary to 'persevere short of realization in a state of quiet reserve'.[1] It must be emphasised that what is offered here is only a concept, not an architectural drawing. However, there are several features which have been carefully configured in order to symbolise their function and placement.

---

[1] SCHWARZ 1938, 218.

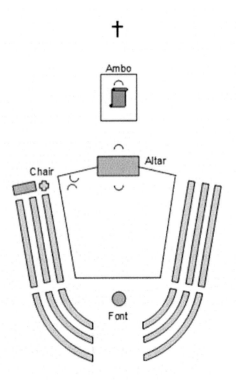

The rounded-V-shaped synaxis or assembly is carefully angled so that it is symbolic of both openness to the God of the beyond, and of the community of its members, priest and people, towards each other, aware also of the Lord in their midst. It may be thought of as a directional version of Schwarz's 'open ring' plan.

Such a polygonal shape may not be practical architecturally. Alternatively, the space may be shaped as a semi-ellipse, a 180° (or less) amphitheatre, or a wide U-shaped design, but preferably not a square format with the people arranged in three blocks, which can separate them rather than unite them.

The *end-point*, represented by †, stands for whatever image or architectural feature marks and symbolises the 'beyond' towards which prayer is addressed to God. It may be easiest to imagine this as the window and cross at St François-de-Molitor (see photo 12). We examined a number of recent examples in chapters 10 and 11.

Whatever means is adopted to represent the end-point, it is important for its symbolism that it should be perceived as distant, as 'beyond'.

The *ambo* is the closest location to the end-point because it is from there that God addresses his people through the reader. Its separation from the pews as a distinct, somewhat separate area can serve to symbolise this – and need not raise a communication problem if there is good sound amplification.

The *altar* is the central focal point (see chapter 5 for the debate about what 'central' might mean). It stands on the threshold of the distinct ambo/end-point space. There is ample space in front of it, creating a sense of spaciousness. This space is also available for coffins at funerals, for wedding couples, and for the Paschal candle at the Easter Vigil. The altar space should preferably stand at the same level as the front benches and be simply delineated by distinctive flooring. The surrounding seating can be gentle tiered to enable good visual sight-lines.

A simple *font*, also serving as a holy-water stoup, is an integral part of the plan, situated near the entrance. If a full-immersion font is desired, it would have to be located in a separate baptistery space.

The *priest's chair* is at the foremost position of the assembly, but is also fully integrated with the people's seating.[2] The priest only uses it as a chair, i.e. for sitting, for one of two reasons: when he is listening to the Word of God and therefore facing the ambo, and when he is, like the

---

[2] If a deacon is taking part, a seat is prepared for him on the priest's right.

people, quietly meditating after Communion or during a lengthy choral piece. On both these occasions, there is no active presidential role in play. However, when he is addressing the people, he steps forward and turns to face them; when leading them in prayer, he turns about and faces the end-point, leading them to do the same.

Neither the chair nor the leadership point are situated on the central axis. The priest is the minister of the liturgy and of the people he leads. As Bouyer stated[3], the central axis of font, altar, ambo and end-point are the significant points of encounter with God during the liturgy, and should not be complicated by yet another focal point.

For the same reason, the *tabernacle* should be to one side, preferably in its own chapel. If local devotion, or national or diocesan authority, requires that it be visible on entry into the church, this will have to be considered in any plan. Ideally, it should not be located at the end-point: the tabernacle contains the sacramental presence of Christ the Mediator as a remembrance of the Mass that has been celebrated at the altar, so it is at the same level of 'threshold'. Liturgical prayer looks beyond the sacrament towards the unseen Father, through the risen Christ who has returned to Him.

Musicians are best accommodated at the end of the pews immediately opposite the priest's chair. The music leader or cantor is then well-placed to direct the music of choir and congregation discreetly from the edge of the altar space.[4]

The Order of Mass with the People: an example

A 'gathering' song is sung for some time before Mass begins, in order to prepare the people spiritually for their transition from the world

---

[3] See above, 138.
[4] Grand pianos and organ consoles should not impinge on the worship area, but be visually discreet.

outside to their special 'liminal' status as God's people, chosen, called and assembled for worship.

The procession of priest and ministers enters by the main entrance and stops at the font, from which they take holy water. They remain there for the Introductory or Penitential Act. The liturgy is still at the stage of 'humble access and approach'. Everyone in the church is partly facing the end-point and partly facing each other, which accords with the opening words of the 'I confess' – 'I confess to almighty God and to you, my brothers and sisters'.

At the end of the Penitential Act, the priest advances to the altar area and kisses the altar[5]. He may incense both ambo and altar: this could take place during the singing of the *Gloria*, when this is appropriate.[6] The acolytes place their candles initially at the ambo, not at the altar.

For the Opening Prayer, the priest steps forward from his chair and faces the assembly from his leadership point to say 'Let us pray'. He then turns towards the end-point and, after a moment of silence, says or sings the prayer. The people, following the priest, should also turn full-face towards the end-point for this and all other prayers. Turning towards the same direction for prayer is traditional, and still standard monastic practice – also for singing the Litany of the Saints at the Easter Vigil and at ordinations.

The reader(s) and psalmist process to the ambo and read/sing the scriptural readings (other than the gospel) from there. A gospel procession takes the deacon (or priest in default) to the ambo for the incensation

---

[5] As in the Extraordinary Form. The Gospel Book, if carried in the entrance procession, is placed on the altar before its incensation.

[6] Alternatively and preferably, a bowl of charcoal within a decorative vessel may be placed in front of the altar before the celebration. At this time, instead of incensing the altar, the priest places incense in the bowl and allows the smoke to rise up: 'Lord, let my prayer be accepted as incense before you' (Ps 141:2). It can be left in place throughout the liturgy and replenished with incense as required to continue its symbolism.

of the Gospel Book and the proclamation of the gospel. The people sing the Gospel Acclamation – and repeat it in short form after the gospel has been read, in order to accompany the return of the procession.

The priest preaches his homily not from the ambo but from his leadership point – or he may opt to do so from the open area in front of the altar.

He leads the Prayers of the Faithful from his leadership point, facing the end-point for the concluding prayer. The invocations can be announced (facing the assembly) by the deacon, or by one or more readers from within the assembly – but not from the ambo.

Signifying the change from the Liturgy of the Word to the Liturgy of the Eucharist, the acolytes transfer their candles from the ambo to either side of the altar. For the procession of gifts, a small table will have been prepared at the side of the entrance. From here the procession advances into the altar space and the priest receives them on the 'western' side. The *berakah* blessing prayers are addressed to God, so the priest turns about and faces across the altar towards the end-point as he says them, preferably silently, while raising the gifts slightly.[7] The priest may incense the offerings and altar; he and the people may subsequently also be incensed. After washing his fingers, he then turns to them and says 'Pray, brethren...'. He says the Prayer over the Offerings over the offerings facing the end-point.

The priest turns to the people for the Preface dialogue. He then turns back and addresses the entire Eucharistic Prayer towards the end-point. At each elevation, he may turn to one side and then the other to show the people the consecrated bread and chalice.[8] Ideally, they should adopt the same prayer gestures as the priest, including standing

---

[7] The first option in the Missal is for quiet recitation of these prayers, without response.

[8] GIRM 150 states that the priest 'shows the host and then the chalice'. This does not forbid him turning to do so.

– if so, they should bow, as concelebrants do, when the priest genuflects at the consecration. However, the proposed V-shaped design allows some natural flexibility so that the people may face either altar or end-point for the Eucharistic Prayer. For the concluding doxology, the priest lifts the paten/ciborium and chalice high as a gesture of offering. The entire assembly make the acclamations.

All stand and turn to face 'east' for the 'Our Father' and continue to do so for the succeeding embolism and acclamation 'For the kingdom...'. For the Sign of Peace, the priest (or deacon) turns to face the people to bid them exchange it.

The priest (and deacon) may now walk halfway round the altar and face the people from the ambo side.[9] In this way, together with the altar ministers, he completes with them a single closed polygon of people ready for communion with their Lord, sacramentally present on the altar, and with each other. He lifts up a large bread and breaks it solemnly in front of them. Since this is the first time that the people will have seen the priest on the 'east' side of the altar, it adds significant attention to this important moment in the Liturgy of the Eucharist. The Fraction begins the sharing with and in the Lord, broken for them and among them. 'Though many, we are One Body.' The people sing the 'Lamb of God' while priest and deacon (and, hopefully, permitted Extraordinary Ministers of Communion) break the other breads ready for sharing.

All now proceeds as customary. For Communion of the faithful, the priest may come forward and stand on the 'west' side of the altar, and have the people process towards him onto the altar space. Alternatively, he may stand back a few paces from the 'east' side of the altar and administer to the people there. Two ministers stand at or near

---

[9] The altar should be no deeper than 70 cm, so that the breads, chalices, etc on the corporal can be accessed from both sides of the altar. The Missal can be removed from the altar at this point if the priest knows his 'Preparation for Communion' prayers by heart.

ORIENTED ASSEMBLY

the ends of the altar to administer chalices. The altar is thus perceived as also the table of the Lord from which He feeds his people.

Alternatively, if there is a single row of people surrounding the altar space, the priest and ministers can approach them and serve them Communion in turn, where they stand. Depending on local conditions, this can be a more effective way of symbolising community sharing.

Remaining hosts are taken to the tabernacle.[10] If intended for Communion of the Sick, this ministry and its recipients might be announced at this point. The 'washing-up' is done at the credence table (behind the priest's chair) or deferred until after Mass.[11]

The Prayer after Communion, blessing and dismissal are said by the priest (and deacon) from his leadership point, facing the end-point or the people accordingly.

Limitations

A great deal depends on the artistic and architectural effectiveness of the symbol chosen for the end-point. We have seen a number of examples of a plain, slender cross (not a crucifix) located near or in front of a window. The absence of a *corpus* on the cross makes it clear that its role is symbolic, for the Lord is risen.

This cross could be back-lit either naturally or artificially. Obviously the direction of the sun in the course of a day in relation to the church's geographical orientation will dictate the size and transparency of the window.

---

[10] It is to be hoped that, in accordance with the Vatican Council's recommendation, fetching hosts *from* the tabernacle can be minimised, so that people normally receive the Eucharistic elements consecrated at the same Mass (cf SC 55). See chapter 11.
[11] GIRM 163.

There is probably a maximum number that could be accommodated in such a ground-plan – perhaps 200. Engaging a larger number than that *as a community* raises the problems of social interaction and participation that were noted by Schwarz and also by us in chapter 10.

Re-ordering existing churches

The template outlined above may well be impractical for many existing churches. The most important feature of any reordering is to situate the altar among the people, to make it truly central among them, as *Inter Œcumenici* paragraph 91 required.

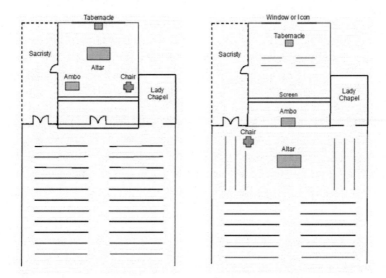

There are many churches in England built from the 1850s to the 1950s which are similar in design to the diagrams shown here: a single-vaulted nave, with a more restricted-width chancel or sanctuary flanked by side altars, or by one side altar and the sacristy. This reflects the pre-Vatican II ethos whereby the sanctuary was 'off limits' to lay people and reserved to the clergy and their all-male servers.

In reacting to the 1974 decree *Inter Œcumenici*, there was a common tendency to simply detach the altar from the 'east' wall and move it only a few feet further into the sanctuary to enable the priest to celebrate Mass facing the people. This failed to make the altar in any way 'central', as originally intended by the Consilium – as we saw in chapter 5[12] – and as later specified in the General Instruction of the Roman Missal ('truly the centre toward which the attention of the whole congregation of the faithfully naturally turns'[13]). We saw in chapter 10 how the unity of the *synaxis* – God's people, ordained and lay, gathered together – requires a single architectural space. The altar is optimally placed at the centre of that space.

An existing architecturally-distinct sanctuary can retain its 'holy area' aura by converting it into a retro-chapel. The removal of the altar will give it additional space and depth. If the tabernacle has traditionally been located at the east end, it may be pastorally advisable to retain it in that position. It may be best to bring it a few feet forward, and install it not on an altar but on a pedestal in a new standalone 'sacrament house', as Schwarz did at Trier.[14] This leaves the wall behind and above it available for a window or icon-type image, as suggested in chapter 10. There can be discreet kneelers and seating for parishioners to access and spend contemplative time near the tabernacle outside liturgical celebrations. It may be possible to install a screen, especially where there are steps, to further distinguish the area as a distinct retro-chapel.

* * *

The Foreword of this book promised no one-size-fits-all answers. The concept described in this chapter is not one, either. It is offered in the hope that it may prompt some creative thinking, for the greater glory of God and the benefit of his holy people.

---

[12] See above, especially 120.
[13] GIRM 299.
[14] See photo 7 and above, 114.

EPILOGUE

Chapter 15

MEETING MYSTERY

> We must be still and still moving
> into another intensity
> for a further union, a deeper communion.

(T. S. Eliot: Four Quartets – Part II: East Coker)

I have arrived at outlining a possible incarnation of liturgical ritual in some detail. That is dangerous. Although I have explained the need for a focus beyond the altar, and eventually specified a potential implementation of it, this book will have been a fruitless effort if it fails to have introduced the reader to something much more important than a draft floor plan – namely, a perception that liturgy offers its participants an awareness of an active divine presence that is expressed by its symbols, but lies also beyond them.

In chapter 1, I attempted to cast light on the nature of liturgy by examining its language, that of ritual. It is time to come full circle in this book by delving further into it.[1]

---

[1] For this Epilogue, I have been much inspired by David Torevell's *Liturgy and the Beauty of the Unknown* (TOREVELL 2016), in which he seeks 'an aesthetic understanding of

Time out of time, space beyond space

When we enter a church – for a liturgical celebration or even privately – we take holy water, reminding ourselves of our baptism, when we first entered the community of the baptised, the holy people of God. The liturgy begins with the Sign of the Cross, the sign under which we were baptised.

> At liturgy, we do not invent or assert our own identity; we *receive* it. That is why Christian worship begins only after all participants agree to act as impersonators, travelling to a 'strange land' under assumed identities, on another's passport: "In the name of the Father, and of the Son, and of the Holy Spirit". The liturgy's first words do not announce who *we* are, but inscribe us in Another.[2]

People gather from out of 'the world' with its social structures to become and be a fellowship, an association of individuals that may not yet be a community, but one that strives for communion with and in God, one in which all its members (including the priest) are of equal status. They have come together to share a common faith, hope and love, and to be united by them in a communion-fellowship that is both symbolic and sacramental, present, experienced and effective now, but yet to be fulfilled.[3]

Liturgical celebrations are thus 'liminal' – literally, 'at a threshold' – in an in-between state where, at least for a short space of time, participants are neither in the world they left behind at the church door, nor in the next world. They belong to a communion-fellowship that is 'in-between times' – the church as locally congregated in this time and

---

worship which releases a transformative movement of the self through liturgical form, allowing an endless and unsatiated encounter with the Unknown' (*id*, 12).
[2] MITCHELL 2006, 45.
[3] This is Victor Turner's '*communitas*': see TURNER 2007.

place and the Church that is over all time and includes the communion of saints.

> The boundary between two worlds is the space liturgy inhabits. 'Another place' is both here and not yet here. The symbolic realism and sacramental signs that liturgy uses offer participants a visible and tangible means to experience this place, which is beyond and yet contained within the rite, allowing them to move towards that for which they long.[4]

We use ritual in this in-between world because there is no alternative. The ritual depicts in symbols the ideal state towards which it points. For the Christian Church this is none other than the celestial city (Rev 21:1-4). As we saw in chapter 2, the art and architecture of Byzantine and Romanesque basilicas illustrated this in transparent symbols, and it is evident to this day in Eastern church art and architecture. The Eucharist, *anamnesis* of the Paschal mystery of Jesus Christ, is the ritual means by which transition to this state is both anticipated and effected.

Time is different in this in-between world. 'The ritual participants emerge from everyday life and its rhythms into a different quality of time that can only be experienced in the ritual and its performance.'[5] For every Mass is an event in salvation-history, one more step in applying the Paschal mystery to the salvation of the world, one more step towards the fulfilment of "thy kingdom come". It is *kairos* time – "Repent for the *kairos* is fulfilled and the kingdom of God is close at hand" (Mk 1:15) – God's time, not common *chronos*, chronological time.

Special time, special place. The place and space of the church is no ordinary place. It is a gateway or threshold to 'another place' beyond it,

---

[4] TOREVELL 2016, 242.
[5] MESSNER 2013, here 303. Cf also HUGHES 2003, 197.

to which we already belong as citizens, though we do not see it.[6] God is present, but He is also absent.

What goes on in this 'liminal' world defies rational explanation. It needs ritual to express it. The liturgy points to an active presence beyond itself, which beckons us to reach out beyond ourselves and allow ourselves to be taken over by it, to be carried along by it, to be grasped by it – or rather, by the Holy Spirit that animates it. We may not feel able to name the sense we have of this divine activity, and this is entirely appropriate: there is a strong tradition of 'apophatic' theology – one that desists from naming God, one that fosters silent contemplation[7]. We met Mrs Murphy in chapter 1 (q.v.).

But can we assume that all worshippers are as enraptured by the liturgy as Mrs Murphy? We live in a world of religious disaffection, disenchantment; Guardini's fears[8] were prophetic. Too many Catholic commentators on liturgy have presumed that what is intended by a liturgical sign is automatically what is perceived by all who observe it.[9] Interpretation of symbols is not just a matter of correct decoding; it is what observers *make* of the symbols according to their own preconceptions and life-view that is decisive for them.

Otto's *mysterium tremendum et fascinans*, even unnamed, stands at the edge of a 'limit' experience, which may be 'awe-ful' or alternatively inexpressibly wonderful – a tragic death, or falling in love, for example. Commonly recognized moments such as these open the way to a realization of a world beyond mundanity, of an otherness that is always there but infrequently averted to. Moreover, these are times when the human subject yearns for some One, some Other One, to cry out to, the One whom Christian believers (and adherents of some other religions)

---

[6] Cf HUGHES 2003, 148-154.
[7] Such reverent reticence is expressed in Judaism by its refusal to pronounce YHWH, and in Moslem mosques by their refusal to admit images, but only calligraphic scripts.
[8] See above, 84.
[9] HUGHES 2003, 229-232.

recognize as the personal God to whom he/she listens and to whom he/she prays. Worship is addressed to a 'thou'. But how many of our liturgical celebrations present this challenge and encounter?[10] Do they really point their participants (or seeking attendees) to an Other that is beyond the priest, the altar and the tabernacle?

The mystical

'Mystery' comes from Greek *muein*, meaning originally 'to shut one's eyes' in order to open them into a new revelation of truth, and thus 'to initiate'. That is the way that St Paul uses 'mystery' – an unfolding of the unspeakable purposes of God (Eph 1:10). As we saw in chapter 9, all creation is a sign of God, and the sacraments are the 'advance guard' in the fulfilment of its ultimate divine destiny.

Mystagogy has found its way into the Roman rites as the concluding stage of the Rite of Christian Initiation of Adults. It is to take place after the new members of the Church have been formally incorporated into it at the Easter Vigil. It is intended to introduce them into 'a fuller and more effective understanding of mysteries through the Gospel message they have learned and *above all through their experience* of the sacraments they have received... Out of this experience... they derive a new perception of the faith, of the Church, and of the world'[11]. Note the preference for experience over rational understanding.

Mystagogy is evidently not something to be limited to newly-received members of the Church, but a constant, lifelong approach to participation in the liturgy. That experience is not just personal, but also communal, shared by all who take part and are united in communion-fellowship by the celebration.

---

[10] Cf HUGHES 2003, 276.
[11] Rite of Christian Initiation of Adults (RCIA), art. 235. Italics mine.

For this to happen in our liturgical celebrations, the symbols must be clearly presented, so that their symbolism can be discerned and appreciated, and thus reveal what they signify. Both identity and difference need to be expressed.[12] Bread for use in the Eucharist is special by being unleavened in Western Church usage, special by being subjected to the rite of *proskomidē* in Eastern usage. It is the same as ordinary bread but also different from it. The wine is poured into silver chalices, not wine glasses. The ritual gestures of Holy Communion say, so to speak, "this is eating and drinking, yes, but of a special kind in a special space-time".[13]

Every sacrament 'both comforts us with presence and confronts us with absence, an irreducible otherness, a mystery'[14]. We saw in chapter 3 how Romano Guardini adopted Edmund Husserl's phenomenological approach to reality, the dialectic or tension between two apparently incompatible existents, a unity in diversity. We have seen the same in Louis-Marie Chauvet's insistence that sacramental presence is also an absence. That approach has been adopted more recently by some philosophers and theologians in search of a deeper understanding of the Eucharist.[15] Jean-Luc Marion sees it as utterly and totally *gift*, to which the only appropriate answer is *kenosis*, a self-emptying to make space for God, to allow ourselves to be grasped, indeed taken over by Him. The experience is not one of our own making; rather, we are overwhelmed by that of which we become conscious. For Jean-Yves Lacoste, sacramental experience is a mysterious non-experience, because it cannot be sensed or articulated within earthly parameters of emotion, affectiveness, objectivity, place or time. 'Sacramental experience presupposes a world where man exists already before God',

---

[12] GERHARDS 2011b, 277.
[13] 'Liturgical meanings need to be both *recognizable* (identifiable) from within the conditions of modernity and yet be clearly *different* from the prevailing axioms of secularism' (HUGHES 2003, 63).
[14] MITCHELL 2001, 89-90.
[15] See GSCHWANDTNER 2019 for an evaluation of the new thinking. See also WALLENFANG 2017 and SCHRIJVERS 2005.

which is not in the present world. Our being-before-God anticipates life beyond death, beyond this *chronos* space-time, in God's *kairos*.

Deeper meaning

Over against this sense of the transcendent 'beyond', there is a danger that because the sacrament of the Eucharist in a special way 'contains' what it signifies (the Real Presence), we may miss the additional meaning that it also points to a fulfilment beyond itself. St Thomas Aquinas makes clear the bridge between the two meanings:

> It was fitting that this sacrament, in which the incarnate Word is contained in order to unite us to himself, be proposed to us under the figure of food, not so that he may be converted into us by his union with us, but rather so that, by our union with him, we may be converted into him.[16]

And by that intimate association with him we become what we are, members of his Body together with all those who share Holy Communion with us.[17] Many people do not wish to be disturbed from their private devotions after receiving Holy Communion, but the greater picture, the broader significance, the finality and purpose of the sacrament is its uniting function, forming the whole community, priest and priestly people, into what we are, the one Body of Christ, sacrament of the Kingdom of God. Perceived in this way, the significance of Holy Communion extends not only beyond the individual or even the assembly, but beyond the walls of the church and into *kairos* time, God's time.

---

[16] St Thomas Aquinas, *IV Sent.* dist. 8, q. 1, a. 3, qla 1. Cf EMERY 2004, here 47.
[17] Until the 12th century the term 'Body of Christ' referred to the Church, and 'mystical Body of Christ' to the Eucharist. As the understanding of sacramental 'Real Presence' developed, the terms came to be swapped. Cf DE LUBAC 2006.

The immanence of God's presence in the liturgy, expressed in so many ways, makes no sense unless it points to God's transcendence. That is why the wider architectural and artistic context in which the liturgy is celebrated is so important. One does not have to be an aesthete to appreciate beauty. The danger, perceived by St Augustine, is to admire the beauty *per se*, in itself, rather than be led through it and by it to what it signifies, what lies beyond words and eyesight. To the believer, all creation must be transparent of God.

> The deep and implicit kinship between the arts (visual and acoustic) and worship lies precisely in the 'boundary pressing' iconicity of the former. These are media which directly effect a sense of 'limit' and of 'transcendence'; hence their long-established role in worship.[18]

Like a Greek chorus, participants in ritual without specific roles to play are sometimes an integral part of the action, at other times drawn into the action being performed by others.

Music faces a particular challenge here.

On the one hand, 'to sing with others, to move as they move in the performance of a ritual, is not merely to symbolize union. It is *in and of itself* to reunite in the reproduction of a larger order... The participants do not simply *communicate* to each other *about* that order but *commune with* each other *within* it.'[19] The style and focus of liturgical music must lie beyond the commonplace. Congregational music has to unite its singers in *worship* of the unseen God. It must be sacramental of who they are and what they are about and whom they are addressing.

On the other hand, there should also be an element of ritual where participants are permitted to stand back, take in what is performed by

---

[18] HUGHES 2003, 169.
[19] RAPPAPORT 1999, 220.

others, and discern its significance. That is written into liturgical ritual by dividing the roles, notably between priest, ministers and people – and this may well include a choir or specialist music resource. The appreciation of beauty requires a degree of detachment from the object described as 'beautiful', to stand back and wonder at it. Ritual participation, even in a dynamic action or event, also includes contemplation, an awareness that words and all human forms of expression should give way to and make space for the ineffable God.

Awareness of 'the Other'

Every human being naturally yearns for what is beyond him/her, looking for fulfilment but never satiated. And God is waiting and longing to respond, to fulfil this encounter. In icons – and in Eucharistic devotion – we can find ourselves being radically *looked at* by God. In chapter 2 we saw how some Romanesque apses contained a window for that very purpose.[20] The same too with light shining through stained or engraved glass.

For our part, we are called to *ascesis* – a *kenosis* or self-emptying to make space for God, to allow ourselves to be grasped, indeed taken over by Him.[21] Indeed, one takes part in ritual not to perform but to be transformed, to lose one's self in the not-self, to 'I' being crossed out to form † – the cross. And for that our model is Jesus Christ himself, who emptied himself in order to be raised to glory (Phil 2:6-11) – and redeemed human nature with him. The kenosis of God in his Son is the *theosis*, the deification of humankind[22], which Jesus the Lord has taken back to heaven with him as its first-fruits. 'And all of us, with unveiled faces, seeing the glory of the Lord as though reflected in a mirror, are being transformed into the same image from one degree of glory to another...' (2 Cor 3:18).

---

[20] TOREVELL 2016, 176. See above, 45.
[21] See FAGERBERG 2004, 121-122, 233-234, and his subsequent writings.
[22] According to Maximus the Confessor: cf id, 187.

Does our liturgy look like 'the glory of the Lord as though reflected in a mirror', the 'epiphany' that Guardini looked for[23]? How can we make it so? How can we make our purview extend through and beyond the altar, and indeed beyond the walls of our churches, to perceive the God who beckons us, even allows us to be transfigured into his image, sacramentally now, and finally beyond the bounds of earthly life?

Return to the world

After the liturgy is over, in contrast to a concert or play, things are not the same as they were before it – or should not be, if its participants have taken its covenant-commitment and sacramental meaning to heart.[24] A transformation has been played out before them and by them in the liturgy, and of this transformation they have become participants, notably by Holy Communion.[25] Now is the *kairos* time to come down from the mountain of transfiguration. 'Go in peace, glorifying the Lord by your life.'

> The mature fruit of mystagogy is an awareness that one's life is being progressively transformed by the holy mysteries into which one is being drawn.[26]

Christians are called to be priests, to transfigure and transform the world into the kingdom of God, to bring it home to the God who made it, loved it and redeemed it. Of that process, the liturgy is a sign and celebration that gives thanks for the continuing work of salvation history, marks a new event within it, and looks forward to eventual fulfilment in God's time and in His own 'other place'.

---

[23] See above, 11.
[24] Cf KAVANAGH 1992, 76.
[25] Cf HUGHES 2003, 170.
[26] Pope Benedict XVI, *Sacramentum Caritatis*, no. 64.

May the Lord Jesus put his hands on our eyes also, for
then we too shall begin to look not at what is seen but at
what is not seen. May he open the eyes that are concerned
not with the present but with what is yet to come, may he
unseal the heart's vision, that we may gaze on God in the
Spirit, through the same Lord, Jesus Christ, whose glory
and power will endure throughout the unending
succession of ages.[27]

---

[27] Origen, *Comm. Genesis*, 46:4.

APPENDICES

Bibliography

Reading List

The literary sources that are quoted in this book are in many languages: English, German, French and Italian. All are listed below. The titles recommended here for further study are available in English; older ones may be found either in libraries or from secondhand dealers, e.g. abebooks.co.uk.

The decrees of the Second Vatican Council are easily accessible on the Vatican website. The version of the *General Instruction of the Roman Missal* specially approved for England & Wales can be obtained from the Liturgy Office of its Bishops' Conference (www. liturgyoffice.org.uk).

For the study of ritual as a human and social phenomenon at the service of religious expression, see RAPPAPORT 1999. For ritual as the basis of liturgy, read especially KAVANAGH 1992 and HUGHES 2003. On its more mystical significance, read TOREVELL 2016.

For the history of liturgy, older books such as KLAUSER 1965 and BOUYER 1967 should be treated with some caution, since more recent research has afforded corrections and new insights. Jungmann's monumental two volumes (JUNGMANN 1951) still command respect.

Paul Bradshaw's more recent contributions to this area are important (see under his name below).

Guardini's *The Spirit of the Liturgy* and *The Church and the Catholic* are still available as a single volume (GUARDINI 1935), as is his *Meditations before Mass* (GUARDINI 2014); so is Schwarz's first book, *Vom Bau der Kirche*, as *The Church Incarnate: The Sacred Function of Christian Architecture* (SCHWARZ 1938).

For comprehensive manuals on the liturgy, see GERHARDS 2017 and KUNZLER 1995.

Many of Joseph Ratzinger's books are relevant to this book (see under his name below). See also LANG 2008.

For the relationship between the priesthood of the laity and the ministerial priesthood, RICHARDS 1995 and O'COLLINS 2010 are important guides.

Regarding the significance of the altar-table, Thomas O'Loughlin's book (O'LOUGHLIN 2015a) affords important new insights on the significance of the Eucharist as a meal.

The symbolism of church space is well explored in Bert Daelemans' *Spiritus Loci* (DAELEMANS 2015).

Official Documents

Encyclical Letter of Pope Pius XII: *Mediator Dei,* 1947

Second Vatican Council (1962-1965):
- Dogmatic Constitution on the Church (*Lumen Gentium – LG*)
- Constitution on the Sacred Liturgy (*Sacrosanctum Concilium – SC*)

- Decree on the Apostolate of the Laity (*Apostolicam Actuositatem – AA*)
- Decree on the Ministry and Life of Priests (*Presbyterorum Ordinis – PO*)

Decree of the Consilium for the Implementation of the Constitution on the Liturgy: *Inter Œcumenici,* 1964

Instruction of the Sacred Congregation of Rites, *Eucharisticum Mysterium,* 1967

Decree of the Sacred Congregation of Rites on Holy Communion and Worship of the Eucharist outside Mass, 1973

Catechism of the Catholic Church, 1994

Congregation for Divine Worship and the Discipline of the Sacraments, Directory on Popular Piety and the Liturgy: Principles and Guidelines, December 2001

General Instruction of the Roman Missal (GIRM), 3rd typical edition, 2002, as amended in 2008: the English translation is dated 2010

Post-Synodal Apostolic Exhortation of Pope Benedict XVI: *Sacramentum caritatis,* 2007

Encyclical Letter of Pope Francis: *Laudato Si',* 2015

Bishops' Conference of England & Wales:
— *The Parish Church: Principles of Liturgical Design and Reordering,* London: Catholic Truth Society, 1984
— *Consecrated for Worship,* London: Catholic Truth Society, 2006

Liturgy Commission of the German Bishops' Conference, *Leitlinien für den Bau und die Ausgestaltung von gottesdienstlichen Räumen*, 5th edition, 2000

United States Conference of Catholic Bishops:
— *Environment and Art in Catholic Worship*, 1977.
— *Built of Living Stones*, 2000.

Books & Articles

BALDOVIN 2008: John F. Baldovin, *Reforming the Liturgy*, Collegeville MN: Liturgical Press, 2008.

BALTHASAR 1988: Hans Urs von Balthasar: *Theo-Drama: Theological Dramatic Theory*, 5 vols, San Francisco: Ignatius Press, 1988-1994.

BALTHASAR 1990: Hans Urs von Balthasar: *Mysterium Paschale*, Edinburgh: T. & T. Clark, 1990.

BARBER 2013: Michael Patrick Barber, 'The New Temple, the New Priesthood, and the New Cult in Luke-Acts', *Letter & Spirit*, 8 (2013), 101-124.

BARKER 2003: Margaret Barker, *The Great High Priest: The Temple Roots of Christian Liturgy*, London: T. & T. Clark, 2003.

BLOWERS 2016: Paul M. Blowers, *Maximus the Confessor: Jesus Christ and the Transfiguration of the World*, Oxford University Press, 2016.

BOUYER 1967: Louis Bouyer, *Liturgy and Architecture*, London: Sheed and Ward, 1967.

BOUYER 1970: Louis Bouyer, *The Decomposition of Catholicism* (trans. C. U. Quinn), London: Sands & Co., 1970.

BOYER 2015: Mark G. Boyer, *The Liturgical Environment: What the Documents Say*, 3rd edition, Collegeville: Liturgical Press, 2015.

BRADSHAW 2007: Paul Bradshaw & John Melloh (eds.), *Foundations in Ritual Studies: a Reader for Students of Christian Worship*, London: SPCK, 2007, 3-8.

BRADSHAW 2010: Paul F. Bradshaw, *Early Christian Worship*, London: SPCK, ²2010.

BRADSHAW 2012: Paul F. Bradshaw & Maxwell E. Johnson, *The Eucharistic Liturgies*, London: SPCK, 2012.

BROWN 2004: David Brown, *God and the Enchantment of Place: Reclaiming Human Experience*, Oxford University Press, 2004.

BUGNINI 1990: Annibale Bugnini, *The Reform of the Liturgy 1948–1975*, Collegeville: Liturgical Press, 1990.

CAMERON-MOWAT 1995: Andrew Cameron-Mowat, 'Liturgical Theology: Who's in Charge?', in *The Way*, 35/4 (1995), 332-341.

CHAUVET 1994: Louis-Marie Chauvet, *Symbol and Sacrament: Sacramental Reinterpretation of Christian Existence*, Collegeville MN: Liturgical Press, 1994.

CHAUVET 2001: Louis-Marie Chauvet, *The Sacraments: The Word of God at the Mercy of the Body*, Collegeville MN: Liturgical Press, 2001.

CRAMER 2006: Burkhard Cramer, 'The Open Ring' in *Rothenfelser Burgbrief*, 1/2006, 13-14.

CRICHTON 1943: J. D. Crichton, 'A Dream-Church', *Music and Liturgy*, 12/3 (1943), 71-75.

CRICHTON 1971: J. D. Crichton, *The Christian Celebration: The Mass*, London: Geoffrey Chapman, 1971.

CRICHTON 1979: J. D. Crichton, H. E. Winstone and J. R. Ainslie (eds), *English Catholic Worship*, London: Geoffrey Chapman, 1979.

CRICHTON 1999: J. D. Crichton, *As it Was: Reminiscences and Prophecies*, Mildenhall: Decani Books, 1999.

DAELEMANS 2015: Bert Daelemans SJ, *Spiritus Loci: a theological method for contemporary church architecture*, Leiden: Brill, 2015.

DANTAS 2020 : João Paulo de Mendonça Dantas, 'L'expression «in persona Christi capitis» et l'identité sacerdotale', in *Communio* 45/1, 2020, 79-97.

DE CHARDIN 1918: Pierre Teilhard de Chardin, *Le Prêtre*, written in 1918 and subsequently renamed 'La Messe sur le monde', *Œuvres*, Paris: Seuil, 1952, vol. 12, 313-333.

DE LUBAC 1986: Henri de Lubac, *The Splendor of the Church*, San Francisco: Ignatius Press, 1986.

DE LUBAC 2006: Henri de Lubac, *Corpus Mysticum: The Eucharist and the Church in the Middle Ages*, London: SCM Press, 2006.

DEBUYST 1968: Frédéric Debuyst, *Modern Architecture and Christian Celebration*, London: Lutterworth Press and Richmond VA: John Knox Press, 1968.

DEBUYST 2008: Frédéric Debuyst, *L'Entrée en Liturgie: Introduction à l'œuvre liturgique de Romano Guardini*, Paris: Éditions du Cerf, 2008.

DODD 1967: William H. Dodd SJ, 'Toward a theology of priesthood', in *Theological Studies*, vol. 28, 683-705.

DOIG 2008: Allan Doig, *Liturgy and Architecture from the Early Church to the Middle Ages*, Farnham: Ashgate, 2008.

DUTHILLEUL 2014 : Jean-Marie Duthilleul, 'L'église nouvelle de la paroisse Saint-François-de-Molitor à Paris', in *Communio* 39/4 (2014), 41-50.

ELLARD 1956: George Ellard, *The Mass in Transition*, Milwaukee: Bruce Publishing Co, 1956.

EMERY 2004: Gilles Emery OP, 'The Ecclesial Fruit of the Eucharist in St. Thomas Aquinas', in *Nova et Vetera*, English Edition, vol. 2, no. 1 (2004), 43-60.

FAGERBERG 2004: David W. Fagerberg, *Theologia Prima: What is Liturgical Theology?*, Chicago: Hillenbrand Books, 2004.

FAGERBERG 2010: David W. Fagerberg, 'What is the Subject Matter of Liturgical Theology?', reprinted in *Roczniki Liturgiczno-Homiletyczne*, 1 (57), 2010.

FAGGIOLI 2012: Massimo Faggioli, *True Reform: Liturgy and Ecclesiology in Sacrosanctum Concilium*, Collegeville: Liturgical Press, 2012.

GALOT 1985: Jean Galot SJ, *Theology of the Priesthood*, San Francisco: Ignatius Press, 1985.

GERHARDS 1999: Albert Gerhards (ed.), *In der Mitte der Versammlung: Liturgische Feierräume*, Trier: Deutsches Liturgisches Institut, 1999.

GERHARDS 2000: Albert Gerhards, 'Versammlung oder Aufbruch? Überlegungen zur Herkunft und Sinngestalt des liturgischen Feierraums', *Gottesdienst* 34 (2000), 65-68.

GERHARDS 2001: Albert Gerhards, '"Blickt nach Osten!" – Die Ausrichtung von Priester und Gemeinde bei der Eucharistie', Martin Klöckener & Arnaud Join-Lambert (eds), *Liturgia et Unitas*, Freiburg/Schweiz: Universitätsverlag, 2001, 197-217.

GERHARDS 2004: Albert Gerhards, 'Teologia dell' Altare', in Boselli, Goffredo (ed.), *L'Altare, mistero di presenza, opera dell' arte*, Bose: Edizioni Qiqajon, 2004, 215-232.

GERHARDS 2011a: Albert Gerhards, *Wo Gott und Welt sich begegnen*, Kevelaer: Butzon & Bercker, 2011.

GERHARDS 2011b: Albert Gerhards, 'Symbol – Ritus – Erfahrung, Liturgie als Quelle von Spiritualität', *Geist und Leben* 84/3 (2011), 269-281.

GERHARDS 2013: Albert Gerhards, 'Liturgischer Raum und Gebetsrichtung', in Stephan Wahle, Helmut Hoping, Winfried Haunerland (eds.), *Römische Messe und Liturgie in der Moderne*, Freiburg im Breisgau: Herder, 2013, 221-242.

GERHARDS 2017: Albert Gerhards and Benedikt Kranemann, *Introduction to the Study of Liturgy*, Collegeville: Liturgical Press, 2017.

GILES 2004: Richard Giles, *Re-pitching the Tent*, Norwich: Canterbury Press, ³2004.

GSCHWANDTNER 2019: Christina M. Gschwandtner, 'Mystery Manifested: Toward a Phenomenology of the Eucharist in Its Liturgical Context', *Religions* 2019, **10**, 315.

GUARDINI 1921: Romano Guardini, 'Über die systematische Methode in der Liturgiewissenschaft', *Jahrbuch für Liturgiewissenschaft*, 1/1, 1921, 97-108.

GUARDINI 1922: Romano Guardini, *Vom Sinn der Kirche*, 1st edn 1922 (5th edn 1990, together with *Die Kirche des Herrn*, Mainz: Matthias-Grünewald-Verlag & Paderborn: Verlag Ferdinand Schöningh).

GUARDINI 1923a: Romano Guardini, *Von Heiligen Zeichen*, 9th edn, Kevelaer, topos Taschenbücher, 2016.

GUARDINI 1923b: Romano Guardini, *Liturgie und liturgische Bildung*, 2nd edn, Mainz: Matthias-Grünewald-Verlag & Paderborn: Verlag Ferdinand Schöningh, 1992.

GUARDINI 1935: Romano Guardini, *The Spirit of the Liturgy*, trans. Ada
Lane, published in *The Church and the Catholic*, London: Sheed &
Ward, 1935.

GUARDINI 1936: Romano Guardini, *Besinnung vor der Feier der Heilige
Messe*, originally published in two volumes by Matthias Grünewald,
Mainz, 1936/9. The English translation, *Meditations before Mass*, by
Elinor Castendyk Briefs was first published by Newman Press,
Westminster MD in 1956. Currently available in two English
editions, one by Sophia Institute Press, Mansfield NH (1993 – but
incomplete), the other by Ave Maria Press, Notre Dame IN, 2014
(used in this book as GUARDINI 2014).

GUARDINI 1950: Romano Guardini, 'Die liturgische Erfahrung und die
Epiphanie'. This paper has appeared in a number of publications. It
is also available in French translation in a volume entitled *Les sens
et la connaissance de Dieu*, Paris: Editions du Cerf, 1954.

GUARDINI 1956: Romano Guardini, *Sacred Signs*, tr. Grace Branham,
St Louis MO: Pio Decimo Press, 1956; CreateSpace Independent
Publishing Platform, 2015.

GUARDINI 1957: Romano Guardini, *La Messe*, French translation of
Besinnung vor der Feier der Heilige Messe by Pie Duployé, Paris:
Editions du Cerf, 1957.

GUARDINI 1964: Romano Guardini, 'Der Kultakt und die gegenwärtige
Aufgabe der Liturgischen Bildung', English translation in
BRADSHAW 2007 (q.v.).

GUARDINI 1965: Romano Guardini, *Die Kirche des Herrn*, 1st edn 1965
(2nd edn 1990, together with *Vom Sinn der Kirche*, Mainz: Matthias-
Grünewald-Verlag & Paderborn: Verlag Ferdinand Schöningh,
1995).

GUARDINI 1995: Romano Guardini, *Stationen und Rückblicken /
Berichte über mein Leben* Mainz: Matthias-Grünewald-Verlag &
Paderborn: Verlag Ferdinand Schöningh, 1995.

GUARDINI 2014: Romano Guardini, *Meditations before Mass*, English
translation by Elinor Castendyk Briefs, Ave Maria Press, Notre
Dame IN, 2014.

GY 2002: Pierre-Marie Gy, in *La Maison-Dieu* 230/2 (2002), 113-20 ; English translation in *Antiphon* 11/1 (2007), 98-102.

HEID 2006: Stefan Heid, 'Gebetshaltung und Ostung in frühchristlicher Zeit', *Rivista di Archeologia Cristiana* 82 (2006 [2008]), 347-404.

HEID 2019: Stefan Heid, *Altar und Kirche: Prinzipien christlicher Liturgie*, Regensburg: Schnell & Steiner, 2019.

HERMANS 1987 : Jo Hermans, 'L'étude de la liturgie comme discipline théologique. Problèmes et méthodes', *Revue théologique de Louvain*, fasc.3, 1987, 337-360.

HILL 1997: Edmund Hill OP (ed.), *The Works of Saint Augustine: Sermons, III/2, Newly Discovered Sermons,* New City Press, NY 1997.

HUGHES 2003: Graham Hughes, *Worship as Meaning: A Liturgical Theology for Late Modernity*, Cambridge University Press, 2003.

JENSEN 2015: Robin M. Jensen, 'Recovering Ancient Ecclesiology: The Place of the Altar and the Orientation of Prayer in the Early Latin Church', in *Worship* 89 (2015), 99-124.

JENSEN 2019: Robin M. Jensen, 'The Symbol and Reality of the Altar in African Sacramental Practice, theology and Ecclesiology', in Cyril Hovorun (ed.), *Sacred Architecture in East and West*, Huffington Ecumenical Institute, Los Angeles, 2019, 37-60.

JUNGMANN 1949: Josef A. Jungmann, *The Early Liturgy to the time of Gregory the Great*, Notre Dame: University of Notre Dame Press, 1959. The contents are translations of lectures given by Fr Jungmann in 1949.

JUNGMANN 1951: Josef A. Jungmann, *The Mass of the Roman Rite (Missarum Sollemnia)*, New York: Benziger, 1951-1955 (2 volumes).

JUNGMANN 1960: Josef A. Jungmann, 'Die Eucharistie als Mitte unserer Frömmigkeit', in *Geist und Leben*, 45/3 (1960), 184-191.

JUNGMANN 1967: Josef A. Jungmann, 'Der neue Altar', in *Der Seelsorger*, 37 (1967), 374-381.

KAVANAGH 1992: Aidan Kavanagh, *On Liturgical Theology*, Collegeville: Liturgical Press, ²1992.

KELLER 1989: Erwin Keller, *Eucharistie und Parusie*, Fribourg University Press, 1989.

KIECKHEFER 2004: Richard Kieckhefer, *Theology in Stone: Church Architecture from Byzantium to Berkeley*, Oxford University Press, 2004.

KILMARTIN 1998: Edward J. Kilmartin SJ, *The Eucharist in the West*, Collegeville: Liturgical Press, 2004.

KIRWAN 2007: Michael Kirwan, 'Eucharist and Sacrifice', *New Blackfriars*, 2007, 213-227.

KLAUSER 1965: Theodor Klauser, *A Short History of the Western Liturgy*, 2nd edn, Oxford University Press, 1979. This is a translation of the 5th German edition, dated 1965.

KRÄMER 2001: Johannes Krämer, 'Offener Raum und orientierte Versammlung', in *Gottesdienst*, 2001/11, 81-83.

KRIEG 1997: Robert A. Krieg CSC, *Romano Guardini: A Precursor of Vatican II*, Notre Dame: University of Notre Dame Press, 1997.

KUNZLER 1995: Michael Kunzler, *Liturgie der Kirche*, Paderborn: Bonifatius Verlag, 1995. English Translation: *The Church's Liturgy,* London: Continuum, 2001.

KWASNIEWSKI 2006: Peter A. Kwasniewski, 'Doing and Speaking in the Person of Christ: Eucharistic Form in the Anaphora of Addai and Mari', *Nova et Vetera,* English Edition, 4/2 (2006), 313–80.

LACOSTE 2004: Jean-Yves Lacoste, *Experience and the Absolute: Disputed Questions on the Humanity of Man*, tr. Mark Raftery-Skehan, New York: Fordham University Press, 2004.

LANG 2008: Uwe Michael Lang, *Turning towards the Lord*, 2nd edition, San Francisco: Ignatius Press, 2008.

LIGIER 1966: Louis Ligier, 'De la cène de Jésus à l'anaphore de l'Église', *La Maison-Dieu,* 87 (1966), 7-51.

LOUTH 1997: Andrew Louth, 'Apophatic Theology and the Liturgy in St Maximus the Confessor', in *Criterion: The Divinity School of the University of Chicago*, vol. 36(3), 1997.

MCCARTHY 2014: Daniel McCarthy OSB & James Leachman OSB, *Come into the Light*, Norwich: Canterbury Press, 2014.

MCGOWAN 2015: Andrew McGowan, 'The Myth of the "Lord's Supper": Paul's Eucharistic Meal Terminology and its Ancient Reception', *Catholic Biblical Quarterly* 77 (2015), 502-520.

MCNAMARA 2009: Denis R. McNamara, *Catholic Church Architecture and the Spirit of the Liturgy*, Chicago: Hillenbrand Books, 2009.

MANNION 2004: M. Francis Mannion, *Masterworks of God: essays in liturgical theory and practice*, Chicago: Hillenbrand Books, 2004.

MARINI 2007: Piero Marini, *A Challenging Reform: Realizing the Vision of the Liturgical Renewal*, Collegeville: Liturgical Press, 2007.

MAZZA 1986: Enrico Mazza, *The Eucharistic Prayers of the Roman Rite*, Collegeville: Liturgical Press, 1986, ²2004.

MESSNER 2003: Reinhard Messner, 'Gebetsrichtung, Altar und die exzentrische Mitte der Gemeinde' in Albert Gerhards, Thomas Sternberg & Walter Zahner (eds), *Communio-Räume, auf der Suche nach der angemessenen Raumgestalt katholischer Liturgie*, Regensburg: Schnell & Steiner, 2003, 27-36.

MESSNER 2013: Reinhard Messner, 'Einige Defizite in der Performance der Eucharistie', in Stephen Wahle, Helmut Hoping & Winfried Haunerland (eds.), *Römische Messe und Liturgie in der Moderne*, Freiburg im Breisgau: Herder, 2013, 297-337.

METZGER 1971: Marcel Metzger, 'La place des liturges à l'autel', *Revue des Sciences Religieuses*, 45/2 (1971), 113-145.

MICHAUD 1945 : M. Michaud, 'La célébration de la Messe face au peuple', *La Maison-Dieu*, 2 (1945), 93-116.

MITCHELL 2001: Nathan D. Mitchell, *Real Presence: The Work of Eucharist*, Chicago: Liturgy Training Publications, 2001.

MITCHELL 2006: Nathan D. Mitchell, *Meeting Mystery*, Maryknoll, NY: Orbis Books, 2006.

MUCK 1961: Herbert Muck, *Sakralbau Heute*, Aschaffenburg: Paul Pattloch Verlag, 1961.

MUCK 1966: Herbert Muck, *Lebendiger Gottesdienst (Heft 12): Die Gestaltung des Kirchenraumes nach der Liturgiereform*, Münster: Verlag Regensberg, 1966.

NAGEL 2011: Alexander Nagel, *The Controversy of Renaissance Art*, University of Chicago Press, 2011.

NICHOLS 1996: Aidan Nichols, *Looking at the Liturgy*, San Francisco: Ignatius Press, 1996.

NUSSBAUM 1965: Otto Nussbaum, *Der Standort des Liturgen am christlichen Altar vor dem Jahre 1000*. Bonn: Hanstein, 1965 (2 volumes).

O'COLLINS 2010: Gerald O'Collins SJ & Michael Keenan Jones, *Christ Our Priest: A Christian Approach to the Priesthood of Christ*, Oxford University Press, 2010.

O'LOUGHLIN 2015a: Thomas O'Loughlin, *The Eucharist: Origins and Contemporary Understandings,* London: Bloomsbury, 2015.

O'LOUGHLIN 2015b: Thomas O'Loughlin, 'Renewing the Liturgy – six simple steps', *The Furrow*, 66/5, May 2015, 269-280.

O'LOUGHLIN 2016: Thomas O'Loughlin, 'Evaluating Liturgy in the Parish', *The Furrow*, 67/9, September 2016, 451-465.

O'LOUGHLIN 2017: Thomas O'Loughlin, 'Facing the Lord's Table – Sacred Space and Our Space', *The Furrow*, 68/10, October 2017, 554-560.

OTTO 1923: Rudolf Otto, *The Idea of the Holy*, Oxford: Oxford University Press, 1923, ²1950.

PACIK 2010: Rudolf Pacik (ed.), new introduction to Pius Parsch & Robert Kramreiter, *Neue Kirchenkunst im Geist der Liturgie*, Würzburg: Echter, ²2010.

PACIK 2012: Rudolf Pacik, 'Kirche und Altarraum in den Vor-Fassungen der Liturgiekonstitution' in S. Haering, J. Hirnsperger, G. Katzinger & W. Rees (eds.), *In mandatis meditari, Festschrift für Hans Paarhammer*, Berlin: Duncker & Humblot, 2012, 357-386.

PARSCH 1939: Pius Parsch, *The Liturgy of the Mass*, Herder, 1939.

PETERSON 1959: E. Peterson, *Frühkirche, Judentum und Gnosis*, Freiburg: Herder, 1959.

POCKNEE 1963: Cyril E. Pocknee, *The Christian Altar*, London: A. R. Mowbray, 1963.

PROCTOR 2014: Robert Proctor, *Building the Modern Church: Roman Catholic Church Architecture in Britain 1955-1975*, London: Routledge, 2014.

RAPPAPORT 1999: Roy A. Rappaport, *Ritual and Religion in the Making of Humanity*, Cambridge University Press, 1999.

RATZINGER 1967: Joseph Ratzinger, 'Catholicism after the Council', tr. P. Russell, in *The Furrow* 18 (1967).

RATZINGER 1986: Joseph Ratzinger, *Das Fest des Glaubens,* Einsiedeln: Johannes Verlag, 1981. English translation: *Feast of Faith*, San Francisco: Ignatius Press, 1986.

RATZINGER 2000: Joseph Ratzinger, *Der Geist der Liturgie. Eine Einführung*, Freiburg-im-Breisgau: Verlag Herder, 2000. English translation by John Saward, *The Spirit of the Liturgy*, San Francisco: Ignatius Press, 2000.

RATZINGER 2014: Joseph Ratzinger, *Opera Omnia: Volume XII*, San Francisco: Ignatius Press, 2014.

REISS 2005: Sheryl E. Reiss (Author) & Kenneth Gouwens (Editor), *The Pontificate of Clement VII: History, Politics, Culture (Catholic Christendom, 1300-1700)*, London: Routledge, 2005.

RICHARDS 1995: Michael Richards, *A People of Priests: The Ministry of the Catholic Church*, London: Darton, Longman & Todd, 1995.

SCHILLING 1969: Albert Schilling, 'Bildhauer und Kirchenbau heute', in Günter Rombold, *Kirchen für die Zukunft bauen*, Vienna/Freiburg/Basel: Herder, 1969, 183-191.

SCHMEMANN 1966: Alexander Schmemann, *The World as Sacrament*, London: Darton, Longman and Todd, 1966.

SCHMEMANN 1987: Alexander Schmemann, *The Eucharist: Sacrament of the Kingdom*, New York: St Vladimir's Seminary Press, 1987.

SCHRIJVERS 2005: Joeri Schrijvers, 'Jean-Yves Lacoste: A Phenomenology of Liturgy', *Heythrop Journal*, June 2005, 314-333.

SCHWARZ 1930: Rudolf Schwarz, 'Erneuerung des Kirchenbaus?', in *Zeitschrift für gestaltende Arbeit*, 5/1930, 552-555.

SCHWARZ 1938: Rudolf Schwarz, *Vom Bau der Kirche*, Verlag Lambert Schneider, Heidelberg, 1938. English translation: *The Church Incarnate: The Sacred Function of Christian Architecture*, trans. Cynthia Harris, Chicago: Henry Regnery Company, 1958, reprinted by Nabu Public Domains, 2011.

SCHWARZ 1960: Rudolf Schwarz, *Kirchenbau: Welt vor der Schwelle*, Heidelberg, Verlag F. H. Kehrle, 1960, reprinted with new introductions in 2007 by Verlag Schnell & Steiner, Regensburg.

SCHWARZ 2004: Rudolf Schwarz, 'Liturgie und Kirchenbau', in *Rothenfelser Burgbrief*, 02/04, 6-16.

SEARLE 2007: Mark Searle, 'Ritual', in Paul Bradshaw and John Melloh (eds.), *Foundations in Ritual Studies: a Reader for Students of Christian Worship*, London: SPCK, 2007.

SEASOLTZ 2005: R. Kevin Seasoltz, *A Sense of the Sacred*, London & New York: Continuum, 2005.

SEASOLTZ 2015: R. Kevin Seasoltz, 'The Christian Church Building', in Julio Bermudez (ed), *Transcending Architecture*, Washington DC: Catholic University of America Press, 2015, 113-129.

SPICHTIG 2017: Peter Spichtig OP, 'New Liturgical Space for a Renewed Liturgy', in Michael Attridge & others (eds), *The Promise of Renewal: Dominicans and Vatican II*, Adelaide: ATF Theology, 2017, 31-47.

TOREVELL 2016: David Torevell, *Liturgy and the Beauty of the Unknown – Another Place*, London: Routledge, ²2016.

TORGERSON 2007: Mark A. Torgerson, *An Architecture of Immanence*, Grand Rapids: William B. Eerdmans Publishing Co, 2007.

TORRANCE 1993: T. F. Torrance, *Royal Priesthood: A Theology of Ordained Ministry*, London: Continuum/T. & T. Clark, 1993.

TORRANCE 1996: T. F. Torrance, *Theology in Reconciliation: Essays Toward Evangelical and Catholic Unity in East and West*, Eugene OR: Wipf & Stock, 1996.

TURNER 2007: Victor Turner, 'Liminality and communitas', Paul Bradshaw & John Melloh (eds), *Foundations in Ritual Studies*, London: SPCK, 2007, 74-85.

VAN BÜHREN 2013: Ralf van Bühren, 'Architettura e Arte al Concilio Vaticano II' in *Nobile Semplicità: liturgia, arte e architettura del Vaticano II*, Bose: Edizioni Qiqajon, 2013, 141-178.

VANHOYE 1977: Albert Vanhoye, 'Common and Ministerial Priesthood', in *Theology Digest*, 25:2 (1977), 157-161.

VANHOYE 1980: Albert Vanhoye, *Old Testament Priests and the New Priest*, Leominster: Gracewing, 2009.

VONIER 1925: Anscar Vonier, *A Key to the Doctrine of the Eucharist*, reprinted by Bethesda MD: Zacchaeus Press, 2003.

WALLENFANG 2017: Donald Wallenfang, *Dialectical Anatomy of the Eucharist: An Étude in Phenomenology*, Eugene OR: Cascade Books, 2017.

WALLRAFF 2001: Martin Wallraff, *Christus verus Sol. Sonnenverehrung und Christentum in der Spätantike*, Münster: Aschendorff, 2001.

WALLRAFF 2006: Martin Wallraff, 'L'Orientamento: Linee Storiche', *Spazio Liturgico e Orientamento*, Bose: Qiqajon, 2006, 167-188.

WEDIG 2015: Mark E. Wedig, 'Ecclesial Architecture and Image', in Julio Bermudez (ed.), *Transcending Architecture*, Washington DC: Catholic University of America Press, 2015, 130-142.

WEISER 2002: Nicolas T. Weiser, *Offenes Zueinander: Räumliche Dimensionen von Kunst und Religion in der Kunst-Station Sankt Peter Köln*, Regensburg: Schnell & Steiner, 2002.

WIKSTRÖM 1993: Owe Wikström, 'Liturgy as Experience – the Psychology of Worship: A Theoretical and Empirical Lacuna', in *Scripta Instituti Donneriani Aboensis*, vol. 15.

WILSON 1990: Christopher Wilson, *The Gothic Cathedral: The Architecture of the Great Church*, London: Thames and Hudson, 1990.

ZAHNER 1992: Walter Zahner, *Rudolf Schwarz – Baumeister der neuen Gemeinde*, Altenberge: Oros Verlag, 1992.

Index of Names & Places

Bottrop, Heilig Kreuz, 108, 114,
211
Bouyer, Louis, 136-142, 153, 225,
228, 235, 241, 242, 262, 288
Boyer, Mark, 150, 288
Bradshaw, Paul, 32, 84, 172-175,
177, 180, 184, 288, 289, 298
Braun, Joseph, 31
Brentwood Cathedral, 220
Brown, David, 213, 214, 289
Buckfast Abbey, 253
Bugnini, Annibale, 118, 289

Cameron-Mowat, Andrew, 13,
289
Carlow, Pastoral Liturgy
Institute, 221
Carthage, 37
Casel, Odo, 52, 70
Castellum Tingitanum, 40
Catechism of the Catholic Church,
4, 167, 169, 184, 287
Charles Borromeo, St, 49, 50
Chauvet, Louis-Marie, 7, 23,
180, 193, 276, 289
Cincinnati, St Monica & St
George, 213
Clifton Cathedral, 218
Cologne, St Engelbert, 211
Cologne-Niehl, 111
Congregation for Divine
Worship, 120, 121, 124, 151,
255, 287
Congregation of Rites, 57, 63,
251, 287

Constantine, 36, 37, 49, 179
Cramer, Burkhard, 238, 239, 289
Crichton, James, 53-54, 58, 59,
132, 217, 289
Cyprian of Carthage, 33, 178,
179
Cyril of Jerusalem, 46

Daelemans, Bert, 199, 201, 204,
209-214, 241, 289
Dalmais, I.-H., 15
Dantas, João Paulo de
Mendonça, 169, 289
de Chardin, Teilhard, 190-192,
289
de Lubac, Henri, 96, 97, 277,
289, 290
Debuyst, Frédéric, 60, 72, 80, 86,
93, 111, 202, 290
Dodd, William H., 160, 169, 290
Doig, Allan, 36, 37, 47, 290
Dölger, Franz Joseph, 29
Douai Abbey, 220
Dülmen, Heilig Kreuz, 209
Durham Cathedral, 45
Duthilleul, Jean-Marie, 208, 240-
242, 290

Eliot, Thomas Stearns, 4, 271
Ellard, George, 58, 290
Emery, Gilles, 277, 290
Eucharisticum Mysterium, 63,
109, 251, 252, 287
Eusebius, 40

Fagerberg, David, 13, 192, 193,
195, 279, 290
Faggioli, Massimo, 31, 290
Francis, Pope
Laudato Si', 190-191, 197, 287
Frankfurt, St Michael's church,
11, 82, 114

Galot, Jean, 160, 163, 164, 290
General Instruction of the
Roman Missal (GIRM), 18,
20, 21, 22, 123, 124, 147, 179,
187, 218, 229, 230, 234, 235,
249, 251, 252, 255, 264, 266,
268, 287
Gerhards, Albert, xii, 8, 19, 41,
43, 45, 116, 170, 188, 196,
210, 222, 224, 226, 229, 231,
232, 237, 244, 246, 276, 290,
291, 295
German Bishops' Conference,
Liturgy Commission, 153, 288
Gibbard, Frederic, 217
Giberti, Gian Matteo, 49
Giles, Richard, 202, 291
Gill, Eric, 54
Goergen, Aloys, 86, 87, 153, 202,
217
Gouwens, Kenneth, 297
Gregory the Great, Pope, 42, 293
Gschwandtner, Christina M.,
276, 291
Guardini, Romano, 11, 17, 20,
52, 54, 59, 60-86, 88, 91, 92,
97, 127, 152, 153, 155, 182,

187, 191, 202, 205, 214, 216,
217, 231, 232, 274, 276, 280,
290, 291, 292, 294
Guéranger, Prosper, 50, 51
Gy, Pierre-Marie, 126, 293

Haunerland, Winfried, 291, 295
Heid, Stefan, 30, 32, 37, 41-45,
141, 144, 172, 175, 178, 182,
293
Hermans, Jo, 67, 293
Herwegen, Ildefons, 52, 54, 65,
67, 88, 217
Hill, Edmund, 38, 39, 40, 165,
178, 293
Holzmeister, Clemens, 56
Hoping, Helmut, 291, 295
Hovorun, Cyril, 293
Howell, Clifford, 22
Hughes, Graham, 15, 245, 273,
274, 275, 276, 278, 280, 293
Husserl, Edmund, 64, 276

Ibaraki, 210
Ignatius of Antioch, 165, 178
Inter Œcumenici, ix, 9, 17, 118,
119, 121, 124, 129-131, 140,
152, 153, 219, 268, 287

Jensen, Robin M., 33, 37, 40,
178, 293
Jerome, St, 233
Jerusalem, Church of the Holy
Sepulchre, 37

Potters Bar, Our Lady and St
  Vincent, 221, 223, 254
Proctor, Robert, 217, 296
Pugin, Augustus Welby, 48

Quickborn, 68, 71, 89

Rappaport, Roy A., 8, 9, 16, 278,
  296
Ratzinger, Joseph, xi, xiii, 23, 25,
  30, 126, 128, 136, 137, 139,
  141-144, 182, 183, 185, 190,
  191, 192, 250, 257, 297
Ravenna
  San Vitale, 41
  Sant' Apollinare in Classe, 41,
    48, 112
  Sant' Apollinare Nuovo, 172
Redhill, St Joseph's Church, 208
Reiss, Sheryl E., 49, 297
Richards, Michael, 160, 297
Rituale Romanum (1614), 50, 122
Ritus Servandus in celebratione
  Missae, 55
Rome
  Lateran basilica, 36, 41
  San Clemente, 41, 228
  San Lorenzo outside the
    Walls, 42
  San Marcello al Corso, 42
  Santa Sabina, 41, 228
  Santo Stefano Rotondo, 37
  SS. Apostoli Basilica, 41
  St Paul's outside the Walls,
    36, 42

St Peter's, 37, 42, 55, 179
Rothenfels, Burg, 59, 68, 69, 71-
  74, 81, 82, 85-87, 89, 92-94,
  96, 108, 110, 119, 153, 202,
  238, 243, 244
Round Lake, Corpus Christi, 221
Ruf, Sep, 87, 217

San Clemente, St Edward the
  Confessor, 208
San Francisco, St Gregory of
  Nyssa, 219
Santarossa, Hella, 209
Sarah, Robert, 151
Scheler, Max, 66
Schildgenossen, 69, 70, 94
Schilling, Albert, 151, 155, 297
Schmemann, Alexander, 192,
  193, 194, 195, 196, 297
Schrijvers, Joeri, 276, 297
Schwarz, Rudolf, 24, 25, 56, 71-
  74, 87-116, 127, 133, 135, 136,
  138, 150, 153, 159, 171, 182,
  187, 202, 204, 206, 211, 216,
  221, 231, 232, 237, 238, 244,
  248, 251, 259, 260, 267, 297,
  298, 299
Searle, Mark, 8, 298
Seasoltz, R. Kevin, 47, 220, 298
Second Vatican Council
  Constitution on the Sacred
    Liturgy, x, 3, 5-7, 12, 17-19,
    22, 76, 81, 117, 183, 196,
    206, 219, 227, 249, 266, 286